The
PRACTICE
— *of* —
KABBALAH

The
PRACTICE
— of —
KABBALAH

MEDITATION IN JUDAISM

STEVEN A. FISDEL

JASON ARONSON INC.
Northvale, New Jersey
London

This book was set in 11 pt. Berkeley Oldstyle.

10 9 8 7 6 5 4 3 2 1

Library of Congress Cataloging-in-Publication Data
Fisdel, Steven A.
    The practice of kabbalah : meditation in Judaism / by Steven A.
Fisdel.
        p.   cm.
    Includes bibliographical references and index.
    ISBN 1-56821-508-8 (alk. paper)
    1. Meditation—Judaism.   2. Cabala.   I. Title.
BM723.F527   1996
296.7'2—dc20   95-51820
                                                 CIP

Manufactured in the United States of America. Jason Aronson Inc. offers books and cassettes. For information and catalog write to Jason Aronson Inc., 230 Livingston Street, Northvale, New Jersey 07647.

"Sanctify to Me, all of the Firstborn, that which opens the womb."
(Exodus 13:2)

May these my firstfruits be acceptable
the Most High, the Holy One, Creator of Heaven and Earth.
Presented in reverence,
may this offering be of benefit and blessing.
Amen.

Contents

The
PRACTICE
— of —
KABBALAH

1

Meditation in Judaism: Purpose and Practice

ON THE NATURE AND PURPOSE OF MEDITATION

"The beginning of Wisdom is Awe of the Lord. All who practice them (the Ways of Wisdom) have great understanding. Praise of Him stands for eternity" (Psalm 111:10).

What the Psalmist is saying so eloquently summarizes the core purpose of Jewish meditation practice. True wisdom is not knowledge. Nor is it comprehension or understanding per se. Wisdom is Knowingness. It is being so closely connected with something at its core level that you are experiencing its light firsthand. There is nothing to know in the cognitive sense. There are no questions and there are no answers. You truly know, because you experience connection and unification. Such direct experience is beyond the level of mind. Rather, it is a direct melding of light with light.

The ultimate objective of meditation in Jewish tradition is to achieve and maintain this direct connection with God and to reach unification with the Light of His Presence in the universe. This is referred to by the Hebrew term *devekut*. This is adhesion to God through direct experience. It is achieved by focus. It is maintained by devotion. The experience is Knowingness.

To achieve Wisdom, one has to practice the Ways of Wisdom. Practicing the Ways of Wisdom involve study, discipline, consistent moral behavior, prayer, devotion, and meditation. The two general terms for meditation in Hebrew point directly to the purpose of meditation and its extreme importance. The terms are *Hitbodedut* and *Hitbonenut*.

Hitbodedut literally means "to be by oneself," "to be completely alone." This describes the reality of meditative practice and experience. When journeying toward God, one may pass through multiple realms of reality and many levels of experience. However, one is making the journey alone. Meditation is an intimately personal, inward process. It is a sacred journey of the Self back toward God, the Source. It is the individual soul moving toward the Core of Being. It is the ultimate inner dialogue. It is a road of experience one travels alone.

The effect of pursuing this journey is a constant recurring one. It is reflected in the term, *Hitbonenut*, meaning "self-understanding," "knowing oneself." The continuing effect, the benefit and purpose of meditation, is the evolution of the Self, the growth and development of the Soul. One evolves by experiencing more and more, on higher and higher levels of existence.

Knowingness of oneself and Knowingness of God are interlocked. They are interactive and mutually supporting of each other. They are the source of the evolution of the soul and the expansion of consciousness. The path to Knowingness is conscious connection to God. The path to connection is meditation. The result of the process is the growth of soul and of consciousness. All who practice the Ways of Wisdom have true understanding. All who have true understanding, Knowingness, remain eternally connected to God. "All who practice it [wisdom] have true understanding. Praise of God stands [endures] for Eternity" (Psalm 111:10).

Wisdom, upon which the Universe is created, originates with the quickening of the soul. When a person is overwhelmed by the majesty of God's work and senses the wonder of that which cannot be expressed, he feels near to the Creator. When one is overpowered by the pure joy of Creation, and praise and blessing become spontaneous, one is indeed close to the very source of life. At that moment, one is standing at the threshold of Wisdom.

Wisdom once approached must be pursued. Sensing God's nearness should lead the soul to the desire to seek out His love. When one explores the universe around him, experiencing wonder and awe at its grandeur, he is giving profound praise to its Creator by the very act of experience. The soul is standing in an eternal moment in close proximity to God's unconditional love. One is at the gates of wisdom and before him lie all of its paths.

The Ways of Wisdom are many, and they are profoundly deep. The Ways of Wisdom are the mystic paths that lead to humility, compassion, self-awareness, and spiritual growth. They are the pathways that connect all levels of reality. They comprise the roads that lead to God's Presence. They are meant to be traveled. As the Psalmist states quite clearly, one who practices them will attain higher consciousness.

Wisdom's beginning point and its end objective are the same: awe of God, the process of eternal praise of the Creator by the soul. Awe of God, connection to the Source, elevates the soul to higher levels of reality, beyond time and space. Following the Ways of Wisdom is the path of spiritual evolution. Pursuing the path is one of action, of doing, and of practice.

What are the Ways of Wisdom? They are study, the practice of justice, meditation, and devotion. Through this course of action comes true inner understanding and spiritual development.

It is the practice of Kabbalah, the practices of meditation drawn from millennia of Wisdom, which will be examined and detailed in this work, for the pursuit of Wisdom, in the fullest sense, requires a thorough knowledge of and deep commitment to meditation and meditative practice. Meditation is the genuine vehicle for attaining Knowingness and for drawing close to God. To experience God and to know self is to praise God within the eternal moment. That is the path of self-evolution. It is the highest obligation of the Soul.

Jewish meditation emerges from the Kabbalah, the Jewish mystic tradition. The term "Kabbalah" itself is very important to understand fully. A complete understanding sheds valuable light on the nature and relevance of the various meditation practices to be discussed, and on their application to one's inner life and personal experience.

First and foremost, the term "Kabbalah" means "reception, receptivity," from the Hebrew verb root signifying to receive or to accept. Receiving involves experiencing. If one receives a gift, for example, one accepts not only the gift, but also the gratitude, respect, or love that prompted it, the spirit in which it was given.

What is received may be solicited or come unsolicited. One may receive in the mail either an item that was ordered or a letter from an old friend. Either way, the act of receiving is an act of acceptance and it involves the recipient in a process, in which he is a participant.

On a spiritual level, receiving is the terminus point. It is the end result of a process. It is the fulfillment. It is the completion. Nothing given really fully exists unless it is received. God sends Life Force through all of Creation. It is simultaneously being received by all Creation and sustaining Creation's very existence. God sends down goodness and it is accepted by all worlds. Man does good and it flows back through all worlds and is received by God. Generating, sending, and receiving are the ebb and flow by which the universe operates.

The more one is willing to open up and receive from above, the more one comes to experience higher realities and intensify the content of life and foster soul development. That is the objective of meditation and practice.

Receiving in its primal form is the reception of Life Force. The great Hasidic master, Rabbi Levi Yitzhak of Berditchev, taught that from the highest level of the universe, the level of Unconditional Love, comes the spiritual influx that sustains all worlds. This influx can be sent down by God to this world or brought down to it by humanity.

The former, that is the Divine influx being sent down, is an act of pure Grace. It is an act of mercy initiated by God out of His love and concern for the whole of Creation. This flow can be received two ways. The first is passively. The influx of Life Force simultaneously streams down, invigorates, and sustains existence at all times. We need do nothing in this regard. This is a continual and primary reality that lies exclusively under God's direction.

There is also an active, participatory route. Through meditation, we can consciously attune our energy and our souls to the influx. To do so is to consciously seek to accept and experience God's unconditional love. This act of intent and focus transforms the reception of God's will from a passive one to an active one. This inner transformation produces revelation. Though the initiation of Grace emanates from God, focusing the heart and soul on it in deep meditation transforms the flow of Life Force, opening up the internal reality, the inner meaning of God's love, and making it manifest.

How is that accomplished? Let us harken back to the revelation at Mount Sinai. The immediacy of God's Presence caused the skies to thunder and the Earth to quake. The natural world reacted physically. It did not simply receive passively. By the same token, Moses and the Israelites reacted affirmatively, declaring, "We will do and we will understand." Confronted with the intensity of God's Presence manifesting, the Israelites responded actively. Confrontation with God requires a response. That response produces revelation in the form of inner understanding.

Revelation on any level, group or individual, is the process of reaching, experiencing, and coming to understand the inner essence of what one receives from God on a continual basis. It is a process that requires effort, clear focus, and the will to search. This process of revelation is the primary focus of Jewish meditation, the practice of Kabbalah. Kabbalist meditation is the receiving of God's abundant flow and the active penetration of the Divine influx, allowing the soul to absorb its inner meaning.

In Kabbalah, the flow of energy that sustains the universe is dual in its direction. It flows both from the Source, God's Will, to the whole of Creation, and upon being received, Creation responds by sending energy back to God. This double flow is intrinsic, as the Kabbalah sees it. God's Grace and mankind's actions form a flow of energy, uniform in both directions.

This dual movement has particularly important implications in relation to humanity. Every time one receives, acts, and comes to understand what has been received, his energy can be channeled constructively. Energy and will can be directed outward toward creation as creativity or upward toward God, manifesting as devotion and resonance with His Will.

According to Levi Yitzhak, the ideal would be to focus one's intentions, actions, and consciousness on the pure joy that God has, when one seeks Him in love and clings to Him with devotion. This intensity opens the gates of Heaven and floods the soul, and indeed all worlds, with light, blessing, and inner peace, meditation being the key to such focus.

As one actively moves toward God, more and more light is received, more love is experienced, and more understanding is gained. Here, the soul is reintegrating with itself. It is healing itself and finding God in the process.

The process itself fosters an increasingly deep relationship. The process of seeking God, climbing the Tree of Life, is that of the evolving relationship between the soul and its source. As the relationship deepens, so does the joy. God rejoices at the effort. The soul is ecstatic about its increasing sense of Self and its growing closeness to the Creator. In summary, the basis of Kabbalah is receiving. However, receiving is not merely reception alone. It is equally receptivity.

Kabbalah is a three-part process. One which is both active and passive. First, one passively receives. Then, one acts on what has been received through doing, through meditation, through learning and teaching. Finally, by so asserting oneself actively, one becomes receptive to experiencing higher levels of reality, to reintegrating and healing the soul, and to returning to God.

THE PROCESS OF MEDITATION

Significantly, the Book of Genesis in describing the Creation makes a very salient point. "In the beginning of God's process of creating the Heavens and the Earth, the Earth was void and unformed. Darkness was on the face of the Deep. The spirit of God hovered over the face of the waters. And God said, 'Let there be light' and there was light" (Genesis 1:1–3).

From God's standpoint, as best we can understand it, Creation is the manifestation of an inner will. Creation is the externalization of the inner thought of God. This thought process is the primordial impulse out of which the universe was created. It is referred to biblically as the chaos or the darkness.

In order for this impulse to be dealt with effectively, God creates the light. Light is the operative, organizational principle within Creation itself. It is the mechanism by which the light was created and by which the creation process is triggered and perpetuated. It is the *Ruach Elohim*, the spirit of God. The creation of light and its subsequent entry into the darkness is for the purpose of ordering and sustaining the Creation. Light's creation is initiated and maintained by the spirit of God, God's breath.

The suggestion of the first couple of lines of Genesis is that God's thought or will to create, to express something, first required the Deep. The Deep was chaotic and needed an organizing principle, which was the light. The light in turn was triggered by the breath of God. God spoke and there was light, speech being an articulation of breath.

In this regard, it is worth recalling the story of the creation of man, which appears later in the following chapter. It says in the second chapter of Genesis (2:7), "And God formed man from the dust of the Earth and breathed into his nostrils a soul of life, man becoming thereby a living being."

Here we find the same principle at work. First, the matter is shaped. Man's form is made out of the clay. However, he is not a living entity until God breathes life into him. Breath is both the mechanical principle of bringing things to life, as well as that which sustains life. Form is animated and sustained by the infusion of breath.

We are all accustomed to viewing breath as life, as the force that sustains it. What is being implied in Genesis is that life itself is a process of activation. This process is a mechanism which not only gives and sustains life, but also connects us directly to God, the source of life.

If one views this as a triangular relationship, there are three inter-related elements. All three represent breathing or breath. One wing of the triangle, the base, would be man's self-expression, the articulation that results from inner will. One side of the triangle is breath as existence, which activates us and allows us to function and express ourselves. The other side is breath as the connection to the Source, the gift of life.

These three elements are integrally locked together, being dimensions of the same reality. From the standpoint of creation, first God breathes life into us. Then, that spiritual energy sustains us. Finally, from that energy we gain consciousness and are able to express ourselves.

This concept has enormous value on a practical level when dealing with meditation. Meditation is induced by breathing. Meditation in turn, can lead us back through ourselves to our inner Self and beyond, directly back to our very connection to God.

Going up through the triangle, one passes first through one's ability for self-expression to the level of connecting with oneself. From there, one proceeds to the point of being with God. This meditative process is facilitated by breath. Breathing is not only primary as a mechanism in meditation, it is the operative trigger within the creative process.

By knowing and utilizing this triangular relationship, one can open the doors to deeper connections with Self and with God. The mechanism, the process, and the reality are very closely related. They are all dimensions of the same experience. Through breathing comes meditation. Meditation focuses on transcending self-expression. That transcendence connects the Self with God.

Now the question arises, how do you utilize breathing to induce entry into a state of meditation? We should follow the example of the primary, life-giving organs, the heart and lungs. They function through a process of repetitive expansion and contraction. The heart expands to take blood in and contracts to pump it out. The lungs expand to take in air and contract to force circulation.

Within this expansion–contraction process, this alternation and the resulting flux of energy is balanced. This equality is critical. The key to inducing a meditative state is through balanced breathing. Understanding that, we can unlock the door to meditative states.

The initial step is to set aside both a time and a place that are conducive to tranquility. One needs an environment in which there will be no external stimuli nor distractions. The prerequisite for meditating is to find a quiet, secure place, at a time where nothing can disturb the process.

Loose-fitting clothing is recommended, so as to allow for the free flow of energy through the body. The body's energy flow can be seriously impeded if one is wearing restrictive clothing of any sort. On a similar note, the flow and distribution of energy within the body via the nervous system is directed through the spinal column. Therefore, it is also important that one meditate in a position in which the spine is straight and unimpeded.

Sitting in a slumped or contorted position will interfere with the efficient flow of energy within the body and this can short circuit effective meditation. One should sit in a comfortable position. Jewish tradition has never required that one necessarily sit in a yogic posture. Any comfortable position will suffice.

Lying down is not necessarily recommended. One is often prone to sleep in such a position and that interferes with the meditative process. Meditation is often an intensely cognitive experience. Sleep will simply deny access to that level.

The next step is to close one's eyes in order to block out any remaining external stimuli. This allows one to focus inwardly. The third step is to start the balanced breathing process. This process of inhaling and exhaling should be cadenced. There needs to be an equality in the length of time one is breathing in and one is breathing out.

An easy way to accomplish this is to sequence one's breathing with a set number of heartbeats. For example, one may want to breathe in to the count of four heartbeats and then out to the same count of four heartbeats. Any even number may be used as long as the cadence is maintained. Moreover, after a short while the subconscious mind will take over the process and it will no longer be necessary to actually count. The heart is an ideal tool because it can act as a subconscious metronome.

Once you are breathing in cadence, you need to release all your thoughts. As one exhales, breathe out all feelings, all thought, all concern, all distractions, all content within the mind. As one inhales, breathe in only nothingness, emptiness. A useful technique is to focus complete attention on the sound of the breath as it flows in and out during the inhalation/exhalation process.

The objective at this point is simply to experience the ebb and flow of one's own energy, without form and without content, then to experience a state of neutrality or void.

To illustrate the induction of a meditative state and experience the state of neutrality, take some time and try the following exercise.

Exercise 1: Neutrality State

1. Close your eyes and breathe in and out to a cadence of four heartbeats in and four out.
2. When comfortable, stop counting and just continue breathing. Listen only to the sound of your breathing.
3. Breathe out all feelings, thoughts, and sensations. As you exhale everything out, only empty space remains.
4. Breathe in pure white light. It fills you entirely. When you are ready, release the white light. You will feel completely tranquil and totally empty. You are in a very secure space with no content at all, just peace and tranquility.
5. Remain in this neutral state as long as you feel comfortable. When ready to leave, count backward from 5 to 1. At the count of one, you will return automatically to normal waking consciousness.

Once you become accustomed to reaching this state, you will be ready to embark on journeys into various meditative states. You will be ready to proceed with the process of meditation.

The objective of meditation in Judaism is self-understanding, self-realization, and connecting with God. One term used to describe meditation in Hebrew is *Hitbonenut*. This refers specifically to the contemplative dimension of meditation. It literally means "the understanding of oneself." If man is indeed created in the image of God, then by understanding one's inner Self, one comprehends aspects of the Divine within and connects with God. Through this dynamic interconnectedness one experiences his relationship to God directly.

The Hebrew term used frequently in kabbalistic literature for meditation is *Hitbodedut*. The term means "being by yourself," "being completely alone." It is important to remember that the Bible says God created man, in the singular. Why doesn't it say that He created mankind or people?

To paraphrase the Rabbis of the Talmud, an individual represents an entire world within himself. If you save the life of one human being, it is as if you have saved the whole world. If you change another person's life you have changed the universe. The mystic view is, that there is no difference between what the individual experiences and what occurs in the world. Each person is a microcosm of the entire universe.

The only individual one can truly understand is oneself. Therefore, God created man in the singular. By knowing oneself, a person comes to know the universe. Understanding that leads to a direct relationship with God.

It states in Genesis (1:27), "And God created Man in His image, in the image of God He created them, both male and female." The implication here is that the human form and the human essence, male and female, is a reflection of God. Understanding oneself as a reflection of God is the gateway to experiencing one's relationship to God.

Hitbonenut, self-understanding, is the objective. *Hitbodedut*, isolation and inner exploration, is the process and the means by which that is accomplished. The ultimate result would be *Yichud*, unification with God Himself, understanding the connection between individual being and the source of all being.

Since the objectives of meditation are sacred in Jewish thought, like any sacred action, it should be sanctified. Meditation, when studied or practiced, should be hallowed and separated from the mundane or the profane. In rabbinic tradition this is done through blessing and prayer.

One should say a blessing prior to entering the meditative state and also one upon emerging from meditation. This sanctifies the action by declaring our intentions, purifying our hearts, acknowledging our dependence on God, and praising His unending mercy toward us.

A very worthwhile practice is to recite a psalm or selection from the prayer book as a way of preparation. Prior to the meditation recite the blessing, *Honen L'Adam Daat*. The blessing in Hebrew is "*Baruch Ata HaShem Eloheinu Melech HaOlam Honen L'Adam Daat*." In English, "Blessed are You O Lord our God, King of the universe, who bestows knowledge on man." I use this blessing, since gaining inner self-knowledge is the objective. Since the goal of all meditation is to unify with God, I feel it appropriate upon emerging from meditation to recite the *Shema* prayer ("Hear, O Israel, the Lord our God the Lord is One"), which affirms the unity of God.

Prayer in general is closely bound up with meditation. One will find for example, that saying the *Maariv*, the evening prayers, prior to meditating, greatly reenforces the experience, giving it a greater personal intensity and thereby sanctifying the process.

An important principle in the practice of Kabbalah is that of *Kavannah*. *Kavannah* literally means direction, intention. In the context of meditation, it refers to the emotional intensity that one focuses on the object of the meditation, in specific, and on God in general. Drawing close and connecting to God stands as the ultimate objective of all meditation.

This principle is central to the whole framework of Jewish meditation and prayer. Kabbalah, its theories, doctrines, and particularly its practice, is predicated on moving in a specific direction. Having one's experience directed to an ultimate objective is the cornerstone, the foundation of all Jewish meditative practice.

The objective is ultimately the unification of Self with God. In Hebrew, this is referred to as *Devekut*, meaning adherence, sticking to, attachment. It is achieved through *Kavannah*. The Hebrew root, *L'Kaven*, means to direct something toward something else. In this context, it is referring to the act of one directing himself toward God.

By so doing, one is embarking on a journey and initiating a process. Meditation is an active principle in Jewish experience, not an altogether receptive one. Though there is a great deal of receptivity involved in the process, the receptive factor only emerges in response to action, direction, and process.

To set a direction is to focus one's energy exclusively on a definable, agreed upon destination. There must be a clear sense of purpose from the very beginning. One must remain focused through the entire process that is initiated at the commencement of the meditation. In moving through a meditation, one experiences a process that leads to the objective. The road and the destination create each other, as it were.

The inner meaning of *Kavannah* is emotional and psychic focus. *Kavannah* is required to harness the intensity of intention that is necessary to create an accessible path to God. It is the power to adhere to Him, as well. Adherence to God presumes the realization of one's self and the strength to remain identified with it.

Traditionally, *Kavannah* has been connected with prayer. To make prayer meaningful, one had to pray with *Kavannah*. Without it prayers were considered to be dead, that is without sufficient energy to reach the Divine Throne. Emotional intensity was required to achieve the objective of allowing the soul to communicate with God through prayer.

In short, as one prays, one has to put heart and soul together into prayer in order to provide it with the validity and spiritual force necessary to achieve communication and unification with God.

In commenting on Song of Songs 8:13, the Rabbis in the *Midrash* made an observation pertinent both to prayer and to meditation. "It is written, 'And you who dwell in the garden, your companions harken to your voice and cause me to hear it.' When Israel is gathered together in the synagogue and reads the Shema (Hear, O Israel, the Lord Our God the Lord is One) in unison, with one mind and one intention, then God says, 'You who dwell in the garden, when you read this way with one voice, I and the angels harken.' But when Israel reads the Shema with distraction, not in unison, some before others and some after, with no *Kavannah*, the Holy Spirit cries out, 'Flee away my Beloved.'"

Seeking understanding, seeking self-realization and the connection between oneself and God is not only an active process, it is a passionate one. The *V'Ahavta* prayer begins, "And you shall love the Lord your God with all your heart, with all your soul and with all your being." This can be understood as a three-stage process, by which one directs energy toward an understanding of self and of God.

1. Love with all your heart. Your emotions need to be focused on these objectives when praying and meditating.
2. With all your soul. One's deep inner sense of longing for understanding and yearning for God needs to be channeled in the process.
3. With all your being. Reach out to God with all your being from the innermost recesses of consciousness. Both self-realization and connection with the Divine require this primal reaching and stretching.

A good preliminary exercise before meditation or prayer would be first to close your eyes. Then, picture your heart opening and let your emotions flow outward. Release any negative emotions first: pain, anger, frustration, and so forth. Let that release trigger a flow of positive emotions: love, joy, whatever may come to the surface.

Next, picture your head opening and let all thoughts, all rational consciousness flow out. There should be two streams, one of emotion emanating from the heart and one of thought, concepts, and imagery flowing from the head, both merging as one river. Let the flow outward continue until you feel a sense of total calm and release. From this point, you may wish to proceed directly into a specific meditation or prayer.

The Rabbis of the *Mishnah* and Talmud used to spend an hour contemplating before they actually commenced prayer, in order to properly ready themselves for the experience. The intention was to gain proper focus and direction. What one focuses on determines what dimension of reality one will experience.

Picture a diamond. The diamond represents reality as a whole, as a totality. There are not only numerous faces on the diamond, but also numerous directions that one can turn the diamond. Each turn exposes a new face and a different light. The diamond has not changed. The viewpoint and perspective have. Focus has shifted and therefore, so has the appearance of the diamond. As one changes the perspective, the color, the level of refraction, and the overall subtlety of how one perceives the diamond also change. Only the focus has altered, not the diamond itself.

Kavannah is the process of establishing focus. Once set, the focus itself becomes the experience. Focusing can be an active or passive process. On the one hand, what is to be sought during a meditation can be determined in advance. An example of this would be to formulate a specific question you want addressed during the meditation. Here, there is an objective, namely greater insight into a problem, issue, or situation.

Another directed approach would be to go into a meditative state seeking a specific experience. For example, one might wish to go into a meditation focusing on the *Sefirah* of *Tiferet*, the central realm of the kabbalist Tree of Life, in order to gain an experience of unconditional love and acceptance.

On the other side of the coin, one can take a receptive approach to a meditation. Here one goes into the meditation completely open, with no expectations. Such total receptivity opens the door for one to draw experience or knowledge to himself. By allowing for all possibilities to be equal, one is paving the way for revelation experiences to take place. This approach is closer to the objectives of biblical prophecy.

It is important to remember that the term "Kabbalah" refers to receptivity. Either way, in meditation of this type, something is being received. Whether one takes an active, directed approach or a passive one—that is, a fixed focus or a flexible one—a receptivity factor operates from both vantage points.

If you take a predetermined course, say by focusing on a question, you must remain open so as to allow the answer to flow in to you from another level of consciousness. Conversely, if you choose an open, fluid focus, you become totally receptive and what needs to be drawn in as understanding or experience will be accepted unconditionally. Either way, you are dealing with Kabbalah. You are receiving from other dimensions, other levels of consciousness. You are receiving from within, as a result of *Kavannah*.

The logical question that arises at this point is, during meditation, what exactly will be coming back to you from the process of *Kavannah*?

The first possibility is that one can receive nonverbal communication in the form of visual images, pictures, color patterns, or in the form of sound, such as music or tonal patterning. All communication on higher levels of consciousness is nonverbal in nature. Moreover, sound patterns are the connective tissue that links the levels of reality together.

If you are receiving flows of images, of color or sound patterns, you are experiencing Jacob's Ladder. You are dealing with that which connects above to below. This allows access and growth, and encompasses movement in both directions. Jacob saw a ladder that was fixed on the ground and yet stretched to the highest Heavens. Angels marched up and down the rungs.

The ladder represents the connective process that allows for communication between the various levels and dimensions of reality. If you consider the structure and function of the ladder, this becomes clearer. The ladder consists of two linear poles, designed to facilitate ascent and descent, yet the poles cannot achieve that objective without the rungs. The rungs hold the two poles in place, as much as the poles determine the order and sequence of the rungs' progression.

The connective tissues between different levels of reality establish both sequence and direction, as well as the interlocking relationships. On a practical level, if one is dealing with music, with sound, with tones, one can use those processes either to progress through different levels of reality or to allow communication from other levels and from other dimensions to reach our consciousness.

Another possibility is to undergo direct experiences in meditation. This may come in the form of emotional flows, the experiencing or re-experiencing of events. It may appear through sensations of different sorts. One can alternately experience a void or even an apparent loss of consciousness.

Here, cognition is the understanding of what has transpired. Assimilating it consciously and learning from it will come often as a delayed reaction to the experience itself. This is because of the intensity involved. An insight, an inspiration, a déjà vu or a sudden clear awareness, is likely to occur after the fact. This time-lapse allows the neurological brain time to process and translate the rush of experience into meaningful cognition and awareness.

One may also experience being somewhere else, directly visiting another place or finding oneself on a different level of reality. Here, communication takes place very vividly on a visual level. This type of encounter bypasses cognitive processes and speaks directly to the intuitive side of self. The logical, rational mind is being sidestepped so as to avoid definition and preconception.

All of these types of meditative experiences are attested to in biblical literature and in Kabbalah. A poignant example would be Moses and the prophets, who were referred to as *Nevi'im*. The term stems in part from the word *L'havi*, "to bring." They were bringing the Word of God directly to the people. Messages were being received from the Divine realm, formulated neurologically, and passed on to the nation. They were the result of direct experience with higher levels of reality to which they made themselves available.

The prophet Samuel was called a *Roeh*, a seer. The prophet Ezekiel and Daniel had visions. Seeing into other dimensions involved not only envisioning the future, but also delving into higher realms of consciousness. Indeed, the chariot vision of Ezekiel laid the very foundation for the development of an entire school of meditative technique.

The Talmud makes frequent reference to the *Bat Kol*, the heavenly voice that speaks from above. Kabbalistic literature and hasidic stories mention great rabbis who were *Maggids*, those who heard voices from beyond and who transmitted the information to others.

The Baal Shem Tov, the founder of the hasidic movement according to numerous stories, went into trance states and reported back what was transpiring on other levels, in Heaven. He reveals the inner hidden meaning of surrounding events.

It is very important to understand that all these types of experience are normal in the meditation process. Much of the practical application of Kabbalah over the centuries was to facilitate *Kavannah*, that is, to establish focus and to experience precisely these phenomena, the intention being to better understand oneself and to draw closer to God by an intimate interaction with His Creation on all levels.

The whole practice of Kabbalah, of which meditation is such an integral part, is designed to train individuals in the techniques and experiences that fulfill this end. The ability to interface with the wonder of Creation is not a gift to the select few, but rather the potential of humanity. The practice of Kabbalah is the drive to explore ourselves and to strengthen our relationship to the Creator by understanding deeply, through personal experience, Creation, and the Creative Process.

2

Biblical Imagery and Spiritual Paradigms

Anyone familiar with the Bible will tell you that one of the fascinations with reading biblical narrative is the strong emotional and spiritual pull that the text exerts on the reader. The strength of the biblical narrative is based on the fact that the text was written as sacred history. The stories were not meant to be simply a record of past events, but also to serve as spiritual paradigms.

The narratives are intended to provide a model for moral and spiritual behavior. One of their most important underlying functions is to embody great spiritual truths. Not only is historical information being transmitted in the biblical stories, but so are profound, universal principles.

In order to achieve these ends, the biblical texts were constructed with great craft and precision. The use of language in the biblical text is concise, yet deep with many layers of meaning and connotation. The literary and poetic style of biblical Hebrew places great reliance on imagery. The visual images the stories create have a very strong impact on the reader's emotions and point the way toward tapping and utilizing one's inner resources.

When one can clearly see the story in the mind's eye, one gains not only a cognitive understanding but also an intuitive sense of the importance of that which is being portrayed. At the same time, a spiritual message is being assimilated on a deep inner level of understanding.

All human interaction conveys messages. What we do, what we say, how we act heavily impact other people on many different levels. A well-constructed story does much the same thing in terms of communicating emotions, values, and spiritual lessons. The authors of the various biblical books understood this principle thoroughly.

The images of Adam and Eve being expelled from the garden, of Joseph's tearful reunion with his brothers, of the drama of the Exodus from Egypt, not only move the reader deeply by their detail and vividness but also impart both consciously and subliminally very powerful spiritual truths.

We cannot help but be affected on profound inner levels of consciousness. When reading and absorbing a narrative, particularly one that contains strong paradigms reflecting universal truths, the reader is affected on several tiers of consciousness. Cognitive, emotional, and spiritual reactions to the material and its inner message all take place simultaneously. An inner alignment occurs that changes the reader from within on many levels of understanding. .

The use of stories and imagery to convey spiritual truths is not simply confined to the Bible. In the Talmud and *Midrash*, for example, the Rabbis made extensive use of parables, stories, and legends. These narratives were designed to help convey specific truths. They were creatively used to illustrate deep spiritual realities that needed to be expressed in a manner that would encompass multiple levels of understanding.

In short, stories that appear in sacred literature are not there merely to entertain or inform. Their deeper purpose is to illustrate spiritual realities and to serve as paradigms and models of behavior that lead to spiritual growth and inner development.

That being the case, an important question arises. What, then, is the difference between hearing or studying a biblical story and meditating on it? Are both important? If so, what distinguishes them and how are they related?

When one hears or reads a story, a transformation takes place. One experiences something new. An often subtle shift occurs internally. Somehow one's understanding of life is changed or at least influenced by what we hear and what we see in our mind's eye. Something remarkable has happened. Consciousness, indeed our very experience of life, is deeply affected. By accepting a story, our inner understanding of what we perceive and our internalized sense of reality is altered. That inner alteration of consciousness cannot help but change our experience of reality.

One learns from stories, because they are condensed experience. We accept them. We internalize them and thereby are transformed by them. Those are the true marks of a good story. The more powerful, the more pertinent a story is, the more impact it has on the reader or listener. The impact, in turn, serves as a catalyst for inner change. If the message truly is a spiritual one, the result is intellectual and emotional development and inner progress.

When one is meditating on a story or a set of sacred visual images, the meditator moves into sacred space. He taps into a new dimension and connects with the spiritual dynamic, the hidden inner core of the story. The meditator becomes attuned to it and begins utilizing the spiritual process behind the story. The universal reality, the paradigm within, becomes clear and usable. The meditator learns to understand and to replicate the process. He can refashion his life in accord with the deeper reality reflected by the story.

Duplicating the underlying process, the internal paradigm of a sacred story produces a deep, inner understanding that surpasses the cognitive and the emotional levels. Here one is not merely assimilating information and processing it internally. More than just being effected subjectively, the meditator is taking the core message and by becoming one with it, transforming it into a spiritual technology.

Both processes, that of accepting a sacred story and that of meditating deeply on it, are very valuable practices, each in their own right. Let us focus for a moment specifically on the latter. Let us center our attention on the process of transformation that is created by meditation. In order to illustrate how sacred stories and sacred images can be used as spiritual paradigms, as a meditation technology, let me give you a few examples.

The first and simplest form of meditation of this type is used for producing behavioral change or behavioral patterning. Let us take the stories of Abraham, for example. Abraham was a man of enormous compassion and of great charity. He risked his own life to argue with God in an attempt to save the people of Sodom and Gomorrah, who had brought down His wrath on themselves. Abraham bent over backwards to be hospitable to any strangers that passed his way. According to legend, he would leave all four sides of his tent open at all times, in order to be able to see any strangers approaching in the distance. That way, he could properly prepare for their arrival.

If one is looking to get in touch with his own sense of compassion, what better person is there to emulate? If one were to seek to enlarge his capacity for assisting his fellow man, these visual images would be very usable in meditation.

The images of sitting in a tent with all four sides open, awaiting the arrival of visitors, picturing oneself as Abraham, entertaining those wandering through the desert, picturing oneself arguing with God to save other people from their own distress, comprise a very potent, meditative pattern. It puts one in touch with compassion, selflessness, service to others, and devotion to God.

Meditating on being like Abraham, and elaborating on the details, is one form of meditation whose objective would be to tap into a universal, spiritual behavior pattern. It allows one to learn compassion and devotion. Subsequently, one is able to assimilate these precious qualities into one's own life experience. By so doing, one is apt to become more internally conditioned to dealing compassionately with other people. This is reenforced by repeating this meditation over a period of time.

The second type of visualization meditation is one that is designed to assist the individual in going through the process of working out something. For example, in the early stages of learning to meditate, one can encounter several distinct psychic and emotional roadblocks. These phenomena can be formidable obstacles. One way to overcome them is through the use of specific meditative patterns.

A good example of a meditation designed to help one through the process of overcoming obstacles would be the story of Elijah in the cave. According to the biblical narrative, Queen Jezebel ordered Elijah's execution and he was forced to escape to the wilderness. Upon arriving there, he sought refuge in a mountain cave and spent the night. In the morning God called to him to come out of the cave.

When Elijah emerged, he witnessed a series of ferocious storms. He endured storms of wind and of fire. After a while, Elijah realized that God was not present in the storms. He did not sense God's Presence in either phenomena. With that realization, the storms ended abruptly and were followed by an earthquake. The Earth shook violently, shattered rocks, and uprooted trees, yet Elijah did not hear God's voice in the earthquake and it subsided. Elijah knew that God was not there either. At that point of cognition, Elijah hears a still small voice within himself and understands that here is where God is to be found.

This story very accurately reflects the stages of obstruction one may go through learning to meditate and seeking God. The first stage,

reflected by the wind storm, is doubt. The initial experiences of meditation can often bring one into realms of consciousness that are not the
normative ones we are familiar with. One can be plagued by both doubt
and uncertainty.

Questions arise. Is what I am seeing another dimension of reality
or is this my own imagination? Have I made a breakthrough or am I
hallucinating? Am I simply losing my mind? How do I know that this is
not just subconscious garbage? Until one learns to shut down the ego,
close off the thinking mind, and accept intuitively what is being experienced, no further progress can be made.

Should one overcome the doubt, the fire storm is often unleashed.
The fire storm represents the onslaught of pain. The purpose of the fire
is actually twofold. Doubt has shaken our old belief system. It has cracked
it, if an individual has passed through the doubt. However, resolving
the doubt has not destroyed the old, unproductive world view. Only
through the fire, the full experiencing of the pain caused by the subconscious acceptance of a distorted view of one's life and experience, is the
damaging, old belief system destroyed.

The fire is the process of the phoenix rising. Out of the ashes emerge
hope and rectification. Yet, one must walk through the flames to reach
this point. Pain destroys the barriers to spiritual growth erected by illusion. Pain is also the consequence of the illusion's demise. When old
belief systems are destroyed, the immediate effect is emotional turmoil.
Long-suppressed emotions crash to the conscious surface. The truth has
to be faced. Pain is the consequent reality. This is the pain of healing.
Skin may burn or itch or throb in pain as the tissue is regenerating. It is
necessary, but it will pass.

Once beyond the pain, one encounters the earthquake. That is fear.
Once one realizes that what one experiences in meditation is very real
in its own right, fear can set in. It may be fear of the unknown, fear of
letting go, fear of losing oneself, or fear of the truth. Regardless of the
form, this is also a formidable barrier.

Fear is the greatest and most all pervasive obstacle a human being
must ever face. Like the hydra, fear has many tentacles. Like a chame-
leon, it takes on many different colorations and weaves itself into the
very fabric of our emotional environment. It can dominate one's life in
ways so subtle and so hidden they are imperceptible to normal waking
consciousness. Yet, in meditation one reaches higher levels of consciousness. The higher one ascends, the more that has been concealed becomes
apparent. Once exposed, it must be faced.

As in life, so in meditation; the greatest obstacle to overcome is fear. Walking through the fire of pain leads to the earthquake of the soul. The old structures, the old buildings, the old, cherished belief system that for so long contained one's view of reality, are destroyed first. That is followed by the breaking open of the very ground on which the foundations of one's beliefs were laid. Out of the chasms that open up erupt the pent-up energies that lay deep beneath the surface.

First, the flood of fears is released. Then, connection is made with the most primal of forces, pure energy of existence itself. When a person reaches this level, that of pure Life Force, unadulterated by fear and superimposed beliefs, then one hears the still, small voice within. One hears the whisper of the Soul.

The way past any of these obstacles is through the process of riding them out. One way to do precisely that is to replicate in meditation the experience of Elijah. By meditating on fleeing to a cave and spending the night, on hearing God call you out of the cave, and by riding out the wind, the fire storm, and the earthquake, through experiencing whatever needs to be felt, one is carried through the process. The result is: the obstacles are removed.

This process may require repeating the meditation in several sessions, over a period of time. That is true for any type of meditation that has a specific objective in mind. It is important always to begin the meditation anew from the very beginning and go as far as one can during any given session. If, for instance, in an earlier session you passed through and completed the experience of the windstorm, during this session you will pass right through the wind and move into the fire, and so forth.

When one reaches the point of feeling the silence, of hearing the still small voice within, one has reached the point of inner connection. The connection with God is finally made, because one has inwardly reached the point of contact with one's deeper Self.

If one is having difficulty in one's life, experiencing profound or debilitating doubts, being shaken by fears to the core of one's being, or undergoing great pain, one can use the story of Elijah in the cave as a meditative process to pass through these difficulties and reach a state of equilibrium.

Another biblical paradigm that can be used to work through the pain and torment caused by an oppressive situation or circumstance, would be that of the crossing of the Red Sea. Here, one should graphically picture oneself standing with the people at the shore of the Red

Sea. Picture Moses standing in the lead and the army of Pharaoh pursuing from behind. As Moses lifts his staff and parts the sea, one should feel the mud and ground underfoot. Smell the distinctive scent of the water and feel the strong winds blowing, as one crosses to dry land. Once on the other side, the waters will close, burying forever the onslaught of the oppressive forces.

This is a good meditation for the reduction of severe stress, for freeing oneself from the effects of oppressive situations, and for the breaking of destructive old behavior patterns.

In short, it is important to understand that sacred stories and parables can be used not only to portray emotional, psychological, and psychic processes but also can be used in meditation as a technological processing tool for healing them.

The third type of visual meditation is drawn from Jewish ritual practice. This type of meditation is designed to focus on spiritual regeneration. A good example of this type of meditation is replicating the experience of immersion in the *mikvah*, the ritual bath.

There are times when people do feel an alienation or separation from God. There are times when people feel that they are being prevented from effectively operating on a spiritual level for whatever reason. There are times as well that people can feel spiritually inadequate or developmentally stuck.

This particular variety of meditation, much like the physical practice of ritual immersion, is designed to purify oneself emotionally and psychologically in order to clear out these types of roadblocks. There should be no obstacles to a soul's communication with God.

One can do this meditation either in the standard method of normal meditation described above or in conjunction with the actual process of physically immersing in the *mikvah*. It is equally effective either way.

Imagine yourself entering a building that is very pleasant, very tranquil, and very serene. As you enter this quiet, sacred place, you will find a room waiting for you, where you will disrobe and prepare yourself for the immersion into the *mikvah*. Upon emerging from the room, you proceed to the edge of the immersion pool. It is a large pool, cut into rock. It is being constantly fed by fresh water from a stream that flows into it.

Take a moment to say a prayer or recollect the verse from Psalms that says, "The soul that you have breathed into me is pure." You will notice that there are several stairs that descend into the *mikvah*. Descend all the stairs until you are totally immersed in the water. Take a moment to sense the utter tranquility of being surrounded by living water. Let all your fears, anxieties, and stress flow out of you and be dissolved in the holy waters. Remain immersed until you feel totally at peace.

At the other end of the pool, you will see stairs that ascend, leading you up and out of the *mikvah*. When you feel ready, climb slowly out of the pool. Once out of the *mikvah*, you will find a beautiful, white robe waiting for you. Put the robe on, and then take some time to feel the light, which is now radiating from you in great abundance. Resonate with the light. It is the light of joy, of purification, of oneness. Conclude the meditation with the blessing: "Blessed are You, O Lord our God, King of the Universe, who restores the soul to life." Then count down from 7 to 0 and return to waking consciousness.

So far, we have explored meditations that replicate processes. Those meditations are designed to reach specific states of consciousness with predetermined objectives. At this point, it would be wise to examine a couple of meditation techniques that are open-ended. That is, they have no predefined objectives or outcomes.

This type of meditation allows for guidance, for information and assistance to come through from other dimensions of reality. Here, one is seeking to find an answer or gain an understanding, rather than to replicate a process and to heal. Under this type of experience, one must be willing to allow himself to be lead somewhere or be open, in order to receive an influx of light and energy from beyond the common, familiar perimeters of conscious reality.

Seeking knowledge and searching for answers are two very primal human needs. There are a couple of biblically derived techniques that can be shared here that address these issues.

If one is seeking to be lead in a new direction, to change the course of one's life and actions, an excellent paradigm to utilize, would be that of the Pillar of Cloud and Fire.

According to the Book of Exodus, when the Jews wandered in the desert for forty years, it was at God's direction. That direction came in the form of a moving pillar. It appeared as a pillar of cloud by day and as a pillar of fire by night. When the Israelites were to break camp and move on, the pillar, which was always visible, would lift up off the ground and move. This was the signal for the Israelites to prepare themselves and follow God's lead to the next destination. When the pillar set down again, the Israelites would rebuild their camp and remain there until the column rose up again.

This sequence provides an appropriate visual image in meditation for those who seek to be lead in the direction of positive life change.

Remember, the ultimate, long-range objective of the wandering in the desert was to lead the Israelites to the Promised Land. Personally replicating such a paradigm leads an individual toward a new, fuller life.

The meditation involved here is very simple and direct. It is as follows:

Desert Meditation

1. Picture yourself in the desert. You may picture yourself alone or with a group of people, whichever is more comfortable. You know where you are and you know where you have been. But you do not know where you are going to be lead to next.

2. Take some time to get a clear visual image of your surroundings. Get a sense of the geography of the desert you are in. What does the sand look like? What does the climate feel like? What sense do you get of the vegetation and animal life?

3. Imagine yourself standing at a specific spot in the desert. Look into the distance and get a clear view of the pillar that is leading the camp. What does the pillar look like? Is it cloud or fire at present? The time of day will correspond to what the pillar is doing.

4. The pillar should appear to be stationary at first. Watch the pillar and wait until you begin to see the pillar lift up and begin to move. As the pillar moves, you follow it. It may move for some time. You should be letting it lead you. Be confident, that you are going to a better place than where you were previously in your life. As you go, feel free to take in all the sights and sounds as the scenery changes.

5. Once the pillar sets down and becomes stationary again, you must stop and rest. Find a comfortable place to sit down and relax. Take an inventory of the surroundings you now find yourself in. How does this place look? What does it feel like? What sense do you have of where you are now? Do you see or feel anything that would indicate what this place may mean or symbolize to you?

6. Look for context clues. Remember, anything you see that strikes you as significant, those images or sensations will provide you with specific data. Once you return to consciousness, those images and symbols will serve as strong mental, emotional, and intuitive indicators of where you need to go next in your life, and what things need to be done specifically.

7. Give yourself the mental instruction that you will retain complete memory of this experience when you awaken. Tell yourself clearly that within a reasonable period of time you will understand fully where you are in your process, and what needs to be done in order for you to move on to the next stage.

Bear in mind that this meditation may need to be repeated a number of times before you reach the Promised Land. You will intuitively know, however, when you have arrived there.

A meditation that seeks specific spiritual information, rather than general direction can also be abstracted from the model of the desert experience. It involves visualizing the Ark of the Covenant, as well as being within the Tent of Meeting. When Moses spoke with God, he would enter the Tent of Meeting and would stand directly in front of the Ark.

The Ark was a large device used to carry the Tablets of the Law that Moses brought down from Mount Sinai. The Ark was a large box covered inside and out with gold. Around the top edges of the Ark was a gold wreath. On top, stood two winged cherubs facing each other. Their wings circled over their heads and almost touched. At the base, rings were in place that held the long staffs that enabled the priests to carry the Ark from place to place.

When the Israelites were encamped, the Ark would remain inside the Tent of Meeting. There, God would speak with Moses. God's voice emerged from between the wings of the two cherubs.

Through meditation, it is possible to put oneself in Moses' place. Using the Ark as a visual image, one can address questions to God or connect with higher spiritual levels, in order to receive information. This received information often pertains directly to spiritual issues and one's own personal quest.

The first stage of this meditation would be to undergo a purification process. This can be accomplished by using the *mikvah* meditation described above, accompanied by either an actual ritual immersion, physically, or a long bath. If one is preparing to stand in God's Presence, it is imperative to be pure. This means both on a physical level, as well as on a meditative and spiritual one.

Next, one should picture entering the circular Tent of Meeting and stationing oneself directly in front of the Ark at a comfortable distance. Then, take some time and feel the energy that is pulsating from the Ark. This energy is very powerful and will effect you strongly. If you feel overwhelmed at all, move back to a more comfortable distance and try it again.

Balance yourself, so that you feel that you are resonating fully with the energy that is reaching you from the Ark. You should be receiving the energy and becoming harmonized with the pulsation. Feel the warmth. Make it part of you.

Once you feel that you are at one with the energy, concentrate your attention on the area above and between the wings of the cherubs. Take a moment to thank God for the privilege of being allowed to ask and to receive important spiritual information. It is important to do this prior to asking anything of God. After giving praise and thanks, you may ask the question that you feel you need to have spiritually addressed. Continue to focus your attention on that same point above the Ark.

Bear in mind that in this meditation you are requesting information from the highest levels. Therefore, questions not of a deep spiritual nature are totally inappropriate.

Stand quietly, and wait patiently to hear the response. The response can come in different forms. It can come as a verbal response, as a flood of emotion, as a sudden insight, or as a specific sensation or series of sensations. Regardless of the form it takes, you need to draw the answer into your heart and into your mind. You have to willingly accept whatever the response is.

Remember to instruct yourself to retain complete, conscious memory of the experience and of the exact details or effects of the response received before returning to full consciousness. The meditation should be ended with a prayer of thanksgiving to God for the blessing of the insight and information received.

In summary, let me reiterate the following points. First, the use of visual imagery in meditation provides the key to experiential awareness. It creates doorways to internal change through a direct process of experiencing other realities and dimensions.

Second, these types of techniques, when properly utilized, allow the meditator to participate in a spiritual paradigm. By experiencing the process, one taps into the universal truth embedded within the model. This experiential processing then provides a deep simultaneous understanding that can only be gained and assimilated on the cognitive, emotional, and spiritual levels as they interconnect with each other.

In other words, sacred stories, because they are behavioral models that contain hidden truths, can be translated into meditative processes that lead directly to spiritual awareness and spiritual growth. The sacred stories provide the paradigm and cloak the inner, concealed truth. Activating the stories through meditation connects the soul to the path that leads to experiencing directly the inner truth.

Visualization of the stories produce the patterns of meditation. It lays out the course the meditator will take. The experience gained in the meditation by following its course completely will lead ultimately to life change and personal transformation.

3

Meditation on the Hebrew Alphabet

Within Jewish tradition, the Hebrew language is referred to as *Leshon HaKodesh*, the holy tongue. This implies a great sacredness that is inherent in the language itself. Hebrew is the language in which God Himself chose to compose the Torah and to transmit it to Israel at Mount Sinai. Moreover, it is the language of the Psalms and that of the Prophets.

In the mystic tradition, not only is the language sacred, but of particular importance are the letters of the alphabet. Not only are the structure and the very words of the sacred tongue revered, but also the alphabet itself. The letters of the Hebrew alphabet are viewed in the Kabbalah as the very foundation of Creation, the central idea being that all twenty-two letters comprising the Hebrew alphabet represent primal forces within the universe. If the universe is a construct, then the Hebrew letters are the building blocks.

The ancients emphasized the concept of the Word, the spoken utterance. The Torah, the Five Books of Moses, reflects this concept frequently. God says something and it is immediately accomplished. The speaking, or articulation, of a thought and the realization of the thought are concomitant. God says something and as He annunciates it, it becomes the Law. It manifests as an enduring reality.

Ancient belief held that speaking, formulating a concept, brought the thought into concrete reality. When one defines something by creating a word, that process brings it into being. In the Genesis story for example, all the animals of the Earth are brought forward and made to pass in front of Adam. Why? So that he could name them. His labels, distinguishing each with a name of its own, provided the animals with their own specific reality.

The animals' reality did not fully exist until names were created to designate them individually. Their identity was created by the act of speech. Moreover, by giving them names, Adam gained mastery and control over them. They were no longer an undifferentiated mass. Each species had its own name and, therefore, its own reality.

The Torah itself begins by saying, "And God said, 'Let there be Light and there was Light.'" The Word creates reality either through articulation or through command. Something is uttered that produces direct results in either case. The biblical concept is that the power of speech is the power of creativity. The Word and Creation are the same thing.

In the Jewish literature of the Greco-Roman period and in subsequent rabbinic literature, the idea was set forth that the Torah, the Law, preexisted the creation of the world. The Torah was thought to have been brought into existence prior to the creation of the universe. This concept has a lot of different ramifications, one being that the Torah is considered to be the blueprint from which the world was fashioned.

This suggests that the underpinning of the universe is moral law. Spiritual force is considered to be the first impetus. It is that which underlies all of Creation. This spiritual intermediary is the Torah, the Law. It is often referred to as "the Word of God." The link between God's will to create and Creation itself is spirit. It is reflected in mankind as spirituality and morality. Spiritual force, then, is the basis for all of Creation. That impetus, which first emerges on the ethereal plane, becomes manifest materially by the Word. God speaks and all comes into existence.

In the human world, man speaks and thoughts are expressed. A person speaks and actions are initiated. Human speech conveys both ideas and commands. A teacher giving a presentation to his class is creating a reality. He is transforming models, diagrams, charts, and pictures from objects into conceptual realities by what he is saying and demonstrating with his speech. His words are conveying thoughts and creating concepts. Understanding is forming new constructs in the minds of those listening.

A thought that is not expressed, does not create anything. It effects nothing. If the door of the office is open and there is a considerable draft, my thinking about it being closed is of no consequence. Yet, if I ask a coworker to close the door, the environment is changed. The word when spoken does create. It creates change. It makes things happen.

On both levels, the Divine and the human, the utterance of the word articulates the will, manifests the spiritual, and brings everything into being. This is expressed poignantly in Hebrew. The Hebrew term *davar*, means a "word" or a "thing." They are linguistically interwoven. They are conceptually the same. Both are assumed to be intimately related. A word spoken has become something. A person, place, or thing is synonymous with its name.

Interestingly enough, the other Hebrew term for "word," which is *Milah*, also tells us something of great importance. *Milah* comes from the Hebrew root *mool*, meaning to circumcise or to cut away. Upon reflection, the message conveyed here becomes clear. Indeed, the message is pertinent to our understanding of the word, as being primal in the process of creation. A word or a thing is something which is cut off. The image is one of something coming into its own by being cut off from its source.

The word creates individual identity. It separates what it is defining from the raw material of pure, undifferentiated thought. When the word is expressed, that which is articulated automatically assumes an independent existence and unique identity. The question arises then, what is the mechanism that forms the word and effects a transformation in the undifferentiated mass from which everything is delineated?

The answer is the alphabet. In the Kabbalah, the letters of the Hebrew alphabet are the primal material of creation. Letters are the elements which compose words. Therefore, they represent the very building blocks from which everything in the universe is constructed. Put together letter patterns and you have words. The formation of the word is its articulation. Once formed, that which it expresses emerges as reality. It is not surprising that the Kabbalah views the twenty-two letters of the alphabet as the primal forces, which interact through configuration to produce everything that exists.

This centrality of the alphabet provides us with an important and powerful tool, which allows us through meditation to access other levels of consciousness. For example, in the Kabbalah, the Law is often spoken of as being black fire on white fire. The scroll on which the Law is inscribed is comprised of white flame. The letters written thereon are described as black fire burning within.

The white flame of the scroll represents universal energy. The internal black flames, the letters, are the condensation of the universal energy into specific forms. It is the interplay of those forms that create reality. Using this image of burning black letters on the background of white flame, in meditation, is a practice hinted at quite often in kabbalist literature.

Using the analogy of hammering a piece of metal on an anvil helps illustrate this concept. The hot metal, burning white, is the undifferentiated mass. Laid upon the anvil, as the metal is struck, the sparks fly. When the hammering is completed, a specific form has been imprinted into the metal. Universal energy, here symbolized by the white hot metal, is subjected to the force of Will. It is being hammered. That creates friction and sparks, which in turn leave behind energy patterns. Boundaries are created, which produce the emergence of form. The black flames, the letters, are the imprint of form.

The Hebrew Alphabet

ה	ד	ג	ב	א
Heh	Dalet	Gimmel	Bet	Aleph
5	4	3	2	1

י	ט	ח	ז	ו
Yud	Tet	Het	Zayin	Vav
10	9	8	7	6

ס	נ	מ	ל	כ
Samekh	Nune	Mem	Lamed	Kaf
60	50	40	30	20

ר	ק	צ	פ	ע
Resh	Kuf	Tzaddi	Pey	Ayin
200	100	90	80	70

ת	ש
Tav	Shin
400	300

MEDITATING ON THE ALPHABET OF CREATION

The importance of the letters in Jewish meditation practice is very clear. If the letters are the building blocks, the primal energies out of which the universe is created, meditating on those letters brings one back to the source of everything. One can penetrate the deeper levels of reality through meditating on a word and its inherent letter patterns. Tap into the source of energy from which something emerged, tap into its name, and one taps into the hidden levels within that reality.

The first and most direct use of the Hebrew letters in meditation would be as gateways. One should concentrate on the letters as a means of reaching the basic energy vortexes within. By focusing on a Hebrew letter in deep meditation, a gateway is opened toward an inner understanding of the dynamic force that comprises the essence of this building block of creation. One gains access to the primal energy of the letter and its inner, underlying significance. To tap into the primal force of the *Aleph*, for example, is also to tap into the *Aleph* force within yourself and within all creation.

By way of illustration, let us say that one wished to focus on the letter *Bet* in order to gain an inner sense of that particular energy vortex. To accomplish this, one could utilize the images of black flame and white fire. This meditative exercise is very simple.

Meditation: Black Fire on White Fire

1. Picture a blank sheet of paper. When ready, concentrate on allowing the letter *Bet* to emerge on the page. You will have a clear image of a white page with a very distinct letter *Bet* imprinted on it.
2. Allow the paper first to assume the dimension and appearance of fire. Once comfortable with that, picture the heat spreading and igniting the letter. Allow the black flame of the *Bet* to emerge.
3. Focus your attention now on the energy, heat, and movement of the white page. Then, move your attention to the intense energy of the letter *Bet*. Allow yourself to be drawn into this primal energy.

This will either put you in touch with this selfsame energy within yourself, or will lead your meditation into a specific direction to some other place or experience. Remember, in abstract meditations, you are allowing yourself to be completely receptive. By tapping into the vortex of *Bet* energy, you are accessing that energy within yourself as well as harmonizing with that primal force within the cosmos. You can be drawn to any locale or dimension where it exists.

Another approach is to meditate with a predetermined objective. For example, the name of the letter, *Bet*, means a "house" or "domicile." It represents, therefore, the ideas of home and family, of protection, of one's internal sense of security. If one were interested in understanding more deeply one's relationship with a family member, for example, meditation on the letter *Bet* would be very valuable. Since *Bet* represents that reality, meditating on a black flaming *Bet* amidst a fiery white paper would provide a gateway toward greater experience and understanding of family relationships.

An alternate technique for accomplishing this same end would be as follows:

Meditation: Connecting with a Letter

1. Visualize the letter *Bet* at a distance, say of 10 to 15 feet in front of you. Picture it as being large and distinct. Study the visual image of the letter carefully.
2. Outline the letter with your inner eye, moving around the entire perimeter of the letter.
3. Allow the letter to start vibrating and pulsating energy. It will produce a distinct light around itself.
4. Draw the energy and the light being produced toward you. Bring it within yourself and harmonize yourself with its pulse. Flow with the light and let it affect you as it will. Experience the energy being transmitted as fully as possible.
5. When you feel the process is finished, release the light and allow it to reintegrate with the letter from which it emerged. Let the letter flow away into the distance and disappear.
6. Wait until the letter has vanished from view and then bring yourself out of the meditation by counting back from 7 to 0.

There is also a technique designed to probe the inner dimensions of what a letter represents. This is accomplished by meditating on the full spelling of the name of the letter. For example, the full spelling of the name of the letter *Bet* is *Bet, Yod, Tav*. It consists of three letters. In meditation, one can explore the inner dimensions of the *Bet* force by focusing on the whole name spelled out. This is what is referred to as the "extended name."

In this meditation, it is necessary to focus on each letter of the name, one at a time. Meditate first on seeing the whole name, *Bet, Yod, Tav*. Next, move to the first letter, *Bet*, and concentrate your attention on it exclusively. When you feel the impetus, move on. Center on the *Yod*, and when ready proceed to the *Tav* and do the same.

The next stage would be to focus on the first two letters of the name together, the *Bet* and the *Yod*. Then, focus on the *Yod* and *Tav* together. Finally, refocus your attention on the entire name again.

You may feel the need to repeat this process more than once. If so, proceed to do so. This can certainly be used as a repetitive concentration cycle. This meditation process will lead to a different type of experience, one in which you are exploring inner dimensions of the *Bet* force, rather than the *Bet* vortex.

Should one wish to go one step further, after finishing the cycle of the meditation, proceed to pronounce the name of the letter over and over again as an oral mantra. Repeat the name *Bet* over and over again out loud. One can chant the mantra by itself or in conjunction with a visualization of the name, held firmly in the mind's eye.

Another way to focus on a Hebrew letter is to study its structure and to contemplate it. Metaphysical meanings will emerge from this type of process. For this exercise, let us use the letter *Aleph*, the first letter of the Hebrew alphabet.

The letter *Aleph* signifies unity. It is the first letter of the alphabet. It is numerically equivalent to the number one. It is the first letter of *Echad*, the Hebrew word for "one." The concept behind the *Aleph* is that of oneness.

In order to gain a sense of the reality of the *Aleph* and its metaphysical significance, one is drawn to study and contemplate the physical structure of the letter. This may be accomplished in several different ways.

The first is to focus intently on the visual image of the letter. Either picture the *Aleph* in your mind while meditating, or fix your gaze upon a printed *Aleph* and contemplate its form. What sense do you get from the letter? What feelings arise? What details about the letter or its construction capture your interest? What do you sense that they mean?

This type of meditation or contemplation allows one to tap into the essence of oneness. For example, one can conceive of the *Aleph* as encompassing two distinct representations of the letter *Yod*, both of which are connected by a bar. This bar acts as a divide, both separating the two *Yod*s as well as holding and positioning them in relation to each other. One sees a *Yod* above the divide and another below it. Moreover, the lower *Yod* is in an inverted position in relation to the one above.

Symbolically, the letter *Yod* represents primal matter. It is the smallest letter of the alphabet. It is also the form out of which all other letters are constructed. The letter *Yod* by extension and enlargement can be made into every letter of the alphabet. *Yod* is the tenth letter of the alphabet, hence numerically ten. Therefore, it represents a higher dimension of "one," the number of beginning, emergence. It is the force of "one" being made functional.

In the letter *Aleph* there is a horizon above which stands a primal force, the *Yod* above the line, and below which primal matter is reflected, in the second *Yod*. There is a *Yod* above and an inverted *Yod* below. This suggests the concept that what is above is reflected below. As there is unity in the higher realms, in the heavens, so there is also unity on the Earth. The unity of the cosmos reflects the unity of the unseen realms beyond it, the unity of the physical body being a reflection of the unity of the soul.

There is great significance in the fact that there exists a barrier that both separates the two levels and yet binds them as well. The image points to the realization that Heaven and Earth are a composite whole, even though there is a divide that keeps them apart. It symbolizes that amidst apparent diversity there is an underlying oneness and that the realm of physical existence is inextricably connected to the spiritual realm.

What is also indicated in the structure of the *Aleph*, in the fact that the lower *Yod* is the inverse of the upper one, is that as one moves up through multiple levels of reality, a continual reversal of polarities takes place. As one ascends the ladder of consciousness to higher levels, each dimension one passes through mirrors that of the one above it in an endless chain of flip-flopping realities.

In experiencing other levels and other dimensions of reality in meditation, this is a very important principle to comprehend. If one passes from our normal physical level of reality to the next level up, one will likely encounter a world that is reversed from our own normal cognitive experience. For example, in moving to a level of consciousness directly above the physical one, what would be tangible and observable at that level may well be our thoughts and feelings, rather than what we do or say. Our actions and their ramifications may only be experienced there internally as inner reality, the opposite of what we experience normally in our day-to-day waking lives.

This pattern would exist up through the "worlds" one would encounter, each level of reality reflecting and reversing both its predecessor and successor. What we are familiar with as reality would not be experienced on the next level up, but rather on the level right beyond it. So traveling up the ladder, every other rung would represent an increasingly more sophisticated dimension of reality that would parallel our own. The intervening ones, being their counterparts, would be the inverse of the preceding level. These inverse realities are increasingly more developed, alternate realities reflecting ours.

Another observation that can be made about the structure of the *Aleph* is that it can be seen as an amalgam of the letters *Bet* and *Tsaddi*. The upper *Yod* melded to the bar forms the letter *Bet*. The lower *Yod* melded to the bar from the other direction forms the letter *Tsaddi*. These two letters, when put together, spell two different yet very pertinent words.

The combination *Bet-Tsaddi* produces the word *Botz*, meaning mud. Mud symbolizes primal matter. From the admixture of Earth and water, all things emerge and develop. The concept here, implicit in the *Aleph*, is that the mud, the primal matter of Creation, both emerges from and reflects the unity of God, the One.

A reversal of the two letters produces the word *Tsav*, meaning turtle. Among the American Indians, particularly in the mythology of the Algonquin, the Iroquois, and the Mohawk, a turtle was responsible for the retrieval of a small ball of mud from the floor of the primal ocean out of which grew Earth. In India, the tortoise supports on its back the four elephants that hold up the world. And in China, the turtle was the symbol for the universe as a whole. The turtle's shell represented the heavens circling the Earth. The Earth, in turn, was seen as the square stomach beneath the shell.

The *Aleph* as a composite of the letters *Tsaddi* and *Bet*, spelling "turtle," would suggest that out of the unity, mud, primordial matter emerges, along with the organizational force that allows matter to be formed into separate entities and systems. The unity of God's purpose unfolds initially as an intertwined dualism. The oneness of God's will first manifests simultaneously, both as undifferentiated matter, on one hand, and the universal organizing principle, on the other. The interaction of the two, subsequently, will create all that is.

Now it is time to move from the structure of the letters to their meanings. By focusing on meaning, we gain access to inner function.

The name of each letter of the alphabet has a specific meaning. By meditating on the letter in conjunction with its meaning, we are lead in a different direction. Meditating on the meaning of a letter focuses our attention and understanding on the process in Creation that is represented by it.

Take the letter *Lamed* for example. One can gain a sense of the power of the *Lamed* and the type of energy it represents, by focusing on the name. The name *Lamed* comes from the verb root *LMD* (*Lamed, Mem, Dalet*), meaning both to teach and to learn. So one of the primary meanings of this letter is "teaching" and "learning." This suggests the concept of experience, since everything we experience in life is a learning process. We learn from doing.

Moreover, learning is also a process of discovery. As such it often leads to shifts in thinking and behavior. Hence, the letter *Lamed* symbolizes different dimensions of human experience. It represents Life Force, learning and knowledge, cumulative experience, and maturation. It can also represent change of thinking and direction.

If one were seeking to strengthen their capacity to learn or to assimilate information, for example, or were working on their ability to convey their ideas to other people more effectively, then meditating on the *Lamed* would be a primary focal point. Meditation on the *Lamed*, which means learning, would be the logical tool for strengthening one's learning ability or teaching capacity.

Conversely, if in the process of meditation one suddenly encounters the appearance of a *Lamed* unexpectedly, it is of use to be able to fall back on an understanding of its meaning. If in a meditation, the letter *Lamed* suddenly appears, one should focus on its meaning in order to interpret the significance of the *Lamed*'s appearance in relationship to the experience.

Each of the letters of the Hebrew alphabet has a name. Each name has a specific meaning. Each meaning has many different ramifications, both on a practical and on a metaphysical level. One should become familiar with each of the letters' names and meanings. By focusing intuitively on the name of a letter and its meaning, the ramifications of a letter in any given context will become clear.

A simple example would be as follows:

One is meditating on a current problem or situation in life. An answer or sense of direction is being sought. The letter *Lamed* emerges. This would suggest that something either needs to be learned or needs to be taught to someone else. In some contexts it could mean that what one needs to go through is necessary as a learning experience. In another context, it may be saying that the answer to the issue being considered requires drawing on past experience or a knowledge base accessible to the meditator. Intuiting the answer comes from placing the meaning of *Lamed* in the context of the question.

There is another application of the principle of extension. It is an understood principle among kabbalists that a Hebrew word represents an inner dimension of the letter it begins with. Any word for example that starts with the letter *Gimmel* will embody a dimension, an aspect, of the *Gimmel* force. Therefore, should a *Gimmel* appear in meditation, one can gain a hold on its significance by utilizing this principle with the following technique.

Meditation: Letter Extension

1. Picture a blank white sheet of paper. Next, visualize a Hebrew letter at the right hand side of the page. Leave room for it to extend itself.
2. Meditate on the chosen letter until you feel a shift in energy. Then, focus your attention to the blank area immediately to the left of the letter.
3. Wait for other letters to emerge. The word that is spelled out in the process will have direct bearing on the earlier meditation and the message that is being transmitted. It should tell you what the letter is meant to symbolize.

For example, let us assume that one is meditating on why he is really dissatisfied with his job. In the meditation, the individual has the sensation, first, of being very cold. As that passes, he feels as if he were marching through a long tunnel. As he emerges from the tunnel, he sees a white light. Amid the light, the letter *Gimmel* appears.

In a subsequent meditation, the meditator seeks to get a sense of what the *Gimmel* actually meant in this particular context. So, he pictures the letter *Gimmel* on a white piece of paper, near the right margin, about halfway down the page. He focuses first on the *Gimmel* and then on the area immediately to its left. By so doing, the word *Gevurah* develops from the *Gimmel* and becomes very distinct. The term means "courage, strength, endurance."

Piecing all the imagery and symbolism together should give one a fair indication of what the meditation is conveying. A possible interpretation would be that the meditator is dissatisfied with the job he has, because he has lost interest.

There is also the feeling of being cold. It could well be that something has happened that makes our meditator feel that he has been left out in the cold, perhaps a change in the work place of some sort.

Passing through the tunnel may suggest the need for going through a transition. It may signal the need to move on. The *Gimmel*, which transformed itself into the word for courage and endurance, would then seem to indicate what is needed in order to accomplish successfully the required process of change. This individual needs to be courageous and to overcome the fear. Persistence in the face of difficulty may be the route to successful change in his case.

If one wishes to gain a sense of what type of courage would be required, or just to get in touch with the sensation, reverse the process. Picture the letters of the word *Gevurah* being, one by one, absorbed back into the *Gimmel*. Meditate on the remaining letter. One should experience the force *Gimmel* exerts as the root of courage.

This is a variation of a similar kabbalist practice that is called *Notarikon*, which means "notation." It presupposes that a word can be an acronym for an entire phrase or sentence. As a meditation, this type of practice is often used to gain insight into something that is being stated or labeled. For example, say a person wishes to gain a deeper understanding of the effect of good in the world. He could take a phrase from the Bible that seems to bear on the subject and condense it into a meditative letter pattern. This would act as a gateway, allowing access to the hidden reality of the operation of good in the world.

Meditation: A *Notarikon* Meditation

A good example of this practice would be to use the phrase from Psalms, "Light is sown for the righteous and joy for the upright of heart."

אור זרוע לצדיק ולישרי לב שמחה

Light is sown for the righteous and for the upright of heart, joy.

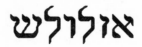

In Hebrew, the phrase is, *"Or zaru'a latzaddik ul'yishrei lev simcha."* Taking the initial letter from each word, I get *Aleph, Zayin, Lamed, Vav, Lamed, Seen.*

I now have *AZLVLS* as a pattern upon which to meditate. Light being created by righteous acts can now be approached experientially, by focusing on this six-letter sequence. By meditating on *AZLVLS*, as if it were a word, I can access the deeper meanings of "light being sown for the righteous." This may come as an understanding of how the righteous manifest good in the world. It may come as a vision of light and benefit being created by someone's righteous action. It may come as a revelation of the effects one's own light has produced in the world. What may come as a result of this meditation is as infinite in possibilities as there are lights in the world and righteous deeds.

Now, it is time to move another step and delve into the geometry of Creation. Let's examine how the letters of the alphabet interact with each other, forming the patterns of Creation.

THE ALPHABET AND GEOMETRIC STRUCTURE

According to *Sefer Yetzirah*, one of the oldest kabbalist texts in existence, there are three Hebrew letters that are referred to as the Mother Letters. That is, these three letters constitute the primary focal points for the entire alphabet, under which all other letters can be subsumed.

The three Mother Letters are the *Aleph*, the *Mem*, and the *Shin*. This trio represents the entire alphabet, for they are the first, middle, and second to last letter of the alphabet respectively. They embody three distinct spiritual principles. *Alef* signifying *Avir*, air or ether, *Mem* representing *Mayim*, water, and *Shin* standing for *e'SH*, fire.

The *Aleph* (air) is the neutral principle. All of creation emerges from the neutral. Neutrality is balance. Neutrality is harmony. *Alef* is movement and direction. It is the motion and directedness of harmony and balance. *Alef* is spiritual force as it operates in the cosmos. It is the breath of life. Being the first letter of the alphabet, it is also the origin of all.

The letter *Aleph* has no sound. It is interesting to note that all of being, all of creation, is predicated on silence, silence being construed as nothingness. All of creation emanates from absolute nothingness. Significantly, *Aleph* is the first letter of the word, *Ayin*, meaning nothingness.

The second letter of the trio, *Mem*, stands in the middle of the alphabet. *Mem*, the first letter of the word *Mayim*, water, represents the principle of fluidity. Here, we have the processes of birth, of sustenance, of change, of emotion, and of development. The *Mem* represents internal movement and transformation.

Mem is receptivity. It receives and reacts, taking impetus in and giving birth, definition, and nurturing to it. It is the receptive force that accepts the creative force, limits it, forms it, and produces reality, an ever-changing reality that continually evolves.

Its counterpart, the last of the three letters, *Shin*, is fire. Fire being creative energy, reflects creation itself. This is the motivation principle, that which activates. *Shin* is the force of ideas, the force of will, the drive to create.

What is interesting is the sequence of the letters in the alphabetic order. *Aleph* is the transcendent principle that emerges first. It is nothing, yet everything emanates from it. *Mem* follows, being the receptive, the passive principle. Last to arrive is the *Shin*, which is creative force. This is the order of their emergence and emanation from God.

When one reverses the order and moves back toward the source, what one encounters is first creative energy. The movement of the energy, in turn, is received and then defined and formed, the final result of the subsequent developmental process being transcendence and unification with the source, the origin. So, movement within the alphabet is circular. One moves through the letters to the final extension of the alphabet, only to reverse course and ultimately reintegrate with the first of the Mother letters, *Aleph*, the One. This constant circular flow is the pattern of creation.

Here we reach a critical point of understanding. This circular flow pattern is very important. Here is one of the chief, underlying concepts regarding creation found in the Kabbalah. It is one that is very pertinent in the application of kabbalistic principles to meditation technique. That is, Creation is a two-way street. It extends itself to its furthest limit, only to return to itself. Creation is the manifestation of Will. The resulting activity of the Will, being manifest, becomes the process of finding its way back to its origin.

The beginning and the end are on one hand reflections of each other and on the other hand, are the same thing, depending on viewpoint. For example, my moving a bicycle off the driveway is the resulting action stemming from my will, my desire to back my car out of the garage and down the driveway to the street. This action, in turn, is the process by which my will is fulfilled. The will itself has no real reality without concrete expression. Notice that the movement here is circular: the action taken is the result of will, and the will is the result of the accomplishment of the action. They are reflections of each other, yet they are also two sides of the same coin. They are two coincident points constituting one reality.

As the Kabbalah points out, a point can expand in two different manners. It can expand in a specific direction and become manifest as a line, or it can expand in all directions simultaneously and become a circle. Linear and circular movement are simply two distinct viewpoints, two dimensions of the development of a point.

Breathing is an excellent, prime example of this duality within unity. Breathing is life. The process is a whole, a unity. Without breath there is no life. Yet, within the unity of the breathing process, there is an external duality: inhalation and exhalation. It is critical to understand, that this duality is really only a reflection, a different expression of the unity. One inhales and as a result, must then exhale. By exhaling one creates, in turn, the need to inhale. You have cause and effect inducing each other. An inhale is the cause of an exhale and the result of the ex-halation, at the same time. They are both distinct from each other in function, but identical in terms of relationship.

By dealing with movement, with the flow of Creation, one is deal-ing with external duality, which reflects and expresses the internal unity of Creation. Duality is the process. Unity is the essence.

The *Aleph-Mem-Shin* trio are focal points representing nature and the primary structure of Creation. *Aleph* is neutrality, balance, the inner unity of Creation. *Mem* and *Shin* are the opposites of water and fire, the interaction between them fueling the energy and movement of Creation. They are reflected in breath and the breathing process. *Mem*, the sound *MM*, is the sound of inhaling. *Shin*, *SH*, is the sound of exhal-ing. *Aleph*, having no sound, is the silence, the balance point, the stop that allows the process to reverse, between breaths. The *Aleph* is one. It is neither the one nor the other. Yet it is also both of them. This is the great mystery of existence.

One is all. The All encompasses the two, which emanate from one, making them both distinct. Yet the two are really one. All that is, is cre-ated out of nothing.

How does a person come to terms with this mystery in meditation? The answer of the Kabbalah is that it comes through focus on the Mother Letters, *Aleph, Mem,* and *Shin.* Let me illustrate by quoting from one of the great early hasidic masters, Rabbi Levi Yitzhak of Bereditchev.

In commenting on the first chapter of the Book of Genesis, Levi Yitzhak draws on a line from the prophet Ezekiel (Ezekiel 1:14) to explain the relationship between nothingness and existence. It reads, "And the creatures burst forth and returned as the appearance of lightning." Levi Yitzhak expounded as follows.

Reality is consciousness moving up and back between existence and nonexistence. Consciousness is focused within the cosmos, which emanates at all times from God.

"Therefore we say that He forms light and creates darkness, not that He formed light and created darkness. Rather, it is in the present tense. For at every moment He forms everything and at every instant He sends an abundance of Life Force to all the living. Everything emanates from the Holy One, Blessed be He, and He is complete within Himself. He is inclusive of everything.

Since man comes from nothing, when he knows that he really is nothing and that there is only the Creator, Blessed be He, the Holy One gives him strength and force." The idea here is that the universe becomes manifest to man, when man realizes he is nothing. God creates the world for man from that frame of reference.

"Moreover, when man looks at himself and does not see the nothingness then he is operating on the level of being, it being only appropriate to refer to the Creator's activity as having formed. That is He created man already." At this point, man is aware of his own existence. Hence, his relationship to God is operating at that moment from the standpoint of existence. There is a constant fluctuation in consciousness between being and nothingness or Non-Being.

"It is said in the writings of Rabbi Isaac Luria that God is King from the standpoint of nothingness. For God is King in the act of giving His children Life Force. He is in the aspect of Nothingness, in that we have nothing except for what the Holy One, Blessed be He, gives His children. The aspect of Nothingness rules and directs everything from above or beyond nature. However, Being directs things from within nature."

Levi Yitzhak goes on to say that the concept "bursting through and returning, like the appearance of lightning" refers to this process of oscillating consciousness between being and nothingness. When we are attuned to nothingness, we open the gate for the Divine influx. When we attune to being, creation unfolds and we understand the inner nature of things.

The *Aleph* is the first letter of the word *Ayin*, nothingness, as well as the first letter of the word *Ani*, "I." Meditating on the *Aleph* becomes the tool for focusing on Being and Nothingness, facilitating deep understanding of the inner connections within reality and the influx of Divine force that sustains it.

There are various techniques by which this may be accomplished. Meditating on the *Aleph-Mem-Shin* is to focus on the duality within the unity of creation and on the creative process. One can meditate on each letter in sequence. Here, one is centering on the realities of the neutral principle, the energy principle, and the principle of receptivity. At the same time, one is exploring the inner relationship between them.

Another alternative is to meditate on the three as a unit, either as a triangle or as circular movement—that is, either *Aleph-Mem-Shin* in continuous rotation or from *Aleph* to *Shin*, and then back again from *Shin* to *Aleph*.

The final approach would be to synchronize the letters with one's breathing pattern. Visualize *Mem* with every inhale, *Aleph* with every pause, and *Shin* with every exhale. Whichever method you choose, remember, combining the rhythm of breath and movement with focus on the visual patterns of the letters in combination with each other will in any of these techniques be the key.

Meditation 1

1. Get in a relaxed and comfortable position. Begin a cadenced breathing pattern, four breaths in and four breaths out.
2. After you feel comfortable and are breathing evenly for a while, breathe in for four counts, stop and hold your breath for two counts, breathe out for four counts and stop for two counts. Continue to maintain this breathing pattern, until you feel ready to move on.
3. Now, listen carefully to your breath as you inhale and exhale. Listen carefully also, to the silence of each stop. Listen just as intently.
4. Then when ready, visualize a *Mem* (מ) as you breathe in. Visualize an *Aleph* (א) every time you stop for two counts and visualize a Shin (ש) as you breathe out.
5. At this point, you may choose to go into a state of free flow and let yourself go. Or you may wish to reach a state of either energy or of tranquility and experience it fully.
6. Bring yourself back to conscious waking reality by saying a prayer of thanksgiving and counting back from 6 to 0.

מ	א	ש
2	3	1
2	3	1
2	3	1
2	3	1

Meditation 2

1. Relax and through balanced breathing, enter a state of relaxation and meditation.
2. Picture three pillars. They are hollow, with light within them. The light may be either transparent or translucent. Each pillar has three parts, a capital at the top, a stalk in the center, and a base at the bottom.
3. When you feel comfortable, picture a *Shin* (ש) sitting on top of the right-hand pillar, an *Aleph* (א) upon the middle pillar, and a *Mem* (מ) on top of the left-hand pillar.
4. Starting with the base of each pillar, send energy up the pillars, one at a time, to the letter at the top. Wait until the letter is fully vibrating or pulsating with energy, prior to moving on to the next pillar.
5. When all three pillars and letters are energized, focus your meditation on the letter that most attracts your interest. Flow with that letter and its energy to wherever it wishes to take you. You may wish to do this with all three letters in sequence.
6. You may wish to end the meditation at this point. If you wish to go one step further, return to the image of the three pillars. Picture all three together. Add energy to the two outer pillars,

the *Shin* and *Mem*. By relaxing and remaining focused on the two external pillars, you will experience different dimensions of the relationship between them.

7. By focusing on the movement of energy from the *Shin* to the *Mem*, you will gain experience of the reality of God's interaction in the world, in Creation, and in the creative process. *Shin-Mem* spell out the Hebrew word *Shem*, meaning "name." In this case, it refers to the Names of God, the dimensions of God's creativity.

8. By focusing on the movement of energy from *Mem* to *Shin*, you will gain a sense of human emotion and its relationship to Creation and creativity. One can heighten their creative capacity and output by so focusing. The letters spell the Hebrew word *mahsh*, meaning "feeling and touching."

9. If you have all three pillars vibrating at an equal rate and center your meditation on the middle pillar, you will experience interrelationship, all the inner connections that link inner and outer reality. If you wish to bring energies into balance, you would also focus your attention in this manner.

10. If you energize the middle pillar, it begins to vibrate more strongly than the two external ones. Focus your meditation on that pillar. Tap into the relationship between man and God, that which is between Creation and God. The middle pillar is governed by the *Aleph*, which is the first letter of the word *Ayin*, meaning "nothingness." This refers to the Nothingness out of which God continually creates the whole of Creation.

11. Steps 7 through 10 are optional. When you feel you have finished your meditation session, return to consciousness by counting backward from 6 to 0. As always, saying a prayer before doing so is very appropriate.

Note: The relationships between the pillars can be understood best by noting the meanings of the letter combinations formed. The relationship between the right and left pillar is (שם), meaning "name" (God's creative presence). The relationship between the left and right pillar is (מש), meaning "feel, touch" (Man's creative presence). The relationship between the middle and right pillars is that of (אש), meaning "fire" (the emergence of Creative Force from the Nothingness). The relationship between the middle and left pillars is that of (אם), "mother," referring to birthing, nurturing, the function of the Mother Letters.

Levi Yitzhak points out that the aspect of Nothingness rules everything beyond nature and that the aspect of Being rules everything within nature. He states that when a person focuses on self-abnegation, sensing the nothingness within that sustains his being, he affirms his ever-present connection with the Creator. When he focuses on his own separate being, a person affirms himself and his own creative potential.

A logical question would be, how does this apply to everyday human experience? What is the practical application of this truth?

According to the *Zohar*, observing the commandments of God is a process that is both the hidden and the revealed. The word for commandment in Hebrew is *mitzvah (MTzVH)*, spelled *Mem, Tzaddi, Vav, Heh*. By a process of letter reversal known as *Atbash*, the equivalent of the first two letters *Mem* and *Tzaddi* necessarily would be replaced by the letters *Yod* and *Heh*. That would transform the word into *YHVH*, the name of God. What was hidden in the commandment (*MTzVH*) is God's name (*YHVH*).

According to Levi Yitzhak, the hidden aspect, God's Name, reflects the Nothingness underlying Creation and the apparent aspect is the revelation, the Divine that is reflected in what we do. The commandment is the relationship of Non-Being with being made manifest.

The central idea here is that man's actions, fulfilling what God expects, is a process of unifying that which is beyond knowledge and beyond our sense of being, with that which is clear, comprehensible, and within our power to achieve.

Atbash Substitution

ה=צ	ד=ק	ג=ר	ב=ש	א=ת
י=מ	ט=נ	ח=ס	ז=ע	ו=פ
		כ=ל		

commandment = מצוה

מ צ וה

יה becomes מצ

remaking the word

יהוה

(The Name of God)

Our ability to do and to achieve creates a link between conscious action and the desire to fulfill God's expectations on the one hand, and our awareness on a deep level of all that is totally beyond our ability to comprehend on the other.

The interplay between Being and Non-Being, knowing and not knowing, between Nothingness and existence is the oscillation of life and of consciousness itself.

How do we connect on a practical level the idea of Being and Non-Being with that of the oscillation of consciousness between them?

The answer is in the doing. To learn more about oneself and to draw closer to God in meditation is an active process. In order to gain an inner knowledge of what God expects from us, one must be in tune with the oscillation of existence, the fluctuation between Non-Being and Being, between consciousness and that which lies beyond it.

The meditations for tuning in to this center around the three Mother Letters. We draw closer to God by learning to harmonize with the oscillation between being and Non-Being. This process is reflected in the nature of the three Mother Letters and in their relationship to each other.

Meditation 3

Accessing the inner Self and experiencing closeness to God through Self or through Creation can be achieved using a very primal meditation of the Mother Letters. Here is how:

1. Close your eyes and relax. Let all emotions, thoughts, and feelings flow out of you until you are completely emptied.
2. Once that is done, spend some time contemplating Nothingness. Focus your complete attention on a void. Consider that the aspect of your being closest to God is beyond time and space.
3. Exhale completely and stop. Do not immediately inhale. Remain in a position of stasis for a couple of seconds before you resume breathing. While in stasis, focus all your attention on this point of Nothingness between inhalation and exhalation.
4. Now, resume a cadenced breathing. Begin listening carefully and fully to the sounds of the breath entering and leaving in sequence. Experience the inrush and outflow of energy.
5. When you are ready, make the sound of *MM* as you breathe in and the sound of *SH* as you breathe out. Use the sounds as a

mantra. Concentrate on the sounds and the energy of the chanting as it develops.

6. At an appropriate point, stop the chanting and resume normal
   breathing. Focus your attention on the silence, the absence of
   sound. Let yourself be carried by the silence.
7. To conclude the meditation, return to normal waking consciousness by counting down from 6 to 0.

In understanding the alphabet and its relationship to structure, one
needs to keep foremost in mind that on the one hand, the Hebrew letters are component parts of the alphabet, and on the other, that the letters by themselves traditionally have numerical correspondences.

Though the letters are self-contained realities, they are also building blocks of all other realities when they interrelate with each other.
The alphabet is the primal structure, that of the natural flow of the Hebrew letters, sequencing the building blocks into a specific general pattern. Each letter has a specific position within the alphabet flow and has
a corresponding numerical value as well.

The numerical structure is simple. *Aleph* through *Tet* represent one
through nine. *Yod* through *Tsaddi* account for ten through ninety, and
Kof through *Tav* signify one hundred through four hundred.

Any sequence of combined letters will either spell out a word or
represent a number—frequently both, since any word will have a corresponding numerical value, if the letters are totaled up.

The alphabet itself is the undifferentiated flow of creation. It is the
sequence of creation as well. When dealing with the undifferentiated flow
of creation or creativity, you encounter the letters in a specific progression, the alphabet, that of sequential unfolding, one number after another.

When a word is created, one is taking elements out of the undifferentiated flow of the alphabet, combining specific forces and creating
defined realities. Those realities emerge both as conceptions and as specific numbers. One creates then both form, words, and pattern, number.

The Life Force of the universe is the flow of the alphabet, the undifferentiated flux, the harmony of numerical sequence. Creativity, formation, takes place when elements are removed from the flux and made
into a construct, either a word or a number. The construct produces
individual, manifest realities.

The process of combining universal forces to create something
specific and individual is reflected verbally and numerically when letters are conjoined into words. This process of creating form, individual

structure, and definition is referred to in Hebrew as Gematria, meaning "geometry."

The implication here is clear. Creative force is an unfolding process of sequence and order, the alphabet and the flow of numbers. Creativity is the construct of elements from that flow into defined interrelating patterns, which produce individualized reality. The selection of elements and their geometric relationship, when combined into words, form a set structure, which in turn produces a specific reality.

The Kabbalah has always maintained that if one understood the numbers and the corresponding geometric relationship within a word or phrase, one would come to see the inner structure of the reality the given term describes. Moreover, one perceives the basis for understanding those connections that bind one individual element in the universe to another.

The best way to understand this principle is through some examples. A simple use of *Gematria* would be "numeric analysis." Let us take the Hebrew word *Emet* ('MT). *Emet* is broken down into three letters, *Aleph* ('), *Mem* (M), and *Tav* (T). Each letter has a numeric value. *Aleph* is 1. *Mem* is 40. *Tav* is 400. Taking a total of all three numbers, one has the sum of 441.

Look at the structure of the number: 4, 4, 1. The number four represents concrete physical reality. Four is symbolized by a square, an enclosure. It completely defines an area, representing borders. We speak of the four directions, the four winds, the four seasons of the year, the four limbs of the body. Even the palm of the hand is square. Four is the number of the physical and the tangible.

Notice that here the number four duplicates itself. The term *Emet*, meaning "truth," is divided into a sequence of three numbers, the first two of which are 4. Reality is duplicated. The first 4 is outer reality, being at the edge and forefront of the word. The second 4 represents inner reality, being in between the 4 and the 1. The word culminates in the number 1, representing unity.

The number 441 indicates something about truth and about the process of arriving at the truth. There are two fours and a one conjoined, the fours representing inner and outer reality, the one representing oneness. Truth, therefore, both internally and externally, is one. It is consistent within itself. Moreover, a person must first deal with both external then with internal reality in order to arrive at the truth, the oneness.

There is a strong message in the number sequence of the word *Emet*, truth. Though truth is consistent within itself, in order to reach it, one must go through a three-stage process—first, of penetrating the outer features of something, then, of coming to terms with the inner dynamics, and finally, of reaching the core, the truth, by understanding the inherent unity of the two.

Now, let us take all three numbers, add them together, and form a base number. Four plus four plus one equal nine. So, the base number of the word *Emet* would be nine.

The number nine represents completion. Nine is the last number before the leap to an additional digit. It completes a cycle. It is the last number in the numerical sequence. On a metaphysical level, this number symbolizes fulfillment. Here, one finds another dimension of truth. One reaches a state of completion, of fulfillment, of integration and integrity on a total level when dealing solely with the truth.

To take this process one step further, let us consider some other words in Hebrew which, like *Emet*, have a numeric total of 441. The assumption of the kabbalists is that there is an internal and indeed intrinsic relationship between any two words or phrases in the Hebrew language that have the same numerical value.

Sister words to *Emet*, that is, those with the same numerical total, would include words such as *Atem*, meaning "all of you," *V'hayiti*, "and I will be," *Talveh*, "you will lend," *Tilveh*, "you will borrow," *T'vatel*, "she will cancel," *Titavel*, "you will be immersed," and *Me'Et*, "from."

The connection between some of these words is self-evident upon reflection. For example, *Emet* (truth) is related to *Me'Et* (from). The implication is that everything comes from the truth. *Emet* is connected to *T'vatel* (she will cancel). *Emet* is a feminine word. Truth will cancel out everything that is not the truth. Truth will ultimately triumph. This is accomplished by total involvement in the truth. *Titavel*, "you shall be immersed, baptized" in the truth.

A further use of the numerical value of *Emet* would be, to equate it with a phrase that has the same value or with one that is logically related. For example, the phrase from Exodus 34:6 reads, "Adonai, Adonai, El Rachum V'Hanun" (ADONAI, ADONAI, Merciful and Compassionate God). The numerical total of the phrase is 451. That is 441 plus 10. Four hundred fifty-one is the value of *Emet*, truth, plus the number of emanations in the process of Creation. God's mercy and compassion is the truth that fills and sustains the entire process of Creation.

Ten represents the stages in the process of Creation, from God's Will to the manifestation of the physical universe. The implication here is that truth moving down through all the levels of emanation, from God's

Will to our level of existence, manifests itself as God's graciousness and compassion. Our experience of Divine truth is as recipients of His Mercy and Compassion as it unfolds in our lives.

Gematria can also be looked at in terms of dimensionality. The first six natural numbers all represent specific geometric shapes. The number one represents a point. Two points produce a line. Three points connected by line is a triangle. Four points form a square, while five make a pentagon and six constitute a hexagon. Four, five, and six have the advantage of having internal diagrams—the cross, the pentacle, and the Star of David, in that order.

Seven is the first number that does not constitute a simple geometric shape. There is movement to a different dimension geometrically. It is not surprising that seven represents *Shabbat*, the Sabbath. "Six days shalt thou labor and do all thy work, but the seventh is the *Shabbat* of the Lord, your God" (Exodus 20:9). Seven represents dimensional leap, transcendence to another level of existence.

The first six numbers represent logical, definable, symmetrical forms. Seven is beyond that pattern. There are six forms, six days of the week in which things are formed and the seventh, the day of rest, the neutrality principle.

The symbolism of each number is also very clear. One is a point. It is focus. Two, a line, represents motion and direction. Three, a triangle, is time and development. It pictures the process of a point extending and becoming a line. It is evolution and creativity. The point is the apex of the triangle and the line is the base. This would suggest that the triangle represents the Time-Space continuum.

Four, the square, is limitation and definition, the restriction and delineation of time and space. Five represents the five senses, perception. Six constitutes the full dimensionality of the three-dimensional world. Our world is duality operating within three dimensions. Hence, there are six facets, forward-backward, up-down, and right-left.

Moreover, The Star of David, the internal geometry of the number six, is constituted by two interlocking triangles, one pointing upward and one downward. Here we have a picture of the interaction of creative forces, two sets of energy interlocking. Human will, emanating from below, expands upward, interlocking and interacting with Divine Will. The Will of God, simultaneously, emanates from above and expands downward. The blending of these two wills is signified by the interaction of the two triangles of the Star.

My point is that *Gematria* represents geometric structure. When meditating or contemplating on Gematria in its structural mode, one can gain insight into the inner meaning of things. It is through the connections that can be seen, or even just sensed, in the patterning of words and phrases, that hidden meaning is revealed.

For example, if we took the word *Makom*, the word for "space," and added up the numeric value of each letter, we would have a total of 186. Add each of the numbers together, 1 plus 8 plus 6, and the sum is 15. 1 plus 5 equals 6. The base number therefore of *Makom*, space, is 6. Six is the number that signifies the interaction of will within all facets of three-dimensional space. In other words, at base level, space reflects itself, the six directions, as well as that which allows for all will to act and react. Quite a contemplative exercise!

Seven, as mentioned, is the rest point, the neutrality point, and the gateway to other dimensions. It is the number of holiness. Eight is, geometrically, two interlocked squares. Eight, therefore, represents the duality of inner and outer existence. It is the interrelationship of inner and outer reality as manifest on the physical plane. Nine, similar to seven, has no simple intrinsic geometric shape. Nine is the last of the single-digit numbers. It stands for fulfillment, completion. This reflects back on the number seven. Where seven is neutrality, nine is totality.

Any word in the Hebrew language has a numerical value. That value, in turn, can be reduced to a base number. There is a geometry to most of those numbers and an inner spiritual meaning to all of them. Both the numeric values and the geometric patterns derived from any word reflect heavily on their spiritual significance and inner meaning. Understanding this principle is the key to many productive variations by which meditation or contemplation can be applied to Hebrew language.

Before delving into the geometry of the *Sefirot* and the meaning implicit in structure, it is important to gain a clear understanding of the nature of the *Sefirot* themselves. This requires careful consideration of the *Sefirot*, the stages of emanation, as the transition and the link between Nothingness and Creation. An understanding of their nature and an exploration of the meditative techniques that involve penetrating them stand at the very core of kabbalist practice. We need to consider them next.

4

The *Sefirot* of Formlessness: Imprinting as the Foundation of Creation

The letters of the Hebrew alphabet are the forces of creativity and transformation. Before one can understand the use of the Hebrew letters in deep meditation, it is important to gain a clear understanding of the nature and process referred to as imprinting. On the highest levels of Creation, the elemental forces of the Hebrew alphabet are seen as impacting directly on primal energy, thereby bringing created forms into existence. This process of imprinting as the foundation for Creation is described carefully in the first chapter of the ancient kabbalist classic, *Sefer Yetzirah* (*The Book of Formation*).

To understand the concept of imprinting, let us use the analogy of visual projection. Picture a slide projector. A slide projector is designed to manifest a picture or visual image on a screen for viewing. It has a powerful lamp or bulb to provide intense light and a lens to focus the image that is being projected.

Without a slide to insert in between the lamp and the lens, the only thing that will be projected onto the screen is blank light. One will see nothing but a blank, illuminated screen. A slide contains an image that is constituted by a pattern, comprised of the interplay between light and shadow. The two forces of light and dark on the slide play off each other. They create form and image, through the contrasts produced by their interaction.

Hebrew letters are often referred to as black fire on white fire. The polarity of light and dark create the primal force that is the Hebrew letter on a cosmic level. The contrast of light and dark interacting forms the letter. Once formed, the power of the letter facilitates bringing things into reality. The letters are the building blocks of Creation.

Different combinations of letters produce different patterns. Each pattern is unique and each represents something specific, some particular reality, waiting to be made manifest in the universe. A letter or a letter pattern is a cosmic slide.

In a projector, the light being generated is undifferentiated. It has substance but no form. It illuminates the screen but produces nothing identifiable or comprehensible. The light facilitates, but it does not create. Something has to act on it before anything is actually created.

The insertion of a slide into the projector completes the process. The undifferentiated light passes through the filter of the slide. By so doing, the light is filtered by the pattern on the slide. The result is that the light conforms to the pattern on the slide. This is imprinting.

The light itself becomes differentiated by passing through the pattern on the slide. It is this pattern that is then projected onto the screen as an identifiable image. In the same manner, if one were to pass a laser beam through a holographic plate, the result of the interaction of the light beam and the pattern on the plate it passes through is the projection of a three dimensional image.

The pattern on the slide or on the holographic plate serve as imprints. The light is imprinted by the filtering and ordering effect of the pattern. It conforms to the pattern and the energy of the light is transformed into an image. Looking at the universe from this perspective, what the Kabbalah is saying is extremely profound.

According to the Kabbalah, God's Will, the will to create, produces Pure Light. This Pure Light is primordial. It is Life Force itself. Life Force runs through the entire fabric of Creation. By nature, this Pure Light is undifferentiated. When it becomes differentiated, Creation comes about as the result. Created essences come into being when the light of Life Force passes through the filter of the *Sefirot* and the Hebrew letters and is thereby imprinted with a pattern. That pattern, energized and sustained by the light, becomes something. It becomes a created essence or being.

In short, according to the *Sefer Yetzirah*, God created two interlocking sets of variables with which to craft Creation. They are the *Sefirot*, the ten dimensions, and the twenty-two letters of the Hebrew alphabet.

The interplay of the *Sefirot* and the letters produce an infinite number of patterns. These patterns act as templates. As the undifferentiated light of Life Force emanates from God's Will and passes through these patterns, it is imprinted. The projection of the imprinted light is Creation. All created things are projections of the Pure Light that have been imprinted by a specific pattern.

SEFER YETZIRAH 1:1

בשלושים ושתיים נתיבות פליאות   1:1
חכמה חקק יה יהוה צבאות
אלהי ישראל אלהיים חיים ומלך עולם
אל שדי רחום וחנון רם ונשא
שוכן עד וקדוש שמו מרום וקדוש הוא
ובורא את עולמו בשלושה ספרים
בספר וספר וספור.

Using thirty-two wondrous paths, *Yah*, Lord of Hosts, God of Israel, Living God, King of the Universe, God Almighty, Merciful and Gracious One, High and Exalted One, The One who Indwells Forever, The One whose Name is Holy, He Who is the Highest and Holy, engraved Wisdom, thereby creating His Universe by three modes of carving, with number (by sequence), with text (with structure) and with story (with content).

That which God is said to be engraving is Wisdom. *Hochmah*, Wisdom, is that upon which God has engraved or imprinted the thirty-two paths. Wisdom is being used here to refer to the eternal knowingness. Wisdom is the pure, undifferentiated light of Creation. In the *Zohar*, the *Sefirah* of *Hochmah* on the Tree of Life is the level of Primordial Light. From the realm of *Hochmah*, Wisdom, flows the Life Force that forms and sustains all subsequent levels of Creation.

Wisdom is Transcendent Knowingness. It stands far beyond mere knowledge. It transcends comprehension completely. It is not an intellectual quality. Wisdom is that inner knowingness, which develops as an immediate result of devotion to God and a direct experience of God's Presence. As it is stated, "The beginning of Wisdom is Awe of God" (Psalm 11:10).

By allowing oneself to transcend the mind and be overawed by God, by connecting with the Divine through devotion, one is suddenly overcome by the pure force of being. Then the door of Wisdom is truly opened. One connects with the Supernal Light and begins the process of experiencing Knowingness. Feeling awe and reverence for God's majesty results from connecting with God through devotion. That in turn leads to establishing connection to Wisdom and learning to experience Knowingness.

Wisdom is equated with Truth. Both Wisdom and Truth are the underlying foundation of all that is created. They are the light that emanates directly from God's will, upon which all is eventually engraved. They are one and the same. They are the hidden light, the original light, the light of Life Force itself.

Wisdom, Knowingness, is buried deep within us all. It is at the very core of our being. Truth, the ultimate reality, underlies our very existence. Moses stated this clearly:

> Indeed, this commandment which I am commanding you this day, is not hidden from you, nor is it far off. It is not in Heaven that you should say, "Who will go up to Heaven and bring it to us, that we may hear it and do it?" Nor is it beyond the Sea, that you should say, "Who will cross the Sea for us to bring it to us, that we may hear it and do it?" Rather, the word is very near to you, in your mouth and in your heart, so that you can do it. (Deuteronomy 30:11–12)

The Psalmist asked God specifically to connect him consciously to the true Wisdom, the Knowingness that results from direct experience of the Divine Life Force within.

הן אמת הפצת בטחות ובסתום חכמה תודיעני. (תהילים 51:8)

> Behold, You have sought (desired) Truth within places that have been covered (plastered) over. So, in the secret places within me, You will make known to me Wisdom. (Psalm 51:8)

The Psalmist is telling us that Truth and Wisdom are the same, and that God seeks to have us all penetrate beyond the obvious, beyond the exterior, to the level of Knowingness. He expresses confidence that by so doing he will gain Divine assistance in reaching and accessing it. God will help him reconnect consciously with the innermost level of existence, Wisdom.

It is Wisdom that the *Sefer Yetzirah* states is imprinted by God, using the thirty-two paths. We are being told that God imprints the total pattern of Creation onto the Primordial Light.

The engraving, the imprinting is both derivative and determinative. The thirty-two paths by which the world is created encompass two sets of variables. First are the ten *Sefirot*, of which one is *Hochmah*, Wisdom. The second set of variables is the Hebrew alphabet, consisting of twenty-two letters. The entire text of *Sefer Yetzirah* elucidates the relation and interplay of these two sets of variables as they interact in the process of Creation.

The Wisdom referred to in the text, refers to the undifferentiated light emanating from God's Will. The light is imprinted with the twenty-two letters of the alphabet, which form the templates of Creation. Each of the ten *Sefirot* act as lenses focusing the light, creating different perspectives of the picture that is ultimately manifest.

The Undifferentiated Light, the *Ain Sof Or* in Hebrew, emerges from the Divine Will, receives its imprinting in *Hochmah*, the *Sefirah* of Wisdom, and is refocused continually as it passes through the lenses of the other *Sefirot*. It is ultimately received by the last *Sefirah*, *Malchut*, and the picture emerges. Reality, as we know it, manifests.

The term in *Sefer Yetzirah* 1:1, *p'leiot*, "wondrous," comes from the root word, *peleh*. The word, *peleh*, does not just mean a miracle per se. It represents something that is supernatural which becomes manifest. The idea of the manifestation of something from the Supernal Realm in the physical universe is a key one. By describing the thirty-two paths as being *p'leiot*, the text here is making it clear that the paths are functional. They are meant to be used.

This can be interpreted practically in a couple of ways. Traditionally, in the kabbalist Tree of Life, twenty-two lines or pathways connected the ten *Sefirot* to each other. The kabbalists named each of the twenty-two pathways with a different letter of the Hebrew alphabet. Meditation then centered on either one of the *Sefirot* individually, or on one of the Hebrew letters that corresponded to a pathway between two *Sefirot*.

Meditation on a specific *Sefirah* drew one into direct experience with an entire level of Creation or with an entire dimension of the process of Creation. Meditation on the letters of the alphabet represented focusing on the connection between two specific *Sefirot*. Hence, the choice. The meditator can choose to focus consciousness on resonating with either the essence of a *Sefirah*, or he can become one with the harmonic that is generated by a letter, which bridges and unites two *Sefirot*. Here, one is both penetrating and experiencing the aspects and dimensions of Creation.

Another way to understand what the *Sefer Yetzirah* is saying would
be that there are two interlocking sets of variables that can and should
be used in meditation. Here, the meditator is being asked to replicate
the process of Creation in meditation practice. Letters and letter patterns form templates. These templates are projected through the *Sefirot*.
Through this process of projection, different realities emerge in Creation.
The number of patterns that can be focused on is infinite.

The focus of one's meditation would be centered on either of two
areas, or on both successively. The first area of concentration would be
on imprinting a letter pattern in the undifferentiated light and exploring the effects. Second, the meditation can be focused on how the imprinted or engraved pattern manifests differently in different *Sefirot*. Both
of these techniques will be described more fully in a later chapter, when
the *Sefirot* themselves are discussed and explored.

An important key to understanding the dynamics of the *Sefirot* is
indicated in this particular verse. It is that of identifying the Names of
God with each of the various *Sefirot*. In referring to God, who as the
Creator does the imprinting, a series of Divine Names are listed. In the
Hebrew, God is first called *Yah*. Thereafter, He is referred to by ten sets
of Names.

ה' צבאות, אלהי ישראל, אלהיים

חיים, מלך עולם, אל שדי,

רחום וחנון, רם ונשא, שוכן עד,

קדוש שמו, מרום וקדוש.

The ten *Sefirot* are represented by pairs of Names. This suggests
that each of the ten emanated *Sefirot* stand as ten different aspects of
God's creative force, and that there are two sides to each of these various realities. The ten *Sefirot*, the emanations that are emerging from God's
Will, are the process of Creation. Each stage of the process reflects a
different aspect of the Divine Will and each has a dual character.

However, *Yah*, God Himself, is transcendent, completely beyond
the process itself. God is the Source, not the process. The process of
Creation reflects God's Will as it moves toward manifestation. What is
interesting is that within the process of Creation, duality is being implied on all levels and at all stages. That is, the dual nature of Creation
is evident from the beginning. Yet it is the duality of Creation, not of
God. God is intimately involved in Creation as the Creator who initiates
and sustains the process but remains outside it.

Since the Hebrew letters are being engraved upon the *Sefirot*, the engraving is not the first stage of the Creation process but the second. Initially, the *Sefirot* are created in order to be acted upon. It is only then that the templates are made by the engraving process of the letters. The process of Creation emerges and unfolds as a result of the letter patterns filtering down, until they reach the last stage: that of reception and manifestation.

The first paired Name of God in the list is "Lord of Hosts." The term "Hosts" implies created essences. The last paired Name is "Most High and Holy." It is apparent that the list is proceeding from the lowest *Sefirah* to the highest. The implication here is that although the created Universe is the end result of Creation, it is first in importance. God's Names, which represent recognition of God, begin with the created worlds and then escalate back up toward the Source. This is also the core objective of meditation, to elevate the soul beyond the purely physical and reattach itself to God, by direct experience.

One can use these Names of God, in this particular order, as mantras, repeating them over again silently, verbally, or in chant. One can use the Names as meditative focal points, as a ladder of ascension back toward God. Equating the paired Names with the various *Sefirot* in this order provides one with meditative access to higher realms. One should advance over time through the stages, through the various Names and *Sefirot*, in the order laid out in the verse. There is a natural progression upward toward greater and greater abstraction and subtlety. View the Names as steps on a ladder. One can only ascend one step at a time. One's footing must be secure on each rung before attempting to move to the next.

MEDITATIONS ON THE SEQUENCED NAMES OF GOD

Method One

1. Start with the Name of God that corresponds to the Tenth and Final *Sefirah*. The Name is pronounced *Adonai Tsva'ot*. Once in a meditative state, repeat the Name over and over again in a rhythmic chant. You may do this out loud or silently to yourself.

2. Repeat the Name over and over again. Concentrate entirely on the sounds as you make them. Then on the Name as a whole.

This should absorb your complete attention. Do not let the mind wander. If you can visualize the Name at the same time, that is all the better. It creates a focal point for your attention.

3. You may wish to stop and focus on silence for a few moments after finishing a cycle of seven repetitions before moving to the next cycle of seven. This is not a required step but can be useful.

4. Once you have a rhythm, and feel comfortable in doing so, let go and flow where the energy takes you. This meditation should be repeated consistently over a period of time, on a regular basis. Once one has become very familiar with this meditation and the places it leads to, move on to the next Name. Repeat this same pattern with the second Name until you are totally familiar with it and move on.

5. Once you have mastered all ten Names, you can move to a more advanced stage. You can meditate on moving up through each of the levels, through each of the Names and experiencing each individual *Sefirah* sequentially, all in the same meditation.

The Names associated with the *Sefirot* are as follows:

Adonai Tzva'ot (Tenth *Sefirah*)	ה' צבאות
Elohai Yisrael (Ninth *Sefirah*)	אלהי ישראל
Elohim Hayyim (Eighth *Sefirah*)	אלהיים חיים
Melech Olam (Seventh *Sefirah*)	מלך עולם
El Shaddai (Sixth *Sefirah*)	אל שדי
Rachum v'Hanun (Fifth *Sefirah*)	רחום וחנון
Ram v'Nisa (Fourth *Sefirah*)	רם ונשא
Shochain Ad (Third *Sefirah*)	שוכן עד
Kadosh Shemo (Second *Sefirah*)	קדוש שמו
Marom v'Kadosh (First *Sefirah*)	מרום וקדוש

Method 2

Visualizing the Names in Hebrew while in meditation is enhanced considerably by the inclusion of color. By visualizing the Hebrew Name as either being a specific color or being visible as black letters on a color field, one can access a specific *Sefirah*, according to the famous sixteenth century kabbalist, Rabbi Moshe Cordevero. According to Cordevero, each of the *Sefirot* has a specific color assigned to it. By connecting God's name with that color, one accesses the Divine dimension of that *Sefirah*. Cordevero used only the Tetragrammaton, the Four Letter Name of God, in relationship to any of the *Sefirot* and their respective colors. However, using the same principle and logic, one can also meditate on the specific Divine Name equated with each of the *Sefirot* by the *Sefer Yetzirah*, by picturing it as being the correct color. In other words, to easily access a given *Sefirah*, or level of the Creation Process, meditate on the corresponding Name in the color of the *Sefirah* itself.

Use the list below for reference.

Sefirot Colors According to *Pardes HaRimmonim* by Rabbi Moshe Cordevero

Tenth *Sefirah*: Blue	ה' צבאות
Ninth *Sefirah*: Orange	אלהי ישראל
Eighth *Sefirah*: Dark Pink	אלהים חיים
Seventh *Sefirah*: Light Pink	מלך עולם
Sixth *Sefirah*: Purple	אל שדי
Fifth *Sefirah*: Red	רחום וחנון
Fourth *Sefirah*: Silver	רם ונשא
Third *Sefirah*: Green	שוכן עד
Second *Sefirah*: White	קדוש שמו
First *Sefirah*: Crystal Clear	מרום וקדוש

Color Correspondence based on the Light Spectrum

Sefirah 10 = Red

Sefirah 9 = Orange

Sefirah 8 = Light Yellow

Sefirah 7 = Dark Yellow

Sefirah 6 = Purple

Sefirah 5 = Light green

Sefirah 4 = Dark Green

Sefirah 3 = Light Blue

Sefirah 2 = Dark Blue

Sefirah 1 = White

AND HE CREATED HIS UNIVERSE
WITH THREE *SEFARIM*

Sefer Yetzirah tells us that by engraving the Thirty-Two Paths in Wisdom, God created the universe in three modalities. The three modalities are sequence (*S'far* is number), structure (*Sefer* is book or text), and content or meaning (*Sippur* is story).

The Hebrew referring to these three modalities looks like this:

ספר ספר ספור

What one notices is that we have the same three-letter root appear three times. The same concept is given three variations of meaning. There are a total of ten letters. This suggests that the ten *Sefirot* are a repetitive process, in which the focus shifts but the underlying reality remains the very same. It also indicates that the ten *Sefirot* are to be grouped together as 3, 3, and 4 respectively.

Here, we have three levels or dimensions interlocked in the emergence of the Universe. The *Samech-Peh-Resh* letter pattern replicates itself three times as the Universe is created. One of the meanings of this verb root, and probably its original meaning, is "to carve." This harkens back to "engraving." What is being replicated is the imprinting. What gets imprinted initially in Wisdom, which duplicates itself and expands into another two dimensions as it advances through the creative process toward final manifestation.

The imprint is formed in the first three *Sefirot*. It replicates itself in a different form in the second triad of *Sefirot*. It coalesces and manifests as the Universe, through the third and last of the *Sefirot*. The final product of this repetitive process is the emergence of the Universe.

The original imprint is that of sequence. Sequence is movement and change. The first stage of imprinting is progression, movement, combination, and evolution. It is sequence, which constitutes the momentum of imprinting as it passes through the *Sefirot*.

In its second phase, the imprint takes on structure and format. Sequence takes on pattern. The geometry of life takes shape. Form emerges in order to contain and give expression to the flow of Life Force with its endless possibilities. Lastly, in its final repetition, the imprint becomes manifest through the taking on of content. Structured Life Force must express itself. It must reveal its inner meaning and reflect its ultimate purpose. Only by so doing, does reality become fully manifest.

What emerges is the created universe. The Hebrew word, *Olam*, has several interlocked meanings that are relevant here for a full understanding of what is being said. On the one hand, it means the world, the physical reality in which we live. It also means eternity, as reflected in *le Olam va'ed*, forever and ever.

The *Olam* is the end product of this tripartite, repetitive process of Creation. The *Olam* is the Time-Space Continuum. Time-Space is being portrayed as the result of a three-stage process that emanates directly from God. It is the product of Supernal Light being imprinted by the Hebrew letters, by sequence, by motion, by change and evolution. The sequence of motion is itself imprinted by structure and design, which in turn is imprinted by expression, articulation, and meaning. Passing through those stages, the Universe of Time-Space emerges and endures. In short, the Universe is pictured as Motion manifesting Time-Space, through a three-fold process whereby the Supernal Light is imprinted with form, structure, and meaning.

The three stages of the imprinting process are a triad of their own. The first stage of *S'far*, Number/Sequence, is active. It is the emergence of form and it is the mechanism by which the undifferentiated Supernal Light is first impacted. It is engraved, given shape.

The secondary level, the middle imprint, *Sefer*, book/text, is that which receives and registers the imprinted light. This function is passive. A text is the structure given to words and ideas. The letters form the words. The words are received by the page and thereby are given organization by being registered. The result is form takes on structure. Words become sentences.

The third stage, the final repetition, the *Sippur*, story/content, is an extension of the two preceding stages and reflects back on the original imprint. A story is an unfolding. A story develops. There is a message and an ultimate point that seeks to be communicated. What was implicit in the beginning, becomes explicit in the end.

Where in the Hebrew *S'far* and *Sefer* both have three letters, the word *Sippur* has four. This fourth letter represents both an extension and a manifestation. A book is an extended form. When fully read, it conveys both a full picture and the meaning within it.

Whereas the first triad, the initial stage of imprinting, is active and the second is passive, the final imprint is both. It receives the totality of the form and structure and then brings it to conclusion, infusing it with meaning and then bringing it to fruition. In the final stage of unfolding, the active and passive principles have united.

Time-Space-Motion is both the product of the process of imprinting and the mechanism by which the hidden meaning behind it is made manifest and understood. In traditional kabbalistic terms, the Supernal Light is imprinted at the level of *Hochmah*. It is understood through the level of *Binah*, processed through the six intermediate *Sefirot*, and manifested in the tenth *Sefirah*, the realm of *Malchut*. It is in the manifestation of the Universe that the meaning hidden in God's Thought and Will are ultimately revealed.

Meditation

1. Get into a comfortable position. Close your eyes and breathe in a balanced fashion, breathing in and out to the same rhythm. Allow yourself with each breath to become more and more relaxed, moving deeper and deeper into a state of tranquility.
2. When you feel ready, picture a large clay tablet. The clay is soft and malleable. It is a very light color. A very pleasing shade.
3. We will meditate on Joy and Transcendence. For this, we will use the Hebrew verb root, *SMH*, to rejoice:

שמח

4. Picture the first letter, *Sin*. Picture it being engraved or stamped into the clay. The letter will appear as very dark black in color and will be embedded into the clay. The contrast between the letter and the clay will be very pronounced. Focus carefully and get a clear and precise image in your mind of the letter. When the letter's image is clearly fixed in your mind, then you are ready to proceed.

5. Repeat the exact same process, first for the second letter, *Mem*, and then for the third letter, *Het*.

6. Now clearly visualize the entire three-letter pattern. Get a feeling for the clay. The clay is the primal matter, the Time-Space continuum, the *Sefer*.

7. Next, focus on the letters. First, focus on each letter individually, in order. Then, create a flow. Move from one letter to the next, repeating the process without interruption, as many times as you feel you want to. This is the sequence. This is structure and progression, the *S'far*.

8. Now, connect emotionally with the whole word. Feel the power, the meaning, the hidden levels of reality contained within it. See where this leads you. This is the *Sippur*, "the story."

9. When you are finished or feel you have gone far enough, count backward from ten to zero. You will awaken to full consciousness at the count of zero.

SEFER YETZIRAH 1:2

עשר ספירות בלי מה ועשרים ושתיים
אותיות יסוד שלוש אמות ושבע
כפולות ושתיים עשרה פשוטות.

There are ten nonsubstantive *Sefirot* and twenty-two letters. The foundation is that of three Mother Letters, with seven double letters and twelve simple letters.

This is a description of the thirty-two paths. The paths are divided into two groups. The ten *Sefirot*, on the one hand, and the letters of the Hebrew alphabet on the other. Together, you have all thirty-two paths.

The *Sefirot* are described as being without substance. The term used here in the Hebrew, *Bli Mah*, literally means "without what." The sense is twofold. The term, employed here, can be interpreted as "nonsubstantive"; that is, as not being matter. It can also imply, "without definition"; that is, as having no form.

The text is defining the Ten *Sefirot* as formless, pure energy. They are portrayed as existing but having no form, structure, or definition. They are pure energies, undifferentiated lights. The *Sefirot* are being spoken of as existing phenomena. They are not Nothingness, "not things." They are nonsubstantive.

That which are forms, that which does constitute structure, are the twenty-two letters of the alphabet. The letters of the Hebrew alphabet have discernable form, specific meaning, and content. The letters have definable shapes. In combination they imply specific meanings. They have distinct sounds. They each represent a given number. The letters are substantive and meaningful.

There is a direct and intimate connection between these two sets of variables, because they are referred to together as the thirty-two paths. The implication is that one can be working with the nonsubstantive *Sefirot* themselves, with the letters themselves, or with a combination of the two interacting with each other. One can focus on pure energy, or on form and structure, or on the interplay of the two.

The paths are labeled as the thirty-two. The paths are the general set. They are the tools by which God creates and by which man can access Creation on deeper levels. Form and Energy are interlocked as two interwoven sets of variables. Form and Energy are subsets of God's creative tools, the paths.

The letters and *Sefirot* have to be seen as inseparable. Form without energy is lifeless, at best. More likely, form without energy ceases to exist. Conversely, energy without form to contain it dissipates. Hence, it would effectively cease to exist as well.

The creative principle, looking at this from a human standpoint, would involve being able to focus one's attention on one set of variables or the other, while understanding that both are intricately interdependent. They are distinguishable in terms of comprehension. They are distinguishable in terms of creative use. But they are not distinguishable in that they are inseparable from each other in reality.

The letters themselves, the forms, are further subdivided. They are broken into three categories. The first are the Mother Letters, the primary principle. They are the three pillars on which all the other letters are built. Next come the seven double letters, followed by the remaining twelve simple letters.

The double letters refer to the letters of the alphabet which are effected by a *dagesh*. A *dagesh* is a dot inserted into the center of the letter for grammatical reasons. These double letters are pronounced differently as a result of the insertion of the dot.

On a metaphysical level, this phenomena of having a letter's sound change by the emergence of the *dagesh* within suggests that these letters, though remaining the same structurally, are changed when their center is activated. These letters have an inner and outer dimension that are distinct from each other. The form remains the same. Yet there is a revealed and a hidden dimension to each of these, one that is emphasized and one that is not.

The Mother Letters are the foundations, the core of the alphabet. The Double Letters are the transformative letters, the letters of duality. The Simple Letters, the remainder of the alphabet, are the tools. These twelve letters are very set, straightforward forms. The seven Double Letters are dual. They have both a manifest and an unmanifested reality. The Mother Letters are the moving forces of the whole alphabet. They are the connective links that define the parameters of the alphabet, as well as bind the letters to the nonsubstantive *Sefirot*.

The three Mother Letters, in combination with the seven Double Letters, harken back to the ten *Sefirot*. Seven and three are ten. In classical kabbalist thought, the *Sefirot* are arranged in three pillars. The seven double letters comprise qualities that are both hidden and revealed. The *Sefirot* are both extant realities, yet nonsubstantive at the same time. They are both hidden and revealed.

Mothers both receive and give. They are impregnated and give birth. They are fortified from the outside and nurture their offspring. The Mother Letters are energized by their interaction with the *Sefirot* and then pass on energy to the other letters of the alphabet. Regarding the Mother Letters, I will have more to say in a subsequent chapter.

The type of meditation one would do with the letters would be influenced very strongly by the category of letter one is working with. If you are focused on a Simple Letter, one of the most effective meditations would be to focus specifically on the letter itself. Should one be working with one of the Double Letters, one can find oneself involved with meditating on the manifest and the concealed aspects of something. To get at the primal meaning behind something, one would use the Mother Letters.

One can choose to meditate on any of the three letter groups, within their own context. Meditating on the Simple Letters can be done by viewing the twelve as letters representing different dimensions of form. One through six are numbers that correspond to the basic shapes in nature, a circle, a plane, a triangle, a square, a pentagon, and a hexagon. Seven breaks the grouping, since there is no simple natural shape to correspond with it. All six shapes have both an inner and outer reality. The outer realities are the circle, the plane, the triangle, the square, the pentagon, and the hexagon. The inner realities, which parallel the outer ones, are the dot or point, the line, the inverse triangle, the cross, the star, and the Shield of David.

The double letters can be meditated on as the seven days of the week, the process of Creation. The Creation process is composed of six active principles of work, of movement, and of the rest principle of the Sabbath. Meditating on the double letters is to tap into the realm of Motion. These letters access the areas of evolution and development, thought and emotion, communication and change. The seventh letter, the *Resh*, is the focal point for rest, reconnection, tranquility.

Meditation upon the Mother Letters focuses on the relationship of the letters to the *Sefirot*. The Mother Letters represent energy being imprinted, primal force being given form. The Mother Letters symbolize the power to imprint. They have the ability to receive Life Force and the capacity to nurture. That is, they are able to pass on the energy and the imprint, through subsequent stages, to the other letters of the alphabet.

The three letters are the three principles of active, passive, and neutral. The light of the *Sefirot* pass through these filters and are qualitatively changed accordingly. Thereafter, the differentiated lights are imprinted further, with form and with content. To meditate on the Mother Letters is to meditate on content beyond form. It is to focus experience directly on the intangible, on the links between energy and form.

Meditating on the Simple Letters is to meditate on the branches of the tree. These letters focus on the vast diversity of detail. With these letters, ramifications can be experienced and explored. To meditate on the Double Letters is to meditate on the trunk of the tree. Here, form and structure are understood and probed. The interlocking connections that build reality are seen clearly through meditation on the Double Letters. To meditate on the Mother Letters is to reach the roots themselves. To meditate on these *Sefirot* is to reach and experience the light that nurtures the tree and makes it visible to the eye.

Meditation on the Interrelationship of the Letter Families

Suppose something has occurred in your life that you wish to understand on a deep level. You wish to know the root cause of the experience, its significance, and the ramifications it has on your life. To accomplish this, it would be useful to meditate on a sequence of letters
that come from the three "families" of letters, as described above.

Before going into the meditation, you should choose one letter from
each group to use in the meditation. You may use your intuition to choose
the letters or do it deliberately with forethought. Let us say that you
choose *Aleph* as the Mother Letter, *Tav* as the Double Letter, and *Samech*
as the Simple Letter. The meditation would proceed as follows:

1. Close your eyes. Breathe deeply and gradually go into the meditative state. Then, completely clear the mind.
2. First, picture the event that you wish to probe and understand.
   Picture it clearly and in vivid detail. Hold the picture.
3. Now, above this picture place the chosen Mother Letter, the
   Aleph. Hold the *Aleph*, along with the original event picture,
   clearly in your mind.
4. Concentrate your attention on the *Aleph*. Let the letter build up
   force. Very shortly, you will see the picture change. The new
   emerging picture is that of the roots of the event. Now, focus
   your attention on the new picture and absorb its details. Gain
   whatever feelings, insights, and information you can. When you
   feel you are complete with it, move to the next step.
5. Now, insert the chosen Double Letter, *Tav*, at the top of the picture. Focus your attention on it and allow it to be energized. The
   picture below will change again. This time it is the true nature of
   the event that is being portrayed. The inner and outer manifestations, the mechanics of the situation, and the hidden motivations
   become apparent.
6. Focus your attention on the new picture and assimilate as much
   of the detail and of the significance as you can. When that process is complete, move on to the last stage.
7. Go back to the top of the picture and insert the chosen Simple
   Letter, the *Samech* in this case. Focus on energizing the *Samech*,
   The last picture to emerge will be that portraying the ramifications of the event in your life and possibly in the lives of others.
   Observe and study this picture closely. Gain whatever you can

from it, in terms of information, intuitive feelings, sensations, and imagery.

8. When you feel complete with that, give yourself the message several times that you will retain full conscious memory of all you have seen, experienced, and understood in this meditation. Tell yourself you will remember and utilize consciously all that you have learned and that will impact your daily life positively.

9. Say a blessing of thanksgiving to God and then bring yourself back to full waking consciousness by counting backward from ten to zero.

SEFER YETZIRAH 1:3

עשר ספירות בלי מה במספר עשר
אצבעות חמש כנגד חמש וברית יחוד
מכוון באמצע במילת הלשון ובמילת
המעור.

There are ten nonsubstantive *Sefirot* in number. Ten fingers, five opposing five. The covenant of unification is directed (focused) in the middle, through the circumcision of the tongue (the word of the tongue) and through the circumcision of the foreskin.

This *Mishnah*, this verse, as well as several of the subsequent ones contained in this chapter, outline specific meditation practices.

The ten nonsubstantive *Sefirot* are mentioned to indicate that these meditations involve drawing on the primal energies of Creation, drawing on that which unites the created world with the Creator. We are told here that this meditation is one of unification. That is, the purpose of this meditation is to unite the individual with God in holy communion, to connect the meditator with God.

The ten *Sefirot* in this meditation practice are represented by the ten fingers of the human hand. The *Sefirot* are pictured as grouped accordingly, in opposing sets of five *Sefirot*. The unification takes place through the meditator focusing and directing his energy and concentration in between the two sets of *Sefirot*.

The phrase "in the middle" suggests two things. First, that the hands each represent one set of five *Sefirot*, and that the center of concentration during the meditation must be in the middle. That is, one's meditative focus must be on the neutral force that connects these pairs of opposites.

One is not to focus attention on the *Sefirot* themselves, but rather on the Divine force that holds them together. The five and five represent the duality of Creation, of the binary forces that push and pull and create the Universe. That is not where the meditative focus is to be put. It is to be centered between them, on the connection, on the underlying Will of God that holds them in balance.

"In the middle" may also be a physical reference. That is, that the hands are to be placed in between the two physical poles mentioned. The hands are to be placed between the mouth and the genitals. Whether this meditation is done standing or sitting, to accomplish this, one would put their arms at their sides and bend them at the elbows. The hands, in turn, would be turned toward each other, with the fingers and thumbs extended and the palms open.

The first step would be to get so positioned. Next, allow energy to flow into the hands. Then the meditator is instructed to direct himself toward the middle. The meditator is to center himself and direct his attention to the middle, to his head and torso.

In all likelihood, one is being directed to focus on the middle of the middle. The torso is the middle point between the two hands. The center of the torso is the heart. One should move the energy generated in the hands to the heart.

The final and most pertinent instruction comes at the end of the verse. The unification is to be achieved by a double circumcision. This concept harkens back to the statement that this process of unification is a covenant. The significance of that statement is monumental.

The Hebrew phrase is signifying that to unify the soul with God's Presence and His Spirit in the Universe is to renew the covenant with God. A covenant is a contract, a binding agreement that links two parties together in mutual responsibility toward each other. Drawing on the primal energy of the Universe, the Supernal Light emanating from God's Will must be taken into the heart and integrated by the individual's capacity for unconditional love. By so doing, a covenant is made between man and God.

Each has a responsibility to the other as a result. The establishment of the covenant presumes that the Divine flow of energy stemming from the *Sefirot* and manifesting in the fingers of the hand will continue. The individual will be blessed with a continual flow of energy from the highest levels. The responsibility of the individual is to let the energy flow through him creatively and benefit others.

The term "circumcision" is used twice here, once in reference to the mouth and once to the male organ. Circumcision represents opening something up. Not only does something that was concealed become revealed, but it also becomes operative. The idea of circumcising the male organ and of uttering something with the tongue both point in the same direction. Something internal is being externalized. Something hidden is being expressed.

In the ancient mind, both the male organ and the word had the power to create. The female organ and the spoken word produced the fruits of creation. The responsibility of the meditator in this covenant arrangement is to be creative, to open up and express what was hidden, letting the light from above flow through him and become manifest.

The last stage of the meditation would be to allow the energy drawn from the hands into the heart flow out through the genitals. At the same time one must open the mouth and speak the word. This is most likely a mantra, possibly the Name of God, possibly a blessing, possibly whatever one is inspired to say.

SEFER YETZIRAH 1:4

עשר ספירות בלי מה עשר ולא תשע
עשר ולא אחת עשרה
הבן בחכמה וחכם בבינה בחון בהם
וחקור מהם והעמד דבר על בוריו
והשב יצר על מכונו.

There are ten nonsubstantive *Sefirot*. Ten, not nine. Ten, not eleven. Understand through Wisdom and be wise through Understanding. Search within them. Examine from them. Arrive at a decision. And seat the *Yetzer* in its place.

The *Sefirot* are the ten lights upon which the patterns formed by the letters are imprinted. The *Sefirot* represent the energy of Creation. That is, all aspects of Creation have their origin in, and owe their existence to, one of these ten lights. The letters of the alphabet are the building blocks of Creation, the forms imprinted on the light. The *Sefirot* are the lights themselves, which are the different manifestations of the Light of Divine Will. These lights are the energy that sustains Creation.

Each of the ten *Sefirot* acts as a lens. The Light stemming from God's decision to create and sustain the Universe passes through ten stages, culminating in the manifested universe. Each *Sefirah* focuses that light somewhat differently. As each *Sefirah* emerges, a new stage in the process of unfolding appears. With each new emergence, with each new stage, the Divine Light is transformed. The Light takes on a new reality. Its focus has shifted and a new color has emerged on the spectrum of light, as it evolves toward physical materialization.

The term *Sefirah* means "counting" or "number." What is implied here is sequence. Light moves through a sequential process, continually refocusing itself and taking on new color. When the full spectrum of color has revealed itself, the outcome is the manifestation of the universe. Starting out as invisible light, the Light of the Divine Will goes through a progression of ten stages, manifesting the various colors or qualities of light before finally solidifying into material reality.

Ten represents the eternal cycle of unfolding that underlies all levels and all aspects of Creation. The text insists that the cycle is a process of ten stages of unfolding, not nine and not eleven. Counting zero and the nine primary integers, the basis of reality is ten. Nine without zero would be a nondynamic system. It could not evolve beyond itself. Eleven already implies movement to a new reality, a new cycle, because it involves multiple digits for the first time, in contradistinction to the other nine integers.

A reality of only nine cannot evolve. A cycle of eleven is an impossibility, because it has crossed the boundary already, toward infinite possibility. A cycle, by definition, cannot be open-ended. Any system in order to exist has to be defined and that means it is closed-ended. Any system that is capable of replication has to have an element of potential growth built into it; hence the zero, the unmanifested infinitude. That is why there are ten *Sefirot*, not nine and not eleven.

According to the Kabbalah, everything in Creation embodies this pattern of ten *Sefirot*. The ten *Sefirot* are the "Pattern of Creation." Everything that exists, replicates this basic pattern on all levels. For the meditator to evolve and grow, one must continually center on this primal reality. Everything is its own system of ten *Sefirot*. The whole pattern of Creation, down to the minutest level, is a self-replicating, self-reflecting system of ten.

These ten *Sefirot* are the focal points of all levels of Creation. They are the ten internal energies, which underlie, sustain, and link together all of Creation. To connect with Creation as a whole or with anything in Creation, the process is the same. One must pass through the portals of the ten *Sefirot*. Through the use of these gateways, the meditator links himself to Creation and to the Creative Process.

How does one utilize the *Sefirot*?

The text answers that question by saying, *Haveyn BeHochmah*, "Understand through Wisdom (*Hochmah*)," and *Hakeym BeVinah*, "Grow wise through Understanding (*Binah*)."

In the sequence of unfolding, *Hochmah* (Wisdom) and *Binah* (Understanding) are the second and third *Sefirot* in the process. They come immediately after the *Sefirah Keter* (Crown). *Keter* is the *Sefirah* of God's Will, signified by hidden light. It is akin to light before it reaches the prism. *Hochmah* and *Binah* are collectively the white light, that is the light that is visible as it hits the prism. The remaining *Sefirot* are the colors of the spectrum revealed as the light passes through the prism. That is why the Kabbalah refers to *Hochmah* and *Binah* as the "Great Father" and the "Great Mother," respectively.

We are instructed to understand through Wisdom and be wise through Understanding. We are being told to gain knowledge by experience, and to experience the knowledge we have so obtained. This is a clear reference to the interrelationship between the second and third *Sefirot*, as well as to their use in meditation. Understanding is gained through the pursuit of knowledge and wisdom is gained through experience. The instruction being given here in *Sefer Yetzirah* is to interweave and combine both processes.

Cognitive understanding and deep, internal knowingness are intimately interconnected. The inference in the text is that the two are inseparable processes. Thought, contemplation, and cognition on the one hand, and experience, expansion, and spiritual growth on the other, must work in harmony with each other as joint processing. Both experience and cognition are deeply and inextricably interrelated.

The meditator is instructed to allow himself to experience fully whatever transpires in the meditation, and subsequently to reflect on it carefully in contemplation. In other words, the first stage is to meditate and experience what comes. The follow-up stage is to contemplate the experience in order to gain an understanding of what has transpired.

Then one is to complete the process by experiencing consciously that which has been comprehended. After contemplating what one has experienced in meditation, some concrete conception or principle should emerge in heart and mind. A true seeker, a true meditator knows that the realization and understanding that has come from contemplating the experience cannot simply be acknowledged. It must be acted upon. It must be brought into one's life and continually reexperienced actively.

This is not to say that the meditative experience itself can be replicated in one's daily life. Rather, the understanding that emerges from contemplating the experience needs to become an active principle in one's thoughts and actions in the external world.

How does that become possible?

The text tells us to search within them (the *Sefirot*) or through them and to investigate from them. Both terms, *behone* (search) and *hakore* (investigate), also mean "to examine." The reader is being instructed to examine things thoroughly by focusing on them through the use of the *Sefirot*.

The text is saying that anything in the universe, be it concrete or abstract, person, place, or thing, thought, action, or potentiality, can be experienced and understood through any or all of the *Sefirot*. By looking at something from the ten vantage points, by focusing on it differently through the various lenses of the *Sefirot*, one will experience it, understand it, and relate to it in a variety of ways. By so doing, one gains greater and greater knowledge of that which is being examined, both cognitively and intimately.

The examination process is being described here two ways. The phrase *Behone Bahem* can be understood as either "search with them" or as "search within them." Either way, the verb refers to internal exploration. Neither reading is mutually exclusive. The meditator is being told to probe into the depths of what is being examined. The internal reality of the thing can be accessed by experiencing it differently through the various *Sefirot*.

By moving something into the *Sefirot* or by focusing one's meditation on the various *Sefirot* within the object of concentration itself, one can experience its inner realities, its inner dimensions and qualities. As one moves from one *Sefirah* to another, the experience of what is being examined, changes. Different internal dimensions reveal themselves to the meditator.

The phrase *hakore meyhem* translates as "investigate from them." Investigation is an external, not an internal, process. Now the instruction is to consider the thing being examined from without as well. Here, the inference is that the *Sefirot* should be used as lenses. One should refocus on the object under examination, by seeing it from the different vantage points of the various *Sefirot*.

The text is implying that meditative experience must be processed. In meditation, experiences will come. Once they do, they need to be contemplated and understood. Once an understanding emerges from the contemplative process, it has to be formulated into a conscious principle or set of principles, in order to be used, in order to effect outside reality. In other words, it must be formatted, so as to become part of the meditator's conscious life. It must become part of his thought and behavior patterns. Without patterns there is no consistent external reality.

The text is stating that these patterns are created by the process of examination. A thought, feeling, concept, image, or letter sequence are all patterns. To actualize the pattern, one must understand it and then determine its details. A pattern can have a multitude of different potential outcomes. For example, the concept of a dress is a pattern. Yet there exist a vast number of possible styles or forms that a dress can take.

The text is instructing the meditator to perfect the details. Once a conception or image appears from contemplating a meditative experience, it is to be examined internally and externally, probed fully, in order to see the inner and outer possibilities. The *Sefirot* act both as different directions from which to approach and reexperience the event, as well as distinct vantage points from which to view it successively.

When the pattern, image, or event is probed and examined by the meditator, not only is one's perception and understanding greater, but the possibilities regarding its physical manifestation are far clearer. The process of crystallizing a practical, working principle that can be integrated into one's daily life from meditational experience and the cognitive understanding derived from it is one of seeing the internal and external possibilities through the *Sefirot*.

Now that the pattern has been explored and examined, one more step must be taken. Now that a number of possibilities for manifestation have presented themselves, it is time for a decision. Having taken the concept of making a dress through the process of exploring different possible designs, one has to be chosen as the pattern to be used to produce the final product.

Sefer Yetzirah outlines the process of bringing something into being as follows. Meditation leads to an experience. Contemplation of the experience leads to a pattern of some sort, be it a concept, image, letter pattern, or whatever. The pattern needs to be examined carefully in order to understand its dynamics and variations. This is done by connecting the pattern to the various energy manifestations of the *Sefirot*. Doing this provides the meditator with multiple possibilities and an understanding of what each possibility represents. Finally, the meditator must decide which of the possible forms the pattern can take, which will become the "official" one.

This direction is rather explicit in the text. The Hebrew reads, *Ha-ameyd davar al buryo*. In the Talmud, that is in Jewish legal literature, this phraseology is very common and means, "to make a definitive decision." This comes normally after long legal discussion has taken place, examining the various precedents and possible interpretations. Once all the findings have been presented and weighed, a final determination on what the law is to be and how it is to be understood and carried out has to be made.

In the context of *Sefer Yetzirah*, this statement instructs the reader to fix whichever of the possible alternative realities one wishes to actualize in one's life. The actualized pattern can be anything, a concept, a belief, an operating principle, a behavior pattern, an event; anything.

The last line of this verse, can be read two ways. Both readings are significant. One reading yields, "Seat the *Yotzer* (the creator, the creative individual; in this case, the meditator) on/at his proper place." This command informs the reader that the process of making a clear decision regarding what potentiality to activate is the final, definitive act, which is not only appropriate but necessary. By deciding, the meditator is completing the process and thereby becoming fully empowered.

An alternate reading would be, "Seat the *Yetzer*, (the form; in this instance, the final pattern) at its dwelling place." Here the instruction would mean that the final stage of this entire process is to take the decided-upon pattern and set it at the point where it would then imprint the light.

The questions arise, "Where is the dwelling place? At what point does one place the pattern?"

The answer is embedded within the Hebrew itself. The term being used for "place or dwelling" is *machon*. *Machon* in kabbalist literature often refers to the sixth of the seven Heavens. In terms of the traditional structure of the kabbalist Tree of Life, there are six *Sefirot* that intervene between the level of Divine Thought and that of the Created Universe. The sixth of these particular *Sefirot* is that of *Yesod*.

The *Sefirah Yesod* is the *Sefirah* immediately preceding that of the final one, *Malchut*, which is the Universe. According to the Kabbalah, *Yesod* collects, condenses, harmonizes, and blends all of the light coming down from the higher *Sefirot*. It is *Yesod* that organizes the light and prepares it for transmission to the universe. To place the final pattern, the one that will imprint the light, within this *Sefirah* makes complete sense.

To illustrate fully what this verse is saying, I would propose the following meditation.

Meditation Process as Derived from *Sefer Yetzirah* 1:4

1. Relax and go into a meditative state. You may wish to meditate on something specific or merely go into meditation and see where it leads you.
2. Let whatever comes work itself through. Flow with the meditation. Allow yourself to experience fully the flow. Participate in the experience totally, as if it were a dream.
3. When you feel you have fully experienced the event or events, focus your attention on some aspect of the experience, some details, the overall feeling, or the imagery. Reflect on it carefully. Try and gain an understanding of what the meaning of the experience is.
4. Next, allow your subconscious to transform the understanding you have come to into a symbol. This can be an image, a picture, a word, a letter, or whatever.
5. Now, picture a row of ten clear globes. Each globe is filled with a different color. Take the symbol and place it into any one of the spheres. A new energy will emerge from the symbol as it harmonizes with the color in the sphere. Connect with the symbol's new energy and see where that takes you. Let it affect you fully. Repeat the process with as many of the spheres as you wish.
6. Having explored the inner realities of the symbol, remove the symbol from the spheres. Replace the ten spheres with ten colored lenses or magnifying glasses. Examine the symbol carefully under any or all of the lenses. Under each lens the symbol will appear differently. It may even change forms or produce multiple forms.
7. Choose the form of the symbol that you most strongly resonate with. Now picture a projector and a screen. The projector has a very high intensity bulb that is burning very brightly. In front of the bulb is a series of six lenses. Each lens focuses the light more narrowly and more precisely. There is a slot and compartment between the last two lenses. The last of the six lenses projects the concentrated light beam onto the screen.

8. Insert the chosen symbol into the compartment. The image will be projected onto the screen. The image will either remain static as a picture or play itself out as a movie. Either way, watch the screen fully. Study it carefully and let it reveal itself to you. When the process is complete and you are ready, exit the meditation.

The pattern you have established will remain in place and continue to fashion that aspect of your reality, until such time as it is changed. It can be changed at any time by repeating this process.

SEFER YETZIRAH 1:5

עשר ספירות בלימה מידתן עשר
שאין הם סוף
עומק ראשית ועומק אחרית
עומק טוב ועומק רע
עומק רום ועומק תחת
עומק מזרח ועומק מערב
עומק צפון ועומק דרום
אדון יחיד אל מלך נאמן
מושל בכולם ממעון קדשו עד עדי עד.

The Ten Nonsubstantive Sefirot, their ten dimensions (attributes) are infinite. (They are) the Depth of Beginning and the Depth of End, the Depth of Good and the Depth of Evil, the Depth of Above and the Depth of Below, the Depth of East and the Depth of West, the Depth of North and the Depth of South. A single master, God the faithful King, rules through all of them from His holy dwelling for all eternity.

In this *Mishnah* of *Sefer Yetzirah*, the ten *Sefirot* are again being paired into five sets of opposites, beginning and end, good and evil, above and below, north and south, and east and west. Five dimensions of reality are being portrayed. The Beginning-End is the dimension of time and of timelessness. The beginning and the end represent process, the unfolding of events over a sequence of time. The point of *Aleph-Tav*, the alpha-omega, is the beginning and the end being the same point. The outcome of a process is implicit in the origin. The purpose, the impetus, hidden within the origin, becomes manifest and tangible at the point of completion.

The duality of good and evil corresponds to the level of morality, the sacred blueprint on which the universe was patterned. In Jewish tradition it is taught that God first created Wisdom, and from that the world was created. In Jewish literature, Wisdom, and the Torah, the Law and the Commandments are interchangeable terms. The Torah is the manifestation of God's will. It is what God expects from humanity. That is moral behavior, spiritual pursuit, the alignment of man's nature, and his actions with the will of God.

The text here states that first God creates timelessness, out of which time emerges, and follows it with the emergence of purpose.

Hence, moral purpose is the Divine construct in the universe. Morality and spiritual focus constitute the imprint. Beginning and End are the process of potential becoming manifest. That is the primal light. Good and Evil are the imprints on spirit, on the light, that result from intention and action.

The emergence of Good and Evil is representative of the Torah. The Torah is the Law of God. It is the articulation of the Divine Will. The patterning of Creation is dependent on God's Will being expressed. God's Will is expressed by moral imperative, the articulation of Divine purpose.

What emerges from the imprint of Divine purpose is the dimension of above and below. As a continuum, above-below represents space and spacial relationship, on the one hand, and the linkage of Heaven and Earth, on the other. In short, God's will, the purpose of Creation, is manifest in the moral-spiritual order of the universe. That order in turn creates the space for all things to exist and connects all worlds, both the seen and the unseen, both the Earth and the heavens, together in an organic whole.

Then, within space, the last two dimensions, north-south and east-west, appear. The north-south access is longitudinal, which from a metaphysical standpoint represents progressive movement, from one point forward or backward to another point. The east-west axis is latitudinal, representing lateral movement. Longitudinal movement is progressive movement, moving to the next step, finding what lies beyond. Latitudinal movement, on the other hand, is exploratory. It delves into the exploration of what has been found.

In summary, the process being portrayed in the text is as follows:

First comes Time, in both its manifestations of timelessness and as the process of unfolding. Time is then imprinted with the articulation of Divine purpose. The imprinting of Time, the process of the expression of infinite possibility through the unfolding of the Divine Will, produces Space and all the worlds that fill it. Finally, within Space emerges internal and external Motion, development, and evolution.

These five dimensions are referred to as "depths." The implication is very clear. Like the depths of the ocean, these dimensions of Creation are not separate realms, but rather they are consecutive layers of the same continuum. One leads to another naturally the further down one travels. Moreover, the depths are meant to be plumbed. To connect with the deep layers of Creation, the reality of existence itself, requires direct exploration and experience.

One can meditate on the continuum of Creation by using the image of the ocean. If you walk forward through the water, moving horizontally at any depth, you will encounter alternating currents of warm and cool water. These are dualities that flow within any of the various depths. If you meditate on moving down deeper and deeper into the ocean of Creation, you will pass through all five levels of existence, Time/Timelessness, Structure/Purpose, Space/Dimensionality, Forward Movement/Evolution, and Lateral Movement/Development. At each of these levels, one will encounter and experience various currents and infinite variation. These are expressions of the duality of Creation, as they manifest according to the laws of that dimension.

This verse makes it clear that the process of exploration is an infinite one. The phrase "they have no end" here in Hebrew is:

אֵין לָהֶם סוֹף

This can be read on two levels. First, that the *Sefirot* are infinite. Second, that all the *Sefirot* are aspects of the *Ain Sof*. That is, all of the *Sefirot* are the interlocking forms of the infinitude of God's will. Probing the Depths of Creation is not only an infinite process, it is an exploration that allows the meditator to experience the dimensions of God's will as manifest in Creation.

All of the *Sefirot* are equal. They are all termed *middot* (measurements, dimensions) in the text. The same term both describes and equates them all. The five dimensions each have two opposite aspects. All are nonsubstantive and infinite, broadly defined realities with endless possibilities for manifestation.

According to the text, not only is the world created out of these *Sefirot*, but God sustains and supervises the universe through them. The *Sefirot* are the vehicles by which God's creative force and His grace and His supervision are all manifest in the universe. God creates, organizes, maintains, and guides the universe all through the *Sefirot*.

God, the Single Ruler of the Universe, is referred to in this verse, as *El Melech Ne'eman* (God, the Faithful King). This term or name for God is not one that is mentioned in the first verse of our text, which portrays God in the active role of Creator. Rather, it is used in connection with God ruling the created universe through the *Sefirot*.

So God creates through the interaction of the *Sefirot* and the letters and, subsequently, rules through the transformed *Sefirot*. God rules as king by being *ne'eman*. Normally this term means "faithful." In this context, there is another dimension implied. The verb root, 'MN, from which the term *ne'eman* is derived, means "to put faith in, to believe, to affirm." *Ne'eman* is in a passive verb form. Therefore, the term *El Melech Ne'eman* can be taken to imply God, the King who operates through the *Sefirot*, is also affirmed through them.

In short, the *Sefirot* are both the vehicles for Creation to take place and for all of Creation to experience and affirm God's creative will as it manifests. In human terms, this means that the process of Creation is not complete, it is unfulfilled, until God's will is experienced, recognized, and acknowledged.

This is the purpose of meditation. Meditation is the vehicle for exploring the multiple levels of existence. By so doing, one continually experiences the hand of God in His handiwork. Those experiences lead to reverence and to acknowledgment of God. By his experience, the meditator perceives the universe more clearly and that expanded perception affirms God as Creator and Ruler. The experience of the meditator leads to affirmation and the affirmation leads to acknowledgment, which is the fulfillment of the purpose of Creation.

God is said to rule from His Holy Place. This can also be read as the "Place of His Holiness." What place is that? The word here used for "place" is *ma'ohn*. The word derives from the verb root 'YN, meaning "to perceive." The implication here is that God rules from the Holy Place, from where He is perceived by Creation.

This implication is reenforced by the term used here for "to all Eternity" (*Ad Adei Ad*). The letters *'Ayin Dalet* can also be read *'Ayd* (a witness). Again, a reference is made to something being seen and affirmed.

Where is this holy place from which God rules and in which God is perceived? The Holy Place is the three levels of Eternity (*Ad Adei Ad*). What are the three Eternities? They are the three Worlds above our Physical World. They are the three Worlds of Formation, Creation, and Emanation, of which more will be said in Chapter 6.

For the meditator, the experience of God's enormous and infinite creative power is found in exploration of the *Sefirot*. One must continually probe the depths of the *Sefirot*, process the multitude of ramifications stemming from their dualities. One becomes exhilarated by the process and thereby affirms the Presence of God in the world, bringing the universe to completion and renewal.

Just as God, the affirmed King, rules the world through the ten *Sefirot*, from His Holy Place of Eternal Perception, so, too, the meditator becomes one with the Single Master by being drawn to God. Drawn to God by perceiving His holiness firsthand in the *Sefirot*, the meditator touches the infinite and the eternal. He thereby effects Creation by the experience itself and by the sense of reverence that subsequently results from it.

5

On Nothingness and Being

The realm of Creation is that of the Ten *Sefirot*, the primordial lights that filter and focus the light of God's Will and manifest the universe. God's creative urge works itself out through the unfolding of the *Sefirot*. Creation, the final result, experiences God as the Creator.

The highest level of Emanation is the *Sefirah* of *Keter*, which is the realm of infinity and infinitude. Out of *Keter*, infinite possibility, all of the other *Sefirot,* and all of Creation flow. The creative Will of God underlies the entirety of Creation, which flows from it and God stands as Creator in relationship to it.

God is also beyond Creation. If God ceased creating, the universe would no longer exist. There would be only God. All worlds would vanish, since Creation is dependent on the Will of God. Our relationship to God is that of creature to the Creator. Only God can truly know God. God Himself completely transcends Creation on the one hand, yet is totally and intimately involved with it as Creator, on the other.

Jewish belief steadfastly affirms that the world was and is continually being created out of Nothingness. Nothingness means "no-thingness." Creation is Being. Nothingness is Non-Being. God creates the world perpetually, forming and sustaining existence from nonexistence.

To quote one of the great Jewish philosophers of the Middle Ages, Rabbi Saadiah Gaon:

Now it is accurately stated, that the objects of sense perception are also to be found existing in Space and Time, in defined form, in delineated quantity, in a fixed position and in changing relationship and other similar conditions. All of these laws considered in this context is the rule that something comes from something. Now if we were going to draw the logical conclusion from these laws and say that things were created from something which existed in Time, Space, form, quantity, position, relationship, etc., everything would have to be considered preexistent, and therefore nothing would remain to be created. Creation would become altogether meaningless. (*Book of Doctrines and Beliefs*, Chapter 1, Section 2).

Simply put, the world is created perpetually by God out of Nothingness. Being or All-Being emerges from the Will of God. The Will of God emerges from God Himself, alone, who is beyond Being.

Saadiah is saying that in our experience as created beings, it is always something being created from something else. That is the law of Creation, the ground rules within Creation, by which things come to exist. However, in the case of Creation itself, this does not apply. God is outside of Creation. He is the Creator of Creation.

To argue that God brings Creation into existence by forming it from something would mean that Time, Space, and Matter were all eternal. If that were so, there would be nothing to create. There would be no Creation, per se. There would be only evolution within eternity. The universe would be eternal. It would be its own creator.

Given that the universe is created from Nothingness, the real question then is, what is the relationship between Nothingness and Creation, between Being and Non-Being? The *Sefer Yetzirah* clearly states that the structure and process of creation are the *Sefirot*. The *Sefirot* are nonsubstantive, yet they exist. The ten *Sefirot* are the dimensions of Being that ultimately constitute Creation, which is the result of the imprinting.

Our question can be phrased, "What is the relationship between the *Ayin* (Nothingness) and the *Sefirot* (Being). An answer to this question can be found in the writings of the great hasidic master, Rabbi Levi Yitzhak of Bereditchev. At the very beginning of his book, *Kedushat HaLevi*, Levi Yitzhak discusses the first verse in Genesis.

כשאדם בא לאין ויודע שהוא כלום

רק שהבורא ברוך הוא נותן בו כח

אז מכנה לשם יתברך בשם בחינות

יוצר דהיינו לשון הוה שגם עתה הוא

יוצר. אכן כשאדם מסתכל בעצמו
ואינו מסתכל באין אז הוא במדרגות
יש אז מכנה לבורא ברוך הוא
רק בחינת יצר דהיינו שברא אותו כבר
ולכן אנו אומרים אשר יצר
את האדם בחכמה דחכמה הוא
מדרגת יש.

When one comes to the Nothingness and knows that he is nothing, rather that only God, Blessed Be He, gives him the force to exist, then the Holy One is called by the name, *Yotzer* ("Creator"). That is reference (to God) in the present tense. (This act is acknowledgment) that He is creating continually. However, when one looks within himself and does not see the Nothingness, then he is within the process (stages) of being. Hence, from this vantage point the Creator, Blessed Be He, is called *Yatzar* (He Who Has Created) since, He has created the individual already (the individual being aware of himself). Therefore, we say that he created man in Wisdom, for Wisdom is the process of Being. (*Kedushat HaLevi*, Chapter 1, page 1)

Levi Yitzhak draws from the Bible and from the liturgy, and stresses the continual creation and sustenance of the universe by God. In his view, when one connects with one's own Nothingness, one links his consciousness directly to the relationship between Non-Being and Being. At that point, one inwardly knows that his existence is based entirely on the Life Force that is continually imparted to him directly by God. To confront Nothingness is the transcendent experience of focusing beyond oneself. To center exclusively on the Life Force, given by God, which underlies all of Creation, is to connect as a created essence with Non-Being. This is to transcend Time and understand God as the transcendent Creator.

Conversely, when one focuses on oneself, one becomes individual. A separateness has been introduced into the equation of consciousness. One's attention is now centered on self-exploration and personal development. This new focus has direction, movement, evolution, and change as major components. The focus on oneself is to experience and to process. This is the basis of existence as Being, in contradistinction to existence connecting as closely as possible with Non-Being.

Levi Yitzhak goes on to say that, whether conscious of it or not, we are guided perpetually, both by the *Ayin* (the Nothingness) and by

Being. The Nothingness is God guiding us from beyond nature, and Being is God's guidance from within nature. The experience with Nothingness and the process of Being are vitally important and are totally interlocked.

He points out that the Hebrew term *BeReyshit*, "In the Beginning," can be understood as *Be Reyshit*, implying two beginnings. The letter *Bet* by itself is the symbol for the number two. What are these two factors that form reality?

The Nothingness and Being. In human terms, these translate into the hidden and the revealed aspects of life. According to Levi Yitzhak, what we do for each other is clear and out in the open. What we do that is pleasing to God is hidden and the ramifications are unknowable on this level.

The world is built on two realities. It is constituted by that which is apparent as cause and effect, and by that which is happening on levels we normally do not or cannot perceive. The *Zohar* says that the Torah and the Divine Commandments are both hidden and revealed. It states that the Law and the Commandments are the manifestation of the Nothingness and Being.

The Torah, the Law, represents the Divine Plan, the impetus and the purpose God has in creating and maintaining the universe. That is the Hidden. The revealed is the Commandments. They are the expectations God has of mankind. It is the revelation of the plan, as it concerns our role in the cosmos. God's Will is reflected in two ways in the universe. One is the hidden dimensions of reality and the ultimate ramifications of our actions. The other is the revealed dimensions of God's grace and our interaction with each other and the world around us.

There is a constant interaction between the two levels of consciousness. The Nothingness extends itself into Being, and being experiences itself and returns to Nothingness. This process of oscillation is, according to Levi Yitzhak, reflected in the phrase,

. והחיות רצוא ושוב

This phrase, taken from Ezekiel's vision (Ezekiel 1:1), literally reads, "And the creatures (life forms) were running up and back."

Levi Yitzhak reads the first word as a singular rather than plural noun. This renders the verse, "And Life Force runs up and back."

Life Force is seen as the connective link between Nothingness and Being. Nothingness continually extends into Being, and Being retreats, returning back to Nothingness in the cycle of existence. The two are interdependent. The source of Being is the Nothingness out of which it is created. Being is the medium by which Nothingness experiences itself. That experience grounds itself back into Nothingness. It is thereby fulfilled and regenerated.

The *Sefer Yetzirah* speaks about this process at greater length.

SEFER YETZIRAH 1:6

עשר ספירות בלי מה צפייתן כמראה
הבזק ותכליתן אין להם קץ
ודברו בהן ברצוא ושוב
ולמאמרו כסופה ירדופו
ולפני כסאו הם משתחווים:

The Ten Nonsubstantive *Sefirot*, the vision of them is as the appearance of lightning and their function is limitless. For His Word is within them, in the running out and returning. As a storm, they will pursue Him to full expression and they will bow down before His throne.

In meditation, the ten *Sefirot* are seen and experienced as a bolt of lightning. Lightning is the sudden unleashing and rapid materialization of unseen force. This force builds up in the clouds and with great, sudden urgency impacts Earth. One sees the manifestation and power of lightning only for an intense moment. Its extension is its appearance. Its retraction is its disappearance. The abruptness and the force of its appearance and subsequent disappearance is what constitutes its existence and its importance.

Lightning is energized by the cloud. It is the manifested expression of the energy hidden within. The lightning rushes forth in brilliant majesty and fulfills itself simply by manifesting. Just as suddenly as it appears, it disappears, returning and reintegrating into the cloud, into the hiddenness from which it came.

By analogy, the text is saying a couple of things about the *Sefirot*, about Being. From our standpoint, that of created beings, the *Sefirot* are the structure and process of existence. Without Being, without the structure it imparts and the processing it brings, we would not exist. The universe would disappear into nonexistence.

The term *TsFYH*, being read "vision," comes from the verb root *TsFH*, which means to see from an elevated position, to look out from a height. So if we read the term as *Tsafayah*, we are talking about seeing something from a higher perspective. From this higher standpoint, one can understand the *Sefirot* as the process of Nothingness expressing itself. It is the Nothingness that remains the constant. The *Sefirot* are the periodic emanations of its power, which manifests itself forcefully and returns to its source.

Consciousness is being portrayed here as a continuing oscillation between Nothingness and Being. Ezekiel's vision of creatures running back and forth is being interpreted as Life Force, manifesting as the *Sefirot*, oscillating between Nothingness, their source, and Being, their manifestation.

Their function, the purpose of the *Sefirot*, is said to be limitless and without end. Being is infinite in a dual sense. First, it has neither beginning nor end. Second, it has limitless potential and the ability to materialize that potential. Being does not begin and end. Rather, it emerges from and then reintegrates into Nothingness. Its existence is its purpose. The purpose is to be the expression of its own limitless potential.

God's Word, His Will, is implicit in the oscillation of the *Sefirot*. This is stated, "His Word is within them as they run forth and return." This connection between God's Will and the oscillation of the *Sefirot* is also implied in the term *ReTs'o*, "running forth." The verb root for this term, on the one hand, could be *RVTs*, meaning "to run" or it could be *RTsH*, meaning "to want." It implies both God's Will as being the hidden force, and the hidden meaning behind the extension of Being, the "running forth."

The "running forth," the extension of Being, is said to be like a flash of lightning. Like a flash of lightning, it is followed immediately by a storm. Being extends itself from Non-Being. As a result, the Process of Being is initiated. Possibilities become realities. The manifested realities then must work themselves out.

The analogy is extended to express the idea that God's Word is followed immediately by its articulation. First, the text uses the term *Davar*, "word," in connection with the flash of lightning and then follows it with the term *Ma'amar*, "utterance," in reference to the pursuant storm.

The idea here is that consciousness has two stages of manifestation. The first stage is the lightning. It is the reality of the *Sefirot*, which are the essence of Being. They are only perceivable when consciousness can connect with its own oscillation between Being and Nothingness. The second stage of consciousness is the storm. The storm is the process of Being unfolding through the movement of consciousness.

Lightning not only presages a storm, it facilitates it. Lightning flashes. Thunder crashes. The atmosphere is charged and the storm ensues. The manifestation of Being emanating from God creates the basis for the articulation of His Will. The result is Movement in Time-Space, the process of life in the created universe.

Being first facilitates Creation and then triggers off the endless process of Creation fulfilling itself, by manifesting its potential and ultimately returning to its source. The Ten *Sefirot* return and bow down in homage and praise, supplicating before the throne of God, His Will.

Being emanates from Nothingness and returns to Nothingness. This flash of Lightning is existence. Within existence, the eternal storm takes place. Potential is both created and actualized in a timeless and unending process. Consciousness oscillates between the Nothingness and Being.

How does one tap into this supreme reality? How does the meditator connect with this oscillation, and why would it be important to do?

Levi Yitzhak explains. "In every moment, all worlds receive sustenance and Life Force from God. It is man however, who initiates [and influences the flow of] this sustenance and transmits it to all the worlds. When a person wants to bring new sustenance to all worlds, he must attach himself to the Level of Nothingness." [This is the level of *Keter*, the level of Infinity, which emerges from the Nothingness. This is the first *Sefirah*. It is the stage of Nothingness within Creation].

This is the level in all universes that is not constricted. When a man nullifies himself completely and attaches his thoughts to Nothingness, then a new sustenance flows to all worlds. This sustenance did not previously exist. A person must fear God to such an extent that his ego is totally nullified. Only then can he attach himself to the Nothingness.

> . . . The individual then [by so doing], attaches the Life Force of all worlds to the Nothingness, which is higher than all worlds. . . . [It is] on the level of where this [the Life Force] has not yet been condensed into the worlds, that it [the Life Force] is attached to the Nothingness. . . . (*Kedushat HaLevi*, section *Bereyshit*).

Connecting with the Nothingness requires the meditator to become nothing. One must void himself out, thereby nullifying his own ego. Once the ego is put into stasis, one empties himself of content and experiences his pure Being. The thought process is put on hold and one's attention is focused solely on the experience of nothingness within Creation. That en-

tails the cessation of all thought, desire, and emotion. One's total focus is
on the Nothingness and on being nothing, but one's own Being.

This connection to the contact point between Being and Nothingness produces an expansion of Life Force. The amount of Life Force that
then reaches to all levels of existence is expanded, and worlds are transformed. This process can be accomplished in meditation or in prayer.

Think of yourself as Nothing and totally forget about yourself when you
pray. Bear in mind solely, that you are praying for the Divine Presence.
You can then enter the World of Thought (the level of Creation), a state
that is beyond time. . . . In order to enter (the level of) the World of
Thought, where all is the same, you must surrender your ego and forget
your concerns. . . .

If you consider yourself as "something," and petition for your own
needs, God cannot clothe Himself in you. God is infinite, and in no way
can a vessel hold Him, a vessel cannot contain Him in any manner what-
soever, the exception being a person, who makes himself like Nothing.
(Rabbi Dov Baer of Mezeritch, from *Maggid Devarav LeYaakov* 159)

When you come to the level of Nothingness, it is here where all your
physical powers (and senses) become nullified. This is the World of Nearness (to God), the Attribute of Wisdom. (*Maggid Devarav LeYaakov* 97)

Both Dov Baer and Levi Yitzhak speak of using prayer and meditation as a means of connecting with the level of Nothingness. The level
of Nothingness is the highest level of the Creation process. It is the level
where God's Will to create emerges from the Nothingness and creates a
level of Nothingness that encompasses Infinity and Purpose, Potential
and Possibility.

By transcending the ego, by moving beyond and nullifying wants,
desires, and needs, one becomes nothing. Becoming as nothing connects
one to the realm of Nothingness. One achieves a state of nothingness and
becomes part of the highest levels of the Creation process, the Will of God.
Spiritually, like attracts like. That part of the process of Creation that is
closest to God, who is beyond Creation, is the level of Divine Will, the
Level of Nothingness, which is a reflection of the Nothingness.

The soul connects with the Will and Presence of God in Creation,
by shedding all, becoming pure and unencumbered, voiding ego, and
nullifying want and desire. One embraces the All by becoming as Nothing. This type of meditation is recommended by Dov Baer of Mezeritch
and Levi Yitzhak of Bereditchev, and is enunciated in the *Sefer Yetzirah*.

SEFER YETZIRAH 1:8

עשר ספירות בלי מה
בלום פיך מלדבר ולבך מלהרהר
ואם רץ פיך לדבר ולבך להרהר
שוב למקום שלכך נאמר
והחיות רצוא ושוב
ועל דבר זה נכרת ברית.

(Regarding meditation on) the Ten Sefirot, stop your mouth from speaking and your heart from pondering. Return to the Source. That is why it is said (in Ezekiel 1), "And the creatures ran forth and then returned." It is on this that a covenant is established.

In order to reach the highest level of Creation, that of Nearness to God, you must emulate it by becoming as nothing. This is accomplished by stopping speech. That is, to refrain in meditation from thinking and expressing thought, and to stop the flow of emotion and desire.

Life Force "runs out." It emerges from the level of Nothingness and establishes the ebb and flow of our experience and our conscious life. That extension manifests itself as our thoughts, perceptions, feelings, and desires. To effectively gain a sense of the underlying unity of our lives and of ourselves, we must "return." That is, we must reconnect with the Nothingness, by temporarily nullifying our thoughts and desires, while in meditation.

We are to meditate first on silencing the thought process and then on quieting the emotional flow. Having accomplished that, we can focus our meditation on reconnecting with the Source, the Will of God. By so doing, we reestablish the covenant, the deep mutual bond between ourselves and God.

In the following verse (*Sefer Yetzirah* 1:9), we are reminded of the extreme importance of that holy bond.

עשר ספירות בלי מה
אחת רוח אלהיים חיים
ברוך ומבורך שמו של חי העולמים
קול ורוח ודבור
והוא רוח הקודש.

The ten nonsubstantive *Sefirot* are one, the spirit of the Living God. Most blessed is the name of the Life of the Worlds, "Voice," "Spirit," and "Speech" and He is the Spirit of Holiness.

The ten *Sefirot* are all interlocking dimensions of the same whole. Collectively, they are one. They are the process of Creation. As a whole, they are the creative power of God in the universe.

The attributes of God's creative force are "voice," capability, and potential, "spirit," Life Force, and "speech," articulation, manifestation. The universe is the result of the infusion of Life Force into the infinite potential produced by God's Will, which in turn brings everything into existence. Behind this whole process stands God's purpose, holiness. Behind it is the Source of Holiness, the Source of Holiness being God Himself.

By voiding ourselves in meditation and transcending our mental and emotional processes, we are able to approximate the Nothingness. By becoming as nothing, we reach the Level of Nothingness in Creation. We become like the Nothing and thereby connect with the infinite, drawing near to God. We connect in this type of meditation with God's Will and Purpose. We experience the holiness. Subsequently, the experience of holiness links the meditator to the Source of Holiness, God's Presence.

Meditation on the Level of Nothingness

1. Relax fully into a state of meditation. Allow the state to continue to deepen, until you are ready to proceed with the next step.
2. As you move deeper into the meditation effortlessly, physical sensation will ebb away. You no longer will be conscious of your body or your physical environment. You will feel no sensation after a while.
3. Moving further inward, you may hear yourself thinking. If so, concentrate on silence. Allow the thought process to slow down and stop. It will do so, if you detach from it.
4. Once you reach silence, if you feel any emotion, picture it being drained from the heart. Let all emotion flow out, until only the heart remains. All will become still.
5. When ready, move into the state of total neutrality. Here you are at peace. You are at the core of your Being, at the point of Nothingness. There is no movement, no processing either intellectually or emotionally. It is as if you are in dreamless sleep, yet you are highly aware of the fact that you are conscious in a dreamless state. There is nothing occurring, yet you are aware of it at the same time.

6. Sense the nearness of God. Sense your Being. Be, but do not become anything. This is the focus of this meditation. Hold it and remain connected with it, as long as you can.

7. When you are ready, begin breathing deeply. As you do, either you will be brought back to full waking consciousness, or you will fall asleep.

8. When you become fully conscious, you can contemplate the experience, or you can choose at a later time to meditate on the experience. By doing either, you will begin to process that which transpired on higher levels that you were not aware of at the time.

This follow-up work to the experience of just being is as important as is the pure joy of making the connection itself. Everything flows from the Nothingness. By connecting to the Level of Nothingness, deep changes take place and one is prepared for future manifestation of the effects. In order to access those changes and activate them in one's life and existence, it is important to become consciously aware of them. This is accomplished by processing the descent into the Level of Nothingness, by independently focusing subsequent meditation sessions on this particular experience of the Level of Nothingness.

When you do process this meditative experience of connecting with the Level of Nothingness, then thoughts, insights, revelations, emotional responses, and new ways of perceiving things often will emerge over time. Remember, everything that manifests, all that we become consciously aware of in our daily lives, originates from the Level of Nothingness, from the Will.

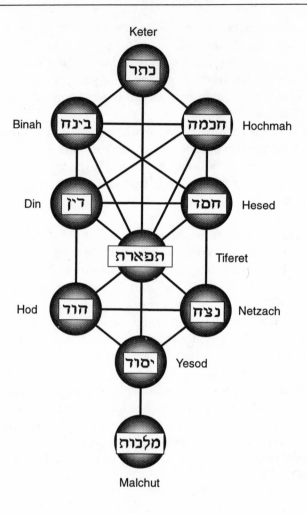

Keter

Binah   Hochmah

Din   Hesed

Tiferet

Hod   Netzach

Yesod

Malchut

6

The Tree of Life:
The Structure of the *Sefirot*

THE UNFOLDING OF THE *SEFIROT*

The process by which God's Will unfolds and moves toward its final manifestation as the created universe is one of unfolding. The *Sefirot* are seen as steps in the process of Emanation. All of Creation is the product of the unfolding of God's Will, as it emanates from Him and reveals itself in stages.

One *Sefirah* is seen as flowing out from its predecessor and, in turn, giving birth to its successor. This course of unfolding is the pattern for development and evolution within all of Creation. In terms of human perception, it is important for us to understand how things are structured. By comprehending form and structure, we develop a frame of reference by which to identify, explore, and understand.

The Tree of Life image is a model of the structure of the *Sefirot* as they interrelate to each other. It is a map of the flow of Unfolding, tracing the evolution of God's creative process from Will to manifestation. The Tree is also the underlying paradigm for all that exists. It is the blueprint for all reality.

So far, we have spoken of the *Ayin*, the Nothingness, that is beyond Creation altogether and is not directly accessible to consciousness. Yet, it is from the Nothingness that God creates the universe, perpetually.

Energy Flow One: Emanation

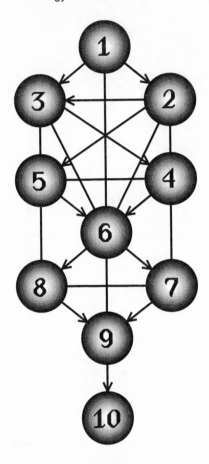

That perpetual urge to create on God's part is the beginning of the process of creation, portrayed by the Kabbalah as the Tree of Life. That urge to create is God's Will. It is the point that separates God as God from God as Creator. This point, God's Will, by its very existence creates infinity. This first *Sefirah* is called *Keter*, the Crown.

Keter represents the emergence of the Creation process. The *Ayin*, the Nothingness, yields the *Ain Sof*, infinity. When God wills, He is extending something from Himself. By so doing, He creates something outside Himself. That is the first *Sefirah*, the first manifestation, *Keter*.

Keter is the hidden of the hidden. It is the emergence of God's Will, His creative urge. It is the infinite, the initiation of all that can and will be. It is infinity, infinitude, and infinite possibility. Yet at this point, no mechanism of any sort exists to bring it to realization. Therefore, it is Will alone. Hence, at this level it is totally and utterly unknowable. It is the Hiddenmost within the realm of the Hidden.

From the *Sefirah* of *Keter*, two additional *Sefirot* emerge. Together, these three will form the Level of Consciousness. This level of the top three *Sefirot* is called the *Arikh Anpin*, the Great Face of God. At this level, the *Sefirot* are an absolute unity. They represent the Will of God emerging and structuring itself to manifest first the process of Creation, and then finally, Creation itself.

A good analogy would be the relationship of the head to the body. When one speaks of the head, one is referring to an integrated whole. It is a unit comprised of important, separate organs. Yet, the organs all function in an interdependent fashion. The sense of taste requires the sense of smell. Sight and sound work closely together to process sensory data. The brain would not be able to program and direct our functioning in the day-to-day outside world if no sense data were being transmitted. Moreover, if you sever the head from the body, life is not possible. The head is a unified whole. Without it the organism cannot exist.

The first *Sefirah* to emerge from *Keter* is that of *Hochmah*. *Hochmah*, Wisdom, is the *Sefirah* that is Life Force. This is the *Sefirah* that produces the energy that underlies all of existence. The *Sefirah* of *Hochmah* is referred to as the "Great Father." Here God's Will produces its first tangible expression. *Hochmah* is the Supernal Light. It is the Light from which all other lights derive their existence. This is the Level of the Great Light, the source of all Life Force.

The Life Force of *Hochmah* is that from which all of the lower *Sefirot* are formed and brought to life. Through it they exist. The Life Force, *Hochmah*, is often called the *Ain Sof Or*, the Light of Infinity. Out of infinite possibility emerges the power to be, the ocean of Being. Infinity requires infinite energy. *Hochmah* is the source of that energy. It is the fountainhead of all light.

Life Force all by itself, however, cannot endure. It cannot endure, unless there is somewhere for it to exist. Life Force needs to be contained. In the material world, this principle could be illustrated by the existence of water. As vapor, the moisture must be housed by the atmosphere, by air. In condensed form as water, it must be contained by the Earth, as a body of water or as moist soil. Without defined space to be received in, the Life Force, water, would not be able to exist.

The function of the third *Sefirah*, the *Sefirah* of *Binah*, is specifically containment. It's function is to receive. The *Sefirah* of *Binah* is the reality of Receptivity. It is the void, the Created Nothingness. It is the ability to receive the Life Force. *Hochmah* is a reflection of *Keter*'s potential, a reflection of Beingness. *Binah* is a reflection of *Keter*'s connection to God as God, its connection to the *Ayin*. *Binah* is a reflection of the Nothingness.

Binah receives the Light, the Life Force of *Hochmah*, and contains it. Binah allows for *Hochmah*'s existence, as well as for its own, by receiving and containing its light. For this reason, *Binah* is called, the "Great Mother."

Hochmah, the second *Sefirah*, is Wisdom. The third *Sefirah*, *Binah*, is Understanding. Wisdom is the broad force of Knowingness, yet it cannot truly exist if not made manifest. What is the manifestation of knowing? To know something. To be aware of the details, to have focal points for the knowingness. When the Knowingness of *Hochmah* is focused, it becomes Knowledge, which is *Binah*.

There is another, closely related reason why *Binah* is known as the "Great Mother." It is within *Binah* that the process of *Tzimtzum* takes place. *Tzimtzum* is the Hebrew word for contraction. According to Kabbalah, in order for Creation to exist there had to be room made for it. If all there was were God, that is all that would be. There would be only God, alone. So God had to create space. This was done by the process referred to as the *Tzimtzum*.

God contracted a small point within Himself, creating a vacated space. It is within this vacated space, the Void, that all of Creation exists. This contraction is within *Binah*. *Binah* is the Void, the vacated space, that is filled with Creation. *Binah* receives the Light, the Life Force of *Hochmah*. It manifests the *Tzimtzum*, the Contraction. Out of the Contraction emerge the remaining seven *Sefirot*.

These seven lower *Sefirot* are referred to as the *Zeir Anpin*, the "Lesser Face of God." The six *Sefirot* between the third, *Binah*, and the last, *Malchut*, are the *Sefirot* that represent the process of Creation. The Upper three *Sefirot* are the process of Will. The following six are the process of production, the last *Sefirah*, *Malchut*, being the end result, the final product.

An analogy here would be that of building a house. *Keter* would represent the homeowner. The future homeowner is seeking a place to live. His desire is strong and he knows what he wants. However, knowing what you want, defining it clearly, getting it done, and having a finished home are different things. They are all elements of a broad process.

The first thing the homeowner must do is to secure the resources. He must have a financier to provide the funding, the energy. That is *Hochmah*. However, all the resources in the world will not accomplish anything without a plan. Hence, the homeowner also needs an architect. Nothing can be built without a blueprint and a structure. That is the function of *Binah*.

The architect, *Binah*, must confer very closely with the homeowner, *Keter*. It is his function to resonate with the desires of his employer and to translate those aspirations into concrete form and expression. Binah articulates the plan implicit in the Will of *Keter*.

Then the resources, the Life Force of *Hochmah*, must be entrusted to *Binah*, who is commissioned to carry out the program. *Binah* will empower others in order to accomplish the task of building the dwelling. *Binah* will oversee their activity and coordinate the effort. The six *Sefirot* of *Hesed*, *Din*, *Tiferet*, *Netzach*, *Hod*, and *Yesod*, are the subcontractors, responsible for getting the work done.

When they are finished, the house, the dwelling, the *Sefirah* of *Malchut* will be ready. It will reflect the intentions and desires of the homeowner, on the one hand, and receive and house him on the other. The *Sefirah* of *Malchut* is the result of the process of Creation, because it is Creation. As Creation, *Malchut*, the tenth *Sefirah*, both reflects the externalization of the Will of God and it serves to receive the Presence of God. It is both house and home.

The fourth and fifth *Sefirot* are *Hesed* and *Din*. *Hesed*, which is the Hebrew word for loving-kindness, is the level of God's Love. This is the energy of God's unconditional love for Creation. It is the level of Grace. This is the energy that sustains. Whereas *Hochmah* is Life Force, the force of Being, *Hesed* is Life Energy, that which sustains life and feeds existence.

This Life Energy is like the light of the sun. Sunlight provides the energy that warms the Earth and makes it habitable. It brings nutrients and produces photosynthesis. It is the source of nourishment and growth. It provides light, the energy by which we are nurtured and grow. It is through light that we are able to see and to function.

Hesed, God's unending and unrestricted Love, is the light that sustains, nourishes, and defines all of the *Sefirot*. And like sunlight, it impacts and affects, nourishes and enlightens all levels of reality with

complete equanimity. Just as the sun shines indiscriminately on everything, on the good and the bad, on the constructive and the destructive,
on the deserving and the undeserving, the light of *Hesed* floods all
levels of all reality with the blessing of God's love and His great goodness. That is why the Kabbalah refers to the *Sefirah* of *Hesed* as the source
of all *Shefa*, God's flow of Abundance and of Goodness.

The predicament of *Hesed* is similar to that of *Hochmah*. God's Light,
His Abundance, His Grace cannot exist without somewhere to go. They
must be received to be fulfilled. Uncontained light simply dissipates into
oblivion. To endure, light needs darkness. It needs to be received. That
is the function of *Din*, the fifth *Sefirah*.

The *Sefirah* of *Din* is the Level of Definition. The term *Din* means
judgment, both in the sense of discernment and also that of decision.
The power of *Din* is that of discrimination, the ability to discern and to
decide. This is the realm of limitation. It is here in the *Sefirah* of *Din*
that definition is imposed and limits are set.

This is a vitally important process. Without limits, without definition, nothing can exist. Darkness needs to impact on light in order for
anything to exist. Blackness and color are both restrictions on the light.
They are the elements by which things are outlined, defined, and therefore, perceived. Without the interplay between light and its counterpart,
dark, there is no definition, no limitation, and hence, no perception. In
pure light, reality is only an unseen potential. A slide has to be placed in
front of a lens for a picture to emerge. Without it, there is only the blank
imagelessness of white light. Though the light is pregnant with possible
meaning, in that state it is stagnant.

On one hand, *Hesed* and *Din* are interdependent. Light must be
received and defined or it dissipates. Darkness without light does not
have the energy to exist. Reality is only perceived and experienced
through the interplay of light and dark contrasting with each other.

On the other hand, light and dark are mutually exclusive. They are
contradicting principles. Dark obscures the light and light dissipates the
dark. As the Hebrew liturgy puts it, God "rolls away the light from
before the dark and the dark from before the light."

Light and Dark emerge at the levels of *Hesed* and *Din*. It is here
that the duality of Creation appears. It is here that the roots of this
dualism lie. There is a duality to the very relationship between *Hesed*
and *Din*. On one hand, *Din* emerges from *Hesed*. Without the Light, Darkness cannot exist. *Din* is the product of *Hesed*. On the other hand, Dark-

ness is the antithesis of Light. Light and Dark nullify each other. They are diametrically opposed to each other. They must coexist but cannot be blended or unified.

This dichotomy of interdependence and antithesis leads to a push–pull relationship between these two great forces. The energy produced by this push–pull relationship is the mechanism by which the entire system, the entire process of Creation, is fueled. Duality by its nature is the law of opposites. One opposite generates the other and the second reflects the first. Neither can exist without the other. Yet as opposites they are opposed by nature to each other. The tension between them, produced by this dichotomy, by the friction of the push–pull, generates the energy by which the entire system is driven.

The question arises then, how is the push–pull controlled? If the push is too strong, the system will explode. If the pull is too strong, the system will implode and self-destruct, the two forces negating each other. How then, does the system survive? What is the mitigating force?

The answer is the *Sefirah* of *Tiferet*.

The *Sefirah* of *Tiferet*, "Splendor," is the pivot of the entire system of the Tree of Life. It stands at the center of the system, both structurally and functionally. It is the crossroad through which all the energy of the Tree is coordinated. The flow of energy is circulated, controlled, and directed through this *Sefirah*.

The *Sefirah* of *Tiferet* receives the energies of the higher *Sefirot* and distributes it to the lower ones. From the opposite direction, it accumulates the refracted energies of the lower *Sefirot* and redirects them back to the higher ones. The *Sefirah* of *Tiferet* is known as the Heart. Like the human heart, *Tiferet* harmonizes expansion and contraction. It draws energy in from all directions and distributes it evenly throughout the entire system of the *Sefirot*, in an unending rhythmic flow.

The chief function of *Tiferet* is to create balance. It receives both the universal energy from *Hesed* and the power of discernment from *Din* and creates the synthesis between the two. It is in *Tiferet* that God's unconditional love is given structure and made into a usable force. God's limitless Grace and the power of differentiation are merged.

It is in *Tiferet* that God's love, His expansiveness in regard to Creation, and His judgment, the power of restriction, limitation, and definition are brought into balance and harmony. This creation of harmony and balance is absolutely essential for the survival and maintenance of Creation.

The power generated by the interaction of opposites fuels the entire system of Creation. At the level of *Hesed* and *Din* duality emerges out of unity. The mutual exclusiveness of the contradicting powers creates a force that could obliterate the entire structure. *Tiferet* draws from both forces and creates harmonization. *Tiferet* transforms the opposing forces from contradictory, mutually hostile ones, to countervailing, contrasting ones.

By holding these opposing forces of light and dark, of expansion and contraction, in check and in balance, the *Sefirah* of *Tiferet* produces the synthesis of energy. The energy modification achieved by *Tiferet* puts energy into a form that can be effectively utilized by the entire Tree, by all of the *Sefirot*. By harmonizing the energy of duality, balance is brought to the entire system. Without this balance, it could not exist.

The next stage of the process occurs at the levels of *Netzach* and *Hod*. It is here that content and form come into being. The two emerge from *Tiferet* and are closely intertwined. There is no reality to content without form. Nor is there meaning to form without content. Form defines content by delineating it. Content enlivens form by filling it with substance. The two are mutually dependent on each other.

Hesed is the fifth *Sefirah*, that of Love, of Universal Energy. The "son" of *Hesed* is the seventh *Sefirah*, *Netzach*. *Netzach* is directly below *Hesed* in the Tree of Life. It is the descendent of *Hesed*. The term *Netzach* literally means "eternity." It refers to the Time-Space continuum. The *Sefirah* of *Netzach* is that of Content. Content is light or energy that has become specialized. Through the mixing of Life Energy with the force of Definition that took place in *Tiferet*, *Netzach* emerged. The light of God's Love has been transformed into the light that imparts content to all created essences.

That content is received by the eighth *Sefirah*, *Hod*. The *Sefirah Hod*, "majesty," is that of Form. The light of content is taken and shaped. It is received into the vessel of form and given a specific definition. *Hod*, the eighth *Sefirah* is the "daughter" of *Din*. Just as *Din* discerns the light of *Hesed* and imparts expression to it, so too does *Hod* interact with *Netzach*. It receives the light of content from *Netzach* and gives it expression through imparting form.

The *Sefirah Tiferet* had to reconcile and harmonize the forces of expansion and contraction in *Hesed* and *Din* and pass the transformed forces on to the next level down, that of *Netzach* and *Hod*. Here again, at the level of *Yesod*, there is a necessity for a harmonization of the forces of form and content. Content must be imparted to form and the resulting form must express and fulfill the content. This is the job of the ninth *Sefirah*, *Yesod*.

The term *Yesod* literally means "foundation." This *Sefirah* is indeed, the foundation of the universe, the last Sefirah, *Malchut*. *Yesod* collects all of the lights and all of the energies of the higher levels and solidifies them into a system, into a unified whole. Content and form, energy and vessel, will and design, light and dark are all synthesized together at the level of *Yesod*.

The purpose behind this process is very clear. Everything is being packaged into its final form, in order to be transmitted to the level of physical Creation. The levels of *Netzach* and *Hod* are the levels of archetype. Along with *Yesod*, this entire level is that of the final imprint, the completion of the design.

The specific function of *Yesod* is to transmit the completed design along with all of its resident energy to the last *Sefirah*, *Malchut*, in order for Creation to manifest and to become material.

Malchut, the tenth *Sefirah*, is totally receptive. It is the only *Sefirah* that has no light of its own. It is the *Sefirah* of Manifest Creation. *Malchut* receives the light, the energy, the form, and the structure of Creation from *Yesod*, which has edited it into its final form. Upon being received by *Malchut*, the image of reality finalized by *Yesod* becomes the concrete materialization of reality. It becomes that which we know and experience as the universe.

Malchut, the level of the physical universe, is the end product of the process of Creation. The process begins at *Keter* with the unexpressed Will of God and concludes with the final, detailed materialization of God's intention, design, and plan. The universe is the final flowering of God's innermost thought.

Like a photographic print, the Level of *Malchut* receives the light of higher *Sefirot* as it passes through the negative of Creation, the final pattern produced by *Yesod*, and once so touched develops into a full, detailed picture. That picture is the material world of the physical universe.

MEDITATING ON THE STRUCTURE OF THE TREE

As important as it is to understand the nature of the *Sefirot*, so too is it necessary to comprehend the structure of the *Sefirot*. The process of the unfolding allows us to see the sequence of the *Sefirot*. It allows us to gain insight into the meaning of the *Sefirot* and to view their evolution

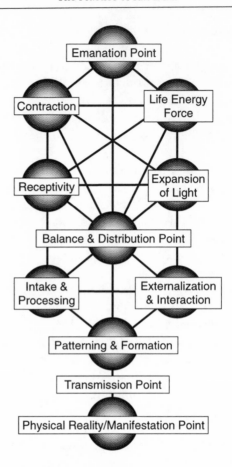

from the unseen to the manifest. We are taught the meaning of the *Sefirot* by watching their progression as they flow from one into other.

In order to understand their interrelationship, the dynamics of the *Sefirot* in relationship to each other, we must come to a clear perspective of the structure of the Tree of Life. The Tree of Life is the organic model, in Kabbalah, of the *Sefirot* as they all interact with and impact on each other.

The Tree of Life is a paradigm. It is a model by which mankind from its standpoint as created being can view and comprehend the various dimensions and levels, implications and realities of Creation itself. The model is an intellectual and psychic construct. It is meant to be a map, outlining the overall structure of the *Sefirot* and illustrating the interconnectedness of the *Sefirot* and their functions.

In actual reality, the *Sefirot* are all distinguishable from each other only in the perceptual sense. No *Sefirah* exists independently of the others. The *Sefirot* are an organic whole.

The process of Creation is a continuum. There is no difference between the beginning and the end. There is no difference between God's Thought and the manifestation of the universe. The end product is implicit in the impetus and the original desire is fulfilled in the final result. The origin, the process, and the resulting product are all the same.

The *Sefirot* represent different vantage points, different views of the whole. A good analogy would be that of a diamond. The diamond is a whole. It is a unified reality. Yet the reality and beauty of the diamond is that it has many different facets. Each face of the diamond reflects the light differently and adds another dimension to it. Turn a diamond in various directions and each new face will present a new appearance, revealing a new dimension of the whole.

The *Sefirot* are called the attributes of God. They reflect different dimensions of God's creative work. They are not God. They are dimensions of God's activity as Creator. The *Sefirot* are not separate realities or independent in any way. They are perceptual views. They are vantage points of observation. The faces of a diamond do not have separate existences. The diamond can exist uncut, but the faces of the diamond are the construction of a finished stone. They are the elements of structure. Their purpose is of great importance, but they have no independent reality.

The Tree of Life diagram is meant to illustrate the inner dynamics of Creation by mapping the gestalt of the *Sefirot* and by allowing us to perceive the interconnectedness and the interaction between these primal forces. Understanding the connections is the key to meditation on the *Sefirot* and on Creation.

One way to understand the *Sefirot* has already been discussed. One can see the flow of the creative process in the progression of the *Sefirot* from *Keter* to *Malchut*. A meditation that connects one to creativity and to the flow of creation is that of moving sequentially through the *Sefirot* in order.

In this meditation, one goes into a meditative state and pictures the Tree of Life. Focusing attention first on the *Sefirah* of *Keter*, one meditates on nothing and on infinity. All form, sensation, thought, and feeling are absent. One hovers in a vast expanse of nothing. One is, but is nothing. When ready, pass to the *Sefirah* of *Hochmah* and focusing there, meditate on sensing one's own Being. Here, the meditator begins to sense motion. One experiences expansion and great joy.

The third stage of the meditation is to focus on the *Sefirah* of *Binah*. Feel the imposition of limitation. Feel Being contract, as it moves toward the process of definition. Picture a point, a dot. Allow energy to be funneled through this point, as the ocean narrows at a specific point and begins to flow as a river.

This will bring the meditator down to the levels of *Hesed* and *Din*. Here, one will encounter duality. There will be a tremendous sensation of push–pull. Experience the Light. Accept the Dark. Focus attention on breathing specifically. Breathe in light and exhale dark. Being has become existence. Feel the power of the Breath of Life.

Moving to the central *Sefirah* of *Tiferet*, one experiences the distribution of energy. Energy flows down from above and is distributed below. Energy is felt rebounding from below and being redirected upward. This is the level of the heart. Move your focus from breathing to the heartbeat. Resonate with the ebb and flow of energy.

This will lead you to the levels of *Netzach* and *Hod*. Here, you begin to perceive clearly that which is uniquely you. Feel the joy of Self, the exhilaration of being who you really are. Allow yourself to see and accept the patterns of your life and the many forms your being takes on, the many hats you wear and the various roles you play.

Then, move on to *Yesod*. Once in *Yesod*, embrace the ego. This is that part of yourself, that element of your soul, that relates to and interacts with the world. Experience how you see yourself. Draw down all the energies from above and bring them into focus. Every aspect of your personality, all the possibilities and ramifications of your conscious life, are experienced and can be explored fully at this level. Take some time for exploration of the present and of the future.

Finally, return to *Malchut*. Descend fully into your physical body. Feel the blood moving through your heart and through your veins. Move your focus through the organs of your body. Breathe with your lungs. Digest with your stomach. Process with your kidneys. Feel through your skin.

Then focus on the senses. See through your eyes. Hear through your ears. Exalt in the experience of discovering your senses as if for the very first time. As a result of this final stage, you will soon return to full consciousness, revived, invigorated, alert, and alive. You will have connected with the whole process of Creation.

STRUCTURES WITHIN THE STRUCTURE

In assessing its internal geometry, one begins to see some of the various structures that lie at the heart of the Tree of Life. One glimpses important elements of the structure inherent within. This is of great importance, because in identifying the internal substructures lies the gate to both a deeper understanding of the *Sefirot* and also to meditation on and utilization of the Tree.

The first way to view the inner structure of the Tree is as four distinct realms of reality. This structure is often referred to as the Four Worlds. The triangle formed by *Keter, Hochmah,* and *Binah* is the highest world, known as *Olam Ha-Atzilut,* the World of Emanation or the World of Nearness. This world is that of God's Will and His Presence in the universe. It is on this level that one connects directly with God.

The World of Emanation is the level of the hidden, the realm of God's immanence. This is the indwelling of God in the universe. It is from this realm that everything ultimately emerges. This is the level of God's purpose. This is the world of pure Being. From man's perspective, this is the place from which the soul emerges. This is the spiritual realm.

The World of Emanation is followed by the *Olam Ha-Beriyah,* the World of Creation. This world consists of the second triangle of *Hesed, Din,* and *Tiferet.* This World of Emanation is the world of primal energies. The forces that will be molded into Creation are created themselves on this level of the Tree. Expansion and contraction, light and dark, energy and limitation, justice and mercy appear on this level. This triad of *Sefirot* produces the great principles which underlie all of Creation. It is here that the primal forces of the universe emerge and are subsequently brought into balance.

The third world, consisting of the *Sefirot* of *Netzach, Hod,* and *Yesod,* is also a triangle. This is the *Olam Ha-Yetzirah,* the World of Formation. This world in large part is a replica of the world above it, and its function is similar. The World of Creation produced and balanced the primal forces of the universe, but imparted to them neither content nor form. That is the function of the World of Formation. In this world, form and content, shape and function, context and reality are crafted. This is the world of prototype.

A question that comes up is that of the repetition of the process of *Hesed-Din-Tiferet* in the following triad of *Netzach-Hod-Yesod*. Why is it necessary to have two worlds, one which seems to replicate its predecessor?

The answer lies in the nature of the gap between the Divine realms of Will and Thought and the lower realms that lead directly to Creation. The highest realm, the World of Emanation, is the realm of Divine Purpose. The lowest world, the World of Doing, is that of Creation itself. The two interceding worlds represent the process that bridges this enormous gulf.

The Process of Creation is handled through the Worlds of Creation and Formation. The latter replicates the former, because the creative procedure is a step-down process. The energies of Creation are brought into being in the World of Creation. However, these forces are of enormous power at this level. They are raw power and must be harnessed and transformed if they are to be received by the physical level without overwhelming and destroying it. The function of the World of Formation is to solidify, control, and transform the raw energy of Creation into usable form.

Let us use an analogy. Let's envision the World of Emanation as the electric company—that is, the corporation itself. At this level all of the planning, financing, and administration is handled. The World of Creation is the power plant that generates all the energy that is converted into electricity. The World of Formation is the network of power stations and regional offices. The World of Doing is the world of the consumer, the end user.

It would be foolhardy, to say the least, to expect that it is either possible or even advisable to plug my living room lamp into a generator. The appliance could not contain such overpowering force and would be obliterated. I must rely on the power station in my area to take in the influx of energy from the generating plant, transform it, distribute it, and send filtered amounts to all of the homes and businesses in my area. Then I can use my lamp by plugging it into the wall socket. That is the step-down process.

The end user in the scheme of Creation is the physical universe. That is the last *Sefirah*. The tenth *Sefirah*, that of *Malchut*, is a world within itself. It is totally self-contained. *Malchut* is the *Olam Ha-Asiyah*, the World of Doing. This is the physical universe. It is the world of manifestation, the world where things exist as concrete functioning essences. Whereas in the World of Formation, archetypes emerge and thoughts take on shape, in the World of Doing the shapes take on solid form and function. This level is the world of action, accomplishment, and development.

The realm of Emanation is the level of Spirit. It is the world of Being. The realm of Creation is the level of Mind. Thought and concept dominate Creation. The World of Formation is the domain of Emotion. Emotion clothes abstract thought with definable form and prepares it for transmission into the World of Doing, where it will be transformed into action. In the World of Doing, *Malchut*, Will, shall be empowered and work itself out fully in concrete form. By doing so, it will experience all of the effects and the ramifications of its own materialization.

In terms of personal exploration, one can meditate separately on each of these four realms or on them collectively, in sequence. When meditating on any of the four worlds, one should focus on the core *Sefirah* within that substructure. It is at the core of each world, the *Sefirah* that acts as the center, that one finds the experience of connecting with its totality. The core *Sefirah* is the integration point of all the forces that constitute any given world.

The core of each world is the *Sefirah* that acts as the fulcrum. The core *Sefirah* of the World of Emanation is *Keter*. Both *Hochmah* and *Binah* flow from it. The pivotal point of the World of Creation is *Tiferet*. *Tiferet* balances and harmonizes the forces of *Hesed* and *Din*. The central *Sefirah* in the World of Formation is *Yesod*, which balances the energies of *Netzach* and *Hod*. The world of Doing is the *Sefirah* of *Malchut*, exclusively. This *Sefirah* is both a complete world within itself, and hence, its own core.

The structure of the *Sefirot* is often seen as that of three columns. The right column is composed of *Hochmah*, *Hesed*, and *Netzach* in descending order. The column on the left is made up of *Binah*, *Din*, and *Hod*. The middle or central column is that comprised of the *Sefirot* of *Keter*, *Tiferet*, *Yesod*, and *Malchut*. The columns, viewed within the structure of the Tree in this manner, are generally referred to as the "Three Pillars."

The Right Pillar is the column of light. It is the pillar of expansion and expansiveness. This is the side of God's mercy. This aspect of the Tree of Life encompasses joy, abundance, grace, and blessing.

Its counterpart is the Left Pillar. The left side of the Tree is that of dark, of receptivity, and of definition. This is the Seat of Judgment. Here, restriction and discipline reign. The Left Pillar is the side of limitation

Central Pillar
Neutrality Principle

Left Pillar
Containment Principle

Right Pillar
Energy Principle

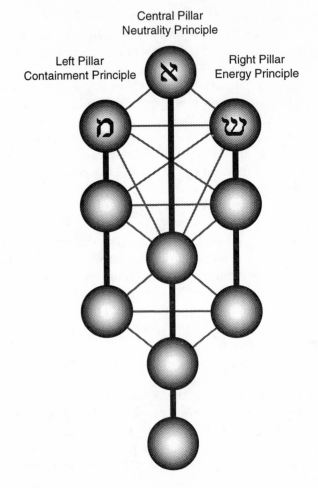

and discernment. It is the point of birth and the ultimate source of development and evolution.

The central Middle Pillar is that of transcendence and balance. It is through the middle, through the neutral principle, that the conflicting forces of light and dark, of expansion and contraction are harmonized and held in working relationship to each other. The central column is the axis, on which the forces of the Tree of Life revolve. This is, therefore, the most appropriate focus for meditation.

The interaction of right and left is like that of a whirlwind. The movement of energy produced by these two opposite and opposing principles is that of a storm. The constant push–pull of expansion and contraction continually create an extremely powerful and endless cycle of revolving energy. To be caught in this storm and exposed to its full fury would be ill-advised and potentially very dangerous.

Proper meditative access to each of the worlds is through concentration on the core *Sefirah* within that world. The pillars on the left and right are countervailing opposites. One cannot exist without the other, yet are mutually exclusive of each other. To focus meditation solely on one of the extremities is to create imbalance and to be potentially drawn into and identified with this imbalance. This leads at best to distortion, at worst to destruction.

Even if one were to somehow escape that dilemma, it is still impossible to perceive the nature and reality of the opposing pillar from the vantage point of its nemesis. One can only see the interrelationship and interdependence from a neutral standpoint.

The center of the storm is the Middle Pillar. Like the inside of a tornado or the eye of a hurricane, it is totally tranquil. Though the outer layer of the Tree of Life, like a storm, is turbulent and ever changing, the inner layer is quiet and at peace. Moreover, the inner core, the Middle Pillar, is the one that directly connects God to Creation. This column is a straight, unobstructed path from *Keter* to *Malchut* and back again.

For the meditator, this is one of the great secrets of spiritual awareness and spiritual growth. The road to God is one of transcendence. It is the inner road of the central *Sefirot*. It is the unobstructed road of inner peace, achieved by harmony and balance, by connecting body, emotion, mind, and soul together, through focus and ascent.

One should move up through the Worlds by focusing meditation on the pivotal center *Sefirot*, thereby taking the road of peace and of transcendence. To move up through the right or through the left creates an imbalance. There is no anchor. One is either caught in unrestricted expansion, which leads eventually to explosion, or in perpetual contraction, which results in implosion. Both can be very damaging and ultimately result in self-destruction.

Trying to balance one's ascent by ping-ponging from the right and left pillar is equally dangerous, because one runs the risk of becoming trapped in the maelstrom. Great destruction takes place in the face of a storm. The key is the Middle Pillar. It is the fulcrum of the Tree of Life and the true path of ascent. One climbs a ladder by stepping on the rungs. The sides of the ladder are only meant to anchor the steps.

The central pillar is the true route for exploration of the *Sefirot*. It is the road of balance. The Middle Pillar is constituted exclusively by core *Sefirot*. This pillar forms the interrelationship of all of those *Sefirot* that harmonize and balance.

By moving through this column of balance and integration one can proceed from *Keter* to *Malchut* and back again, viewing the right and left columns from the standpoint of neutrality. This can be done in either of two ways. One is to move sequentially through all of the *Sefirot*, centering one's meditation on the middle *Sefirot*, or by moving in meditation exclusively up and down the Middle Pillar. Whichever path you choose, the true focus of meditation in reference to the Tree of Life must be through the core *Sefirot*.

So now let us explore several meditations of varying complexities that use the Tree of Life and focus on the *Sefirot*.

7

Meditations on the *Sefirot*

There is great, practical importance in learning to use the Tree of Life and the *Sefirot*, the blueprint of all of Creation, in meditation and in contemplation. Therefore, the following chapter is dedicated solely to illustrating a number of applicable meditations. Each of these chosen meditations access a different dimension of the Tree of Life and serves a specialized purpose. Each is a specific meditative focus.

In order to reach the levels of consciousness normally accessed through these practices, the meditator first must move into a deep state of meditation. In all cases, this can be done in the same manner. For the experienced meditator, moving into a deep state of meditation is a rapid and familiar process. For those new to meditation, the following preliminary steps can be followed to induce the meditative state.

PRELIMINARY STEPS:
INDUCING THE MEDITATIVE STATE

1. Relax and clear all thoughts from the mind. Picture a clear, endless field of blue. This ocean of blue is serene, comfortable, and accepting. Let all thoughts, images, feelings, and so on melt

into this ocean of blue energy. Breathe evenly and deeply. Inhale and exhale in a slow and balanced manner, moving deeper into relaxation and quiet with every breath.

2. Go into a deep state of meditation by slowly counting backward from 10 to 0. With each count, you will go deeper into a state of tranquility and calm. You will move further and further into a deep meditative state. At a certain point, you will know you are ready to proceed with the meditation.

It is important to understand that meditation is not a thought process. There is no thinking involved, only experiencing. Meditation, in Jewish tradition, is an intuitive, free-flowing, creative process. For that reason, one must clearly understand and must be completely familiar with each of the meditation sequences before attempting to do them. Trying to remember what you are supposed to do next, while you are in a meditative state, will only disrupt the meditation or hinder it. You must already know what the sequence is prior to using it in meditation.

It is best to study each of the following meditations carefully before attempting them. After going over them several times, do a dry run. Close your eyes and picture the entire process. Do this consciously. Become very familiar with this process before attempting to duplicate it in meditation. Once this is second nature, then it will replicate itself automatically. In meditation, the focus of attention should be on the experience, not on the process of reaching it.

If the mind is already programmed, the meditation becomes the vehicle for reaching and experiencing other levels of consciousness. The mind is then free to absorb and assimilate, to learn and grow. Learning the meditations before doing them creates the program internally. When meditating, the process is then either fully or semiautomatic. One is able to focus attention on what is happening and so is freed from having to worry about making anything occur.

The first two meditations, presented next, involve reaching into oneself. They are designed to access different perspectives of both inner and outer reality, by connecting with higher dimensions of oneself. The first meditation moves consciousness up through all of the Four Worlds within oneself, allowing one to view and experience reality through very distinct lenses. The second meditation explores experiencing consciousness from various vantage points within the body itself, each area of the body representing a unique form of consciousness.

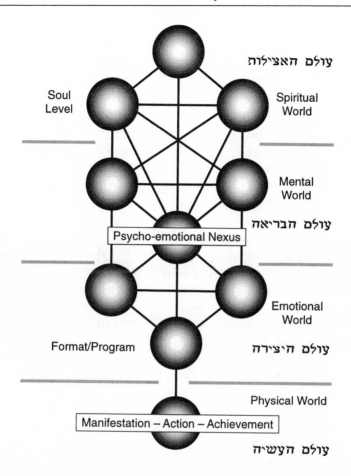

Meditation One: Ascension through the Four Worlds

1. Relax and enter the meditative state fully. When ready, proceed to the next step.
2. Picture a very large, transparent globe in front of you. This globe is the size of a room. It is filled with a quality of light specifically its own.
3. Move into the globe. Take some time to feel the energy of the globe. Become comfortable with the light. This globe is the *Sefirah* of *Malchut*, the realm of your physical existence. Let the energy around you permeate you.

4. As the energy moves through you, let it concentrate wherever in the body it wishes to. As it centers itself on its journey through the body, concentrate your attention on those points. What do you sense from these energy centers? What comes to you? What do you experience there? Take time to do this. Focus on each center individually. Move on to the next center only when you feel you are finished with the current one. Continue doing this until all of the centers of concentrated energy have been explored.

5. The physical plane also encompasses your conscious environment and your physical life in general. The energy in the globe houses memories of all your actions and of all the resulting interactions and implications as they occur on this level. Tapping into this energy allows one to experience and to explore one's conscious, day-to-day life in an expanded manner. Take a moment and focus your attention on the energy around you. What sensations, insights, or understandings come to you? What are you experiencing differently? What does all of this tell you about your life? Take some time to explore. You are in *Malchut*, the World of Doing.

6. It is now time to move on. Count up from zero to four. At the count of four, you will find yourself rising into an equally large globe, directly above this one. You will reach this globe on the fourth count. This is the *Sefirah* of *Yesod*. This is the core *Sefirah* of the World of Formation. This is the level of form and content. This is the realm of emotion. The energy found on this level of the Tree of Life is multifaceted. It is composed of a great many colors.

7. Look directly above. You will see two equally large globes there. One will be to the right and one will be to the left. They are the *Sefirot* of *Netzach* and *Hod*, respectively. Take some time and watch the energies that are pulsating within each of these *Sefirot*. Observe them carefully and get familiar with them. When ready, simultaneously draw a comfortable amount of each *Sefirah*'s energy down into *Yesod*.

8. Allow the energies to be mixed and blended. Become one with the balanced, refined energies. These are your emotional energies. Here in *Yesod* they are being patterned into a gestalt. This emotional gestalt defines much of your life experience. Take a few moments and harmonize with your emotions. Get

in touch with what you are feeling. Sense the inner connections between your emotions and the patterns that they are playing out in your life. Explore this realm thoroughly. Take as much time as you need.

9. Now, move up to the next *Sefirah*, directly above *Yesod*. This is the *Sefirah* of *Tiferet*. Count to six. You will find yourself centered in *Tiferet* on the sixth count. *Tiferet* is the hub of existence. All energy flows through this *Sefirah*, coming and going in all directions. Here is where the higher and lower realms meet and integrate. Experience the very flow of life. Energy is drawn in from all levels of the Tree of Life. Here, it is redirected and redistributed from this central juncture to all parts of one's being.

10. *Tiferet* is the core *Sefirah* of the World of Creation. This is the realm of the mind. It is the level of thought and purpose. On this level, cognition, understanding, motive, and choice all reside. Here, is the level of perception and self-awareness. In order to explore one's sense of self, one's life purpose, one's perceptions of reality, and one's alternatives, one must focus on this level of Tree within this *Sefirah*.

11. This is accomplished by replicating the pattern used below in *Yesod*. One must first focus attention on the two *Sefirot* to the upper right and the upper left, the *Sefirot* of *Hesed* and *Din*. Observe the dynamics of duality. Watch the push–pull of Creation. Sense the enormous power generated by the interaction of dependence, the drive toward independence, and the reality of interdependence. When ready, draw comfortable, equal amounts of energy from each of these two *Sefirot* into *Tiferet*.

12. Harmonize with the energies, as they achieve balance in *Tiferet*. Connect with the forces of expansion and contraction, as they are brought into equilibrium. Remain in harmony with the flow of the energy. Take time to experience the free flow of thought and perception. Become one with your thoughts and your processes. What do you sense about yourself? What are you comprehending about life and purpose? What are the real choices that lie open to you in your life? Take the opportunity now to explore this realm fully and completely, before moving to the highest realm of pure Being.

13. It is time to ascend to the highest realm, the World of Emanation. Picture a great globe of brilliant, clear light directly above.

This is the *Sefirah* of *Keter*. This is not only the core *Sefirah* of the level of *Atzilut*, Emanation, it is the origin point of all that you are. This is the level of pure Being. This is the level of the soul. If you look down to the right and down to the left, you will see the *Sefirot* of *Hochmah* and *Binah*.

14. Center in *Keter*. Focus on the Nothingness. Sense your pure, undefined Being, your intimate connection with God. By focusing your attention next on *Hochmah*, below and to the right, you will begin to feel the oscillation of consciousness between Being and Non-Being, between the Supernal Light of the soul and the Nothingness of God's Will from which it emerges and to which it is always connected. Then, by focusing next on the *Sefirah* of *Binah* on the lower left, one experiences the core of one's consciousness, the soul becoming conscious of itself.

15. This triad of *Sefirot* is the level of Soul. This is the spiritual realm of Being. Explore the three facets of this realm carefully and experience them fully. This can be accomplished by moving sequentially through each of the three *Sefirot* or through the agency of *Keter* alone. When finished, take a moment to look down and to reconnect with all of the lower *Sefirot* from this exalted position. This can be done either through *Keter* or through *Binah*.

    Position yourself in either *Sefirah*, then gaze down on all of the movement, energy, and activity taking place in the Tree below. Gain a sense of the spiritual meaning of all that is transpiring below, from the higher perspective of the soul.

16. Conclude the meditation by counting down from 10 to 0. With the count of 7, you will reach *Tiferet*. On the count of 4, you will reach *Yesod*. On the count of 1, you will reach *Malchut*, and at the point of 0, you will awaken from the meditation completely.

In the following meditation, movement into and through various organs of the body serves as gateways to the various *Sefirot*. By focusing attention within an organ, one opens up passage into the *Sefirah* with which it corresponds.

Resonating with the energy of the heart, one becomes attuned to the higher reality of the heart. That act opens up a gate into the *Sefirah* of *Tiferet*. Once inside *Tiferet*, one may explore the realities of the *Sefirah* itself, or connect with the level of *Tiferet* within anything in Creation.

In the following meditation, entrance will be into the *Sefirah* of *Tiferet* specifically. However, any *Sefirah* can be entered by using the exact same meditation format. Below is a list of the traditional correspondences between the parts of the human body and the various *Sefirot*.

Keter: The crown of the head. The apex of the cerebral cortex.

Hochmah: The right side of the brain.

Binah: The left side of the brain.

Hesed: The right lung.

Din: The left lung.

Tiferet: The heart.

Netzach: Liver and right kidney.

Hod: Spleen and left kidney.

Yesod: Stomach and digestive system.

Malchut: Genitals and reproductive system.

Meditation Two: Reaching the *Sefirot* through the Body

1. Get comfortable, in a relaxed position. Move into a deep state of meditation. When ready, proceed to the meditation itself.
2. Focus your consciousness at the very crown of the head. On the count from 1 to 6, move down through the head, neck, and upper torso, until you arrive at the heart. Enter the heart on the seventh count.
3. Spend time in the heart itself. Move gradually through the heart. Feel the movement of the blood, the pulsation of the energy. Listen to the sound of the heartbeat. Look, listen, and feel. What do you sense? What do you come to know from this experience?
4. Pass out of the heart, as if through a gateway. The journey through the heart is a passage through a series of corridors. One emerges from the corridors into the realm of *Tiferet*. There, one encounters a vast field of color. Pass through it, to wherever it shall take you.
5. Let yourself loose. At this point, the journey will conduct itself. Allow yourself to experience whatever happens. Let everything unfold. Savor the experience fully. Then, before exiting, tell yourself that you will retain a complete, conscious memory of

the experience. Tell yourself that you will be able to recall this state at will, at any time in the future.

6. When ready, you may return to full waking consciousness by counting from 10 to 1. You will reach the crown of the head on the count of 3 and awaken on the count of 1.

The *Sefer Yetzirah* speaks extensively about the thirty-two paths. The thirty-two paths are the interplay between the *Sefirot* and the letters of the Hebrew alphabet. The process of the thirty-two paths is one of exploring the dimensions of Creation and of creativity.

There are two different ways one can view and interpret the interplay of the *Sefirot* and the alphabet as one explores the dynamics of Creation. One way is to see the twenty-two letters of the alphabet as corresponding to the twenty-two lines or pathways that connect the *Sefirot* together in the Tree of Life. The other is to view the impact of each letter of the alphabet on the *Sefirot* from within each *Sefirah*. The next two meditations illustrate techniques representing both of these approaches.

Meditation Three: The Letters as Pathways

For the sake of clarity and consistency, it is easiest to use the three Mother Letters, *Aleph*, *Mem*, and *Shin*, as examples in these exercises. The Mother Letters are the primal forces fueling the entire alphabet. They are the most powerful and the most central of all letters. Moreover, they embody the three basic principles which stand at the structural base of the Tree of Life.

Aleph embodies the principle of neutrality and balance. *Mem* represents the passive principle of receptivity and depth. The *Shin* is the letter of action, movement, and creativity. Together, they form the fundamental triad of existence as is signified in the Tree of Life structure.

The Tree of Life model reflects a universe that is powered and sustained through duality. The universe exists as a balance between opposites. As opposites, the right and the left pillars define the parameters of the Tree, on one hand. On the other, because they are opposites and therefore exclusive of each other, their mutual existence is totally dependent on the neutrality and on the harmony of the central pillar.

This interdependent relationship between the right column and the left infuses Creation with life. The turbulent oscillation between them, between expansion and contraction, produces a spinout from the neutral center of the Middle Pillar. The alternation of attraction and repulsion resulting from the opposition of these two pillars, set them in constant revolution around the neutral central pillar. This whirlwind movement produces both the energy of the universe, and is that which produces the fullness of Creation, by its very movement.

The connection between the expansive right and the contractive left is one of the most mysterious and one of the most important elements of Creation and the creative process. This intimate and awesome conjunction of polar opposites can be explored carefully through meditation on the three Mother Letters.

According to Rabbi Isaac Luria, the *Ari*, each of the three Mother Letters constitutes the connection, the pathway, between the six polarized *Sefirot*. According to the *Ari*, the path between the *Sefirah* of *Hochmah* and the *Sefirah* of *Binah* is the letter *Shin*. The corridor between *Hesed* and *Din* is the letter *Aleph*. The third path bridging right and left, the *Mem*, unites the *Sefirot* of *Netzach* and *Gevurah*.

Any pathway, any line between two *Sefirot*, should be understood as a corridor. Such a corridor both links the two *Sefirot* and leads directly from one *Sefirah* to the other and back again. Meditating on a letter as a pathway between two *Sefirot* can reveal many dimensions of their interrelationship.

This type of meditation can allow one to experience the very transformation of energy. The flow of energy through the Tree gains in quality and substance, as it evolves from the form and imprint of one *Sefirah* and passes into that of the next. Using a letter as a guide, one becomes one with the flow of universal energy, as it evolves and takes on new layers of richness and meaning, as it flows from one *Sefirah* into another.

In short, a letter represents a pathway between two *Sefirot*. The letter can be seen either as a link between the two *Sefirot* or as a path leading from one to the other. Viewing the letter as a link allows one to explore the significance of the various dimensions of the relationship between the two connected letters. Approaching the letter as pathway permits one to follow the corridor from one *Sefirah* to the next and to experience the evolution that takes place in the process of moving from one to the other.

Meditation A

1. Go into the meditative state. Picture the *Sefirah* of *Hesed* in front of you to your right and the *Sefirah* of *Din* before you to your left. Notice the bridge that connects them.
2. On the bridge is the letter *Aleph*. Focus your attention on the *Aleph*. Move the *Aleph* to any point on the bridge. Each point on the bridge represents a different and distinct aspect of the relationship between the two *Sefirot*.

3. With the *Aleph* positioned at a specific juncture, observe how the two *Sefirot* interact. What does this point on the bridge tell you about their relationship? Now reposition and focus the letter at another point on the bridge. As the energy changes, what do you see? What do you hear? What do you feel? What do you come to know about the interaction of these two *Sefirot*?

4. You may wish to move the *Aleph* any number of times during the meditation. When finished with the experience, count backward from 10 to 0 and return to full consciousness.

Meditation B

1. Enter into the meditative state. Visualize yourself in a huge, bright green globe. This is the *Sefirah* of *Hesed*. Picture yourself approaching the gate that exits from *Hesed*. Laid out before you is a long tunnel. Facing you is a very large *Aleph*, pulsating with energy. It is there to guide you through the tunnel to the gate of *Din*.

2. As the *Aleph* moves, follow it. Allow yourself to be drawn effortlessly along as you move through the tunnel. As you move, first focus your attention on the *Aleph*. Then focus on yourself. How is the *Aleph* changing as it goes? How are you changing? What are you experiencing as you progress gradually toward the realm of *Din*?

3. Monitor your feelings carefully. Pay close attention to the sensations you are experiencing and to the events that are transpiring on the journey. Conclude the exercise upon reaching the gate of *Din*. Before exiting, tell yourself that you will retain complete memory of this experience and all you have learned.

4. When you are ready, exit from the meditation by counting down from 10 to 0.

In a similar manner, the various dimensions and aspects of a *Sefirah* itself can be explored via the use of a Hebrew letter. Since *Aleph* is a neutral force, and also the most inclusive of any letter in the alphabet, let us meditate on the *Sefirah* of *Hesed*, by using the *Aleph*.

Picture an immense circle before you. This circle is filled with an endless field of green. In the center of the circle, on the field of green is the letter *Aleph*. Focus your meditation on the *Aleph* and on the green light and green energy that permeates it and the environment all around it.

There are two different approaches you can take at this point. One method is to focus your attention and to contemplate intensively on the green field within the *Sefirah*. This connects you with the workings of *Hesed*. Then, concentrate even more carefully on the *Aleph* in the middle of the green field. By so doing, after a while, you will be linked to the *Aleph*. You will experience the power of the *Aleph*, acting within *Hesed*. The reality and the nature of the *Sefirah* of *Hesed* and the effect of the *Aleph* within *Hesed* will eventually impact you. You will feel the ramifications of their interaction. Let them work themselves through you. When you have experienced and assimilated as much as can be handled at this time, exit from the meditation.

The other approach is to enter the field of *Hesed*, drawing the *Aleph* into your heart and allowing yourself to float. Let the *Aleph* carry you through the vast green expanse of *Hesed*. Allow yourself to accept and acknowledge whatever may come. Become one with the flow and at peace with the experience. Again, when you are ready, simply exit the meditation.

Taking either approach, any Hebrew letter can be so used in exploring the nature and function of any given *Sefirah*. As far as the pathways are concerned, however, each letter represents a specific bridge between two defined *Sefirot*. They are bridges rather than methods of examining *Sefirot* per se.

In exploring the nature and content of a *Sefirah*, one has a choice. So it is important to choose carefully and consciously. Inside the *Sefirot*, the letters act as guides, acting on the energy of the *Sefirah*, filtering certain experiences and making clear specific realities.

Choosing a specific letter as a gateway to understanding a *Sefirah* is like being taken on a tour of a city. What the tour will be like, what one sees, and what one experiences will be different depending on who is leading the tour. The tour guide may be a professional. He may be a relative or a friend. He may be a business contact or salesperson. Each will have his own style, viewpoint, and set of priorities. The city will be the same. The tours, however, will not.

THE *SEFIROT* AS CONCENTRIC CIRCLES

The interrelationship of the *Sefirot* in early kabbalist literature is sometimes pictured as concentric circles. The innermost circle can be either *Keter* or *Malchut*, and correspondingly, *Malchut* or *Keter* would be the outermost one. This depends strictly on viewpoint. *Keter* to *Malchut* would be the projection of Creation, or the Self, outward from the core. Movement from *Malchut* to *Keter* would be that of inward movement from the outside into the core. This would, for example, be a paradigm for introspection.

This particular geometric view of the *Sefirot* is also very useful as a model for meditation. Its applications are immediately obvious. If one wishes to move deeper into oneself for purposes of self-exploration, the model of the concentric *Sefirot* is a perfect vehicle for doing so. The same is true if one seeks to project some aspect of oneself out into the world.

Before utilizing the concentric circle pattern of the *Sefirot*, it is important to understand what this pattern represents. What does it mean to have the ten *Sefirot* arranged as concentric circles? What significance lies behind this model of the *Sefirot*?

The geometry of the concentric *Sefirot* tells us a good deal about the totality of being. A set of concentric circles is a complete, integrated whole. Each *Sefirah* is a layer within the whole. Each *Sefirah* is distinct, having its own definition, yet all the *Sefirot* are the same in structure, form, and substance.

A good analogy would be that of an onion. When an onion is cut in half, one sees that it is comprised of layers. Each layer replicates the earlier layers but is distinct from the others, representing a new, more advanced level of growth. Each layer by itself is onion. The onion itself is a composite of all the layers, encompassed by a dry outer covering. To remove any of the layers would be to shatter the onion into pieces. What constitutes an onion is the unified totality of all its levels of growth.

The *Sefirot* can be seen the same way. All of the *Sefirot* are equal. All of the *Sefirot* are nonsubstantive. There is growth and development implied in their geometric relationship to each other. One *Sefirah* emanates from the other. They each reflect what has come before and what will come next. The *Sefirot* are all an interlocked unity of equal elements and dimensionality, reflecting different aspects of the same whole. There are exactly ten *Sefirot*, not nine and not eleven. Zero through nine is a complete set. It is the set of all the elemental numbers. No number is more important than its neighbors. No number can be missing from the set.

Consider that the diagram of a set of concentric circles can be a two-dimensional portrayal of a three-dimensional reality. What the three-dimensional shape represented would be depends on one's viewpoint. If one were viewing the geometry of the circles from above, in three-dimensional space, one would be seeing a cone. Viewing it conversely from the other direction—"below," if you will—one sees a funnel. From the third standpoint, observing it from a parallel position, one perceives a tunnel or corridor.

All three of these images can be used effectively in meditation. The image of the funnel is one of introspection and internalization. Conversely, the cone can be used to project that which is within outward toward manifestation. This is the model of revelation, self-expression, and interrelationship. The tunnel or corridor is the paradigm for movement, evolution, and processing. Which model one chooses to use is based on the objective of the meditation. Both are sefirotic models, merely with different vantage points.

The life of the soul on all levels of existence is that of experience and self-development. All three of these meditative approaches to the *Sefirot* foster that evolutionary growth. This is the true use of the *Sefirot*, self-exploration. By experiencing the dimensions of self through inner search, through self-expression, and through self-process, we come to know ourselves. By connecting with who we are, we grow and thereby fulfill the highest purpose of existence, serving God continually through self-realization and growth.

Meditation Four: Moving into Oneself

1. Relax and enter into the meditative state.
2. Count slowly from 1 to 10. In progressing through the numbers, feel yourself becoming lighter and lighter, and rising into the air. Reach a comfortable point for hovering at the number 10, then hover in space for a while, until ready to proceed.
3. Below you will be a large funnel. The funnel has ten levels that are contiguous. Each level narrows as it descends and each is smaller than the level from which it came. Each level is another *Sefirah*, another dimension of your being. The highest stage, at the top of the funnel, is that of *Malchut*. The narrow end at the bottom of the funnel is the level of *Keter*.
4. Move down progressively through the funnel. Move deeper, one stage at a time, farther and farther into the funnel of the *Sefirot*. Allow yourself to experience whatever occurs, at each successive level. Your focus should become greater and greater in clarity. You should experience more increased focus as you move down through the levels of self.
5. At the bottom of the funnel, what you experience is often the most concrete and the most detailed. The answers one seeks can, and often do, appear on several levels as one descends. How-

ever, the complete synthesis, the totality of the experience and all the information meant to be understood on the deepest level, is achieved at this last stage, that of *Keter*, the level of Essence.

6. Focus your attention on encompassing, absorbing, and assimilating this condensed, core material. It is through connecting with the core, with the very essence of something, that it is later understood on the innermost level of Being. Something has to be experienced on the deepest level before its meaning and ramifications can be processed.

7. When finished, exit the meditation by counting backward from 10 to 0.

Energy Flow Two: Revolution

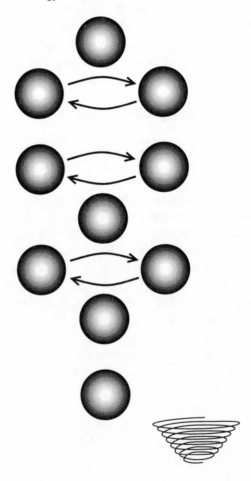

Meditation Five: Projecting Self into the World

1. Relax and enter into the meditative state. Spend some time, moving into a state of great inner peace and tranquility.
2. Move your consciousness, either to a point at the very back of the brain or to a point deep within the center of the heart, depending on where your intuition tells you to start.
3. Take some time and let the energy at this point build up and become strong.
4. Allow the energy, resident at this point, to expand in the form of a growing cone. It should expand forward toward the center of your forehead. Each stage of expansion will enlarge the cone and move its base closer to the forehead. Each stage is another *Sefirah*. The base of the cone will reach the forehead at the ninth stage, the level of *Yesod*.
5. The cone will complete itself outside of the head, some distance in front of you. That is the level of *Malchut*. Allow the energy being generated by the origin point within to flow freely through the cone. Eventually a visual image, sights and sounds, or a set of feelings will emerge in front of you, on the base of the cone. This is the image of something within you that is seeking to manifest. It may already be in the process of working itself out in the world. Some part of you either is emerging or is seeking to express itself outwardly.
6. It may be of great benefit to examine what is manifesting. At this point, one can learn from it. One can come to terms with it. One can even alter it, if need be. Let your instinct and intuition tell you what need be done, if anything.
7. When you are through with the meditation, move back into yourself. Return to full waking consciousness by counting backward from 10 to 0.

Meditation Six: Walking through the Levels of Self

1. Relax fully and breathe deeply, slowly entering a deep state of meditation, a deep state of peace and serenity.
2. When ready, picture a large tunnel before you. There is a circular gate at the mouth of each end of the tunnel. There are eight similar circular gates within the tunnel, all at equal intervals from each other. At the count of seven, enter the first

gate. You will find yourself in a field of red light. This is the
area of *Malchut*, your physical existence and daily conscious
life. Take some time to explore this area. When ready, position yourself in front of the second gate.

3. Upon entering the second gate, you enter into the realm of
orange energy. This is the *Sefirah* of *Yesod*. At this juncture
you are exploring the imprints and patterns that affect your
life, your experiences, and the way you perceive things.
Explore carefully.

4. When ready, enter the third and then the fourth gates. These
are the levels of *Hod* and then, *Netzach*. This is the realm of
dreams, hopes, aspirations, and desires. Spend some time here
before moving to the next, central level. The area of the third
gate will be yellow. That of the fourth gate will be bright
yellow.

5. Emergence through the gate brings you to the field of golden
energy, the level of the heart, the level of *Tiferet*. You have
arrived at the seat of all your emotions. This is where mind
and emotion meet. This is the central point of the tunnel and
the very fulcrum of one's existence. Particular attention should
be given to the exploration and experience of *Tiferet*. Only after
you have fully connected with the energies here should you
attempt to move on.

6. Passing through the next two gates will bring you first to the
Sefirah of *Din*, and subsequently, to that of *Hesed*. The realm
of *Din* will possess an energy field of green. The *Sefirah* of *Hesed*
will have an energy of bright green. These segments of the
tunnel are the level of duality and generation. Here is the realm
of your thoughts, your beliefs, and your plans. This is the
cognitive level of existence. Take some time to explore this
realm and to process what you find.

7. Entering the next gates, those of *Binah* and *Hochmah*, allows
you access to the levels of understanding and wisdom. This is
the realm of the True Mind. Here, one moves beyond thinking and thought. Within these *Sefirot* one experiences inner
knowledge and knowingness. Within this realm lies the
impetus of one's life and one's life purpose. Harmonize with
this energy. These are the fields of blue, the energies of tranquility and peace.

8. Exiting the tunnel, one reaches the infinite white light of *Self*. One arrives at *Keter*, that which is truly you, beyond time and space. Here is the level of Being. Here is the Self. Here is the core of existence, the intimate connection with God and with all that is. Be who you are. Rejoice.

9. When you feel that you are ready, return to normal, waking consciousness by counting backward from 10 to 0. Because of the extremely powerful effects that this particular meditation can have, it is wise to take a moment after awakening to reground yourself physically. This can be done easily, by moving energy. Do some stretching exercise. Walk around the room. Touch something. Perhaps even have a bite to eat or something to drink.

10. Say a blessing thanking God for this experience and for just being.

8

Contemplation and Meditation
on Hebrew Verb Roots

In Kabbalah, the triad or triangle is of primary importance. As has been illustrated already, the Tree of Life has three triads of *Sefirot* comprising the upper worlds. The Tree is also structured into three vertical pillars. In the upper worlds, each pillar has three *Sefirot*, leading down toward *Malchut*.

There are also three Mother Letters, upon which the entire alphabet is structured and upon which the twenty-two paths connecting the *Sefirot* are dependent. The *Sefer Yetzirah* states that the Mother Letters give birth to the Fathers, the three principles. These principles, expansion, contraction, and neutrality, are the basis for the entire alphabet. All the remaining letters are referred to as the descendants.

Kabbalah ascribes to the Mother Letters the role of organizing principle. Each Mother Letter is viewed as the force best characterizing the underlying, unifying principle behind each pillar of the Tree of Life.

The Middle Pillar of *Keter*, *Tiferet*, *Yesod*, and *Malchut* is that of neutrality and of balance. It is governed by the letter *Aleph*, *Aleph* being air. The right pillar, which is the side of energy, creativity, and expansion, is characterized by *Shin*, fire. *Mem*, water, governs the left side of the Tree. The left pillar is that of existence, receptivity, and definition.

The *Aleph* stands at the apex of the Tree of Life. It is the emanation point of the middle pillar. In conjunction with *Keter*, the *Aleph* serves as both the origin of all, on one hand, and as the balance point mediating between the *Shin* and the *Mem*, on the other. The *Aleph* is One. It is the source and the ultimate unity of all Creation. Below it stand the *Shin* and the *Mem*, fire and water. They represent the great duality, the principles of yin and yang, out of which the movement of the universe is produced.

Shin-Mem together spell the Hebrew word for "name." United to the source, to God's Will, is God's Name. The level of *Aleph* gives birth to the level of *Shin-Mem*, the Name. This Great Duality is not only the origin of Creation, it is the force that generates and sustains it. The duality of fire and water is the interplay of the primal principles of Creation, out of which the whole process of Creation emerges. This interplay is the Name.

The interaction of *Shin* and *Mem* is the foundation of differentiation. To name something is to give it a separate identity and existence. The infinite multiplicity of God's intention is manifest first in the Name. From the Name all Creation flows.

Everything in the universe, according to the Kabbalah, has a name. The name of something is the constellation of energy formed by the patterns of Hebrew letters in conjunction with one another. The pattern formed by *Aleph-Dalet-Mem* (*ADaM*), for example, is that of mankind. The conjunction of *Aleph-Resh-Yod-Heh* (*ARYeH*) is the energy pattern that produces the reality of the lion.

Letter patterns form energy vortexes that create realities. So it is logical that contemplation of letter groupings that constitute names, if done in conjunction with the Mother Letters pattern, would allow the meditator to pierce deeply into the vast hidden layers of meaning concealed within the name.

How is that accomplished? The three Mother Letters spawn the Fathers, the three principles. Each of these principles first appear in the uppermost triad of the Tree of Life. *Aleph* is equated with *Keter*, *Shin* with *Hochmah*, and *Mem* with *Binah*. *Aleph* gives birth to the neutral principle, air. *Shin* produces fire, the principle of energy, and *Mem*, water, the principle of transformation.

One meditates or contemplates, depending on level of comfort, on one letter of the pattern within each of the *Sefirot*. For example, if one were meditating on growth or development, one would use the verb root *Gimmel-Dalet-Lamed*. The *Gimmel* would be placed in the first *Sefirah*,

Keter, the *Dalet* in *Hochmah*, and the *Lamed* in *Binah*. What lies at the core of growth is the *Gimmel* force, understood in the context of the neutral middle pillar. The expansive, external side of growth is reflected by the *Dalet* force governing the right pillar. The internal, developmental side of growth is grasped by meditation on the *Lamed* force dominating the left pillar of the Tree.

This process presupposes that the name being meditated on is three letters. It also assumes that the first letter of the pattern will correspond to *Keter*, or the neutrality/balance principle. Hence, the second letter will correspond to *Hochmah*, the active principle, and the third to *Binah*, the receptive principle. The levels of meaning would then be derived from contemplation and meditation on what each letter, connected to its specific principle in this pattern, implies. Moreover, meditation on the sequence of letters, on the geometric relationship between the letters, on the overall gestalt of the pattern, and so on would yield further levels of meaning and insight.

Are all nouns or names in Hebrew three letters? Obviously not. However, all verb roots are. That fact is crucial to our discussion here.

The entire Hebrew language is based largely on the verb as the central, pivotal element of its very structure. At the base of any verb, there is a verb root. A Hebrew verb root has three letters, always. Only verbs taken from foreign languages may have a four-letter root. From the verb root, all forms of the verb are built. Verb forms encompass gender, number, and person, as well as past, present, and future tenses. In biblical Hebrew, they can also contain subject and direct object pronouns.

Moreover, the vast majority of nouns, adjectives, and adverbs are all built directly and predictably from the verb root. The verb root is the basis of 95 percent of the Hebrew language. The key to truly understanding the Hebrew language, its structure, its psychology, its inner meaning, and its metaphysical depth is through the verb root.

The verb root, therefore, has a very deep and abiding significance in meditation practice. It is the primary pattern that emerges from the alphabet and forms the basis of reality on multiple levels of consciousness.

The letters themselves are the primal building blocks or energies, which when combined together into patterns or words, create reality. The letter combinations produce focus. The result of this focus is reality. Verb roots are the most essential, elemental realities. Derivative realities, articulated verbs, nouns, adjectives, and adverbs are all formed from them. Meditation on the verb root is the key to experiencing the hidden depths of human action and process. It is the gateway to deeper understandings of all of the forms and realities that derive from them, also.

To illustrate this contemplative and meditative process, let us use the verb root *Shin-Mem-Resh* (*ShMR*), which means "to guard, to protect, to keep, to observe." Some derivative words from this root include *Shemirah*, "guard duty," *Shemirat Shabbat*, "observance of the Sabbath," *Shimurim*, "canned goods," *Shemurah*, "preservation."

To gain a deeper sense of what guarding or keeping watch represents, one should contemplate the verb root. One method of doing so is to focus consciously on the meaning of each of the three root letters, in sequence, then to allow the information to coalesce into a new understanding or insight. Perhaps an illustration of this approach would be helpful.

A CONTEMPLATION ON THE VERB
ROOT *SHIN-MEM-RESH*

Among its many meanings, the verb root *ShMR* is used to refer to keeping or observing the biblical commandments. *Shemirat Shabbat* is the observance of the Sabbath, for example, the term *Shemirah* deriving from the root *ShMR*. The observance of the commandments, acting in accord with God's expectations of us, is a primary, fundamental principle within Jewish belief and practice. It is certainly an extremely pertinent focus upon which to meditate.

In using a verb root as a meditation, the first stage is that of contemplation. Contemplation, that is, deep concentration and focus of thought on the verb root, provides the gateway to the meditation. Contemplating each letter of the verb root, and extracting hidden meaning from them, gives one the raw material to focus on in meditation. Once focused, the meditation leads one into very deep levels of experience.

One of the meanings of the first letter of the verb root *Shin* is that of the soul. Of the three parts of the soul, the two active elements are the *Neshamah* and *Nefesh*. Both contain the letter *Shin*. In both instances, the Sh sound, the *Shin*, dominates the articulated pronunciations. As Mother Letters, the *Shin* and *Mem* are the two active elements of the Tree of Life, the right and left pillars. The third element of the soul, the passive one, *Ruach*, meaning "spirit," does not contain a *Shin*. Rather, this passive element of the soul, *Ruach*, begins with a *Resh*, the third letter of the verb root *ShMR*.

It is therefore obvious that somehow all parts of the soul are involved in the process of keeping, observing, and guarding. One clear example would be keeping and observing the commandments. "Guarding"or "keeping" (*ShMR*) is characterized in Hebrew as a progression from *Shin* to *Mem* to *Resh*. Fire (*Shin*) is emotional involvement, passion, and expression. In the process of "keeping," this leads to Water (*Mem*). The Water is internalization. It is also the flow of life. Action leads to internal change. The *Mem* progresses ultimately to *Resh*, the Mind. Understanding on the deepest level is the result of observing and preserving.

Shin-Mem-Resh represents on one hand a conjunction of all three elements of the soul. On the other hand, it also is a progression of events that impact on the soul. An important implication here is that "keeping the commandments" involves the entire soul. The soul is engaged actively at first, through intention, motivation, and doing. Ultimately, as a result of the process, the soul is affected by the impact produced by the enacted commandment.

The entire process emanates from the *Shin*, the soul, and in the end, helps mold and enrich it. The shape of the *Shin*, with its three branches, characterizes the three components of the soul, the *Neshamah* (the innermost Being), the *Ruach* (the domain of movement, development, and imprint), and the *Nefesh* (the ego and personality). The three branches of the *Shin* extend upward from a common base toward Heaven. They reach toward higher levels of reality and consciousness.

The beginning of the keeping the commandments, remaining in touch with what God expects of the individual, resides within the soul itself. The *Shin* is also the first letter of the word *Shalom*, peace. The root of *Shalom*, *Shin-Lamed-Mem* (*ShLM*), means to complete, to make whole. So the beginning of the process of observing or keeping the commandments is rooted in the desire of the soul to complete something and to become more whole, more integrated. It is the soul's longing for God. The soul seeking to reconnect with God yearns for completion.

That yearning leads to the second stage of the process, symbolized by the letter *Mem*. The *Mem* signifies water, *Mayim*, in Hebrew. Water is the element of change, transformation, and evolution. Water, in its natural state, is always moving. It ebbs and flows. It streams and pulses. It churns and cleanses. In its yearning for completion, the soul extends itself toward God. This act of extension, in turn, triggers change and internal transformation. There is inner movement within the soul, which transforms it.

What is transformed is the yearning for completion. What was yearning in the *Shin*, has been transformed by the *Mem* into the *Resh*. The last stage of our process is the *Resh* principle. The letter *Resh* is the initial letter of the word *Reshith*, meaning "the beginning." To commence something is to initiate a process. By keeping something sacred, by observing the commandments, by preserving the integrity of one's relationship with God, one transforms the yearning for completion from a potential into an active process.

Resh is also the first letter of the word *rosh*, "head." The head symbolizes thought. The first two letters of the verb root, *ShMR*, are *Shin-Mem*. This combination of letters spells out the word *shem*, meaning "a name." When you give something a name, you are defining it. So the process that is initiated by the transformation of yearning into action is one of thought, definition, and limitation. To observe the commandments of God is to begin an active process of continual thought and reflection. It produces a constant effort at defining, redefining, and delineating the limits of one's actions, with the objective of seeking completion.

Hence, one way to understand the observance of the commandments is the meeting of God's expectations. Viewing this through the perspective of the verb root, *Shin-Mem-Resh*, fulfilling what God wants is a process. Rooted in the soul is the yearning to be more complete and to experience reconnection. As the yearning extends itself, a transformation occurs. The soul evolves and grows through thought, contemplation, and meditation. These processes move the soul through cycles of completion and closer toward God. Yearning has been transformed from a passive state into concrete action.

Another auxiliary interpretation would follow from viewing all of the letters of the verb root as principles. The *Shin*, as mentioned earlier, represents the principle of fire. The *Mem* represents the principle of water. Both of these elements oppose each other by nature. Yet in the verb root, *ShMR*, the *Shin* and *Mem* are conjoined. They are followed by the *Resh*. These two principles of creation, energy, and receptivity are joined together and held in balance by the presence and force of the *Resh*. The *Resh* is, on one hand, the seventh of the double letters, the neutral principle. On the other hand, it also symbolizes the head, the center of thought, contemplation, and meditation.

Shin-Mem-Resh, to keep, to guard, to preserve, then is connected directly to the three pillars of the Tree of Life. The right and left pillars of expansion/energy and limitation/receptivity are brought together by the neutral center pillar, which holds them in place and balances their forces to allow the universe to exist. This balance is preserved by keeping one's obligations to God, by doing what God expects. "Observing the Commandments" maintains the central focus and balance that allows the universe to exist.

Moreover, the inner reality of what God expects from us, the key to fully understanding the deeper levels of the commandments and what their implications are, comes through thought, contemplation, and meditation. As it is expressed in the Bible,

" כי אם בתורת ה חפצו ובתורתו יהגה יומם ולילה. "

"For if one's desire is for the ordinances of God, he meditates on His Law, day and night"(Psalm 1:2).

In the external world, for something to warrant being guarded or protected, it must be considered valuable. On the internal level, for something to be truly cherished and preserved, one must understand its direct connection with the soul, the source from which it derives its worth. What one keeps within and cherishes is tied directly to the *Shin*, the soul.

Drawing on the power of the soul, one is lead to experience the *Mem*. One must allow that which is harbored within, one's feelings, thoughts, and beliefs, to change and evolve, if they are to continue to exist and to grow. Room must be made for continuity and development. Energized by the force of the soul, what one feels, thinks, believes, experiences, and accepts, are protected and kept alive by evolution and growth.

Evolution, in turn, needs purpose and direction. Unless there is planning, analysis, self-expression, and increased knowledge forging its direction and molding its course, evolution deteriorates into disintegration and dissipation. Therefore, the centrality of thought and the harmonizing neutrality of contemplation and meditation are required to ensure the growth and development of what one keeps and understands of life experience. That is the element of *Resh*.

That which one preserves (*ShMR*) within—our thoughts, memories, beliefs, and so forth—are linked to the soul and energized by it. The energy produced transforms these perceptions into something very valuable to the individual holding them. The transformed energy propels their growth and evolution. One's emotional, intellectual, and spiritual development is now guided by thought, contemplation, and meditation. Such is the process of the verb root *Shin-Mem-Resh*.

The foregoing interpretations of *ShMR* are by no means exclusive of the verb root, or exhaustive. They are simply examples of the process of abstracting inner meaning from a Hebrew verb root by contemplation. Focus can be centered on the meaning of the individual letters, their sequential relationship, their interplay as a total concept, or all three.

The material derived from contemplation is often very fertile ground on which to center a meditation. For example, any of the insights detailed above in reference to the verb root *Shin-Mem-Resh* may productively serve as focal points of meditation. A simple way to accomplish this would be to take a specific insight that was gained in contemplation and formulate it as a sentence. For example, "A concept takes on spiritual force and great personal importance, when internalized and attached to the soul."

That statement is a formalized concept derived from the insight received during contemplation of the *ShMR* verb root. This formulation can now serve as a meditative focus of its own. One can then meditate on the reality of what the spiritual impact of guarding a specific belief within oneself actually is. One simply repeats the sentence over and over as a mantra and focuses on the images or sensations produced by the recitation. The repetition of the concept generates the energy. The energy is transformed into sensation or imagery. The imagery symbolizes the inner reality.

THE VERB ROOT AS THE PILLARS OF THE TREE

Another meditative technique that can be used with the three letter verb root is that of correspondence. Each of the three letters of the root can be seen to correspond with one of the three pillars of the Tree of Life. In short, the first letter of the root can be seen as the central pillar or the *Aleph* force, the second as the right pillar, the *Shin*, and the third letter of the root as the *Mem* force, the left pillar.

As is reflected clearly in the structure of the Tree of Life, one of the most fundamental principles of existence is that of the triune relationship of left, center, and right. All of life is seen by the Kabbalah as predicated on a tripartite pattern. Duality, which is the energy for all of Creation, is maintained by the medium of neutrality, which keeps the opposing forces in balance and in check.

By equating each letter of a verb root with a pillar of the Tree of Life, one can penetrate into deeper levels of existence. Among the Four Worlds of the Kabbalah, the physical world is referred to as the "World of Doing." The universe is the realm of action, the domain of manifestation and accomplishment. Verbs are the words we use to denote action. Meditating on the verb root is to focus on and explore the vast network of ramifications implicit in a specific dimension of physical reality.

For example, were one to take the verb root *Nune-Tav-Nune*, "to give," and meditate on it, one would find themselves exploring infinite dimensions and subdivisions of the reality of giving. That may manifest as anything, from a deepening understanding into the nature of charity, to experiencing the ramifications of an altruistic action. This can be accomplished by picturing the Tree of Life in front of you. Place the first letter of the verb root, the *Nune*, in the *Sefirah* of *Keter*. Then, place the second letter, the *Tav*, in *Hochmah*, to the right, and the third, the second *Nune*, in *Binah*, to the left.

Let the energy of each letter expand and flow downward, encompassing and filling each of the *Sefirot* below it. You may wish to use a different color for each of the three energies. When all of the *Sefirot* have been filled with the light of their pillar, focus your attention on the energy buildup in the *Sefirah* of *Tiferet*. When you are ready, pull some of the energy being produced into your heart. Keep the connection with *Tiferet*, and leave the channel open as long as you need to. You will begin to feel and experience specific aspects of the reality of "giving," as well as how it manifests and operates in the universe.

Should you wish to delve further into the realm of this action, center your attention on the letters themselves in the top three *Sefirot*. Everything that exists has an inner and outer dimension. When attempting to gain a sense of this inner to outer relationship in a specific area of human endeavor, the verb root is again of great use on a contemplative/meditative level.

At this level of the *Arikh Anpin*, the Great Face of God, *Keter-Hochmah-Binah*, one is dealing with the core of reality. This is the level of Will. It is the level of the Hidden. It is the level of connection to God. At this supreme level, any specific reality, any energy force, is in a state of unity. The first letter of the root, in the *Aleph* position in *Keter*, represents the origin, the innermost reality of the concept. By direct extension, the letters in *Hochmah* and *Binah* are the forces that will eventually manifest as the outward reality of the energy pattern.

By way of example, let us examine the verb root *Nune-Tav-Nune*, "to give," in this light.

The first *Nune* of this verb root would be in the *Aleph* position. That would signify that the spiritual origin, the hidden reality of giving, is that of the *Nune* force. To gain a clearer sense of what the *Nune* force represents, one can contemplate the numerologic total of the fully spelled out name of the letter,

נ ו ן

The name *Nune* has the numerical value of 106. One hundred six is also the numerical value for:

"Your Servants" (*Avadekha*)   עבדיך

"As God" (*Ke-Elohim*)   כאלהים

"Line" (*Kav*)   קו

According to the great kabbalist Rabbi Isaac Luria, the creation of the lower six *Sefirot* takes place in part from the penetration of the light of *Hochmah* into the vacated space in *Binah*. The vacated space is produced by the contraction that takes place in *Binah* to allow room for Creation to come about. This penetration of the light into the vacated space is referred to as the *Kav*, "the line."

This tells us that giving in its truest sense is the directed, focused flow of Divine energy into the void. Giving is a replication of the interaction that triggers creation itself. True giving is the act of providing light. By giving, the giver becomes "like God."

When inserting the verb root for "gives"(*NTN*) into the top three *Sefirot*, the first *Nune* goes in *Keter*, the *Tav* in *Hochmah*, and the second *Nune* in *Binah*. The fact that the *Nune* reproduces itself in *Binah*, the third root letter position, suggests that once an emptiness is filled with light, it in turn becomes a transmitter of light and replicates the process again.

The inner reality represented by the *Nune* in *Keter* means that the origin of giving is in the very act of God's Will manifesting in the first place. Its replication in *Binah* makes it clear that giving replicates Divine Grace on all levels of reality. The inner and outer aspects are the same. Giving on an external level directly reflects and makes manifest the inner reality of God's grace and God's Will. When human beings truly give of themselves, they truly express the reality of the core purpose of the universe. When so doing, we are then truly functioning as "Your servants," servants of God.

The other *Sefirah* comprising the external dimension, that of *Hochmah*, contains the letter *Tav*. *Tav* is the last letter of the alphabet. As such, it is often equated with the last *Sefirah*, *Malchut*. *Tav* as a letter represents the physical plane. In the verb root for giving, *NTN*, the *Tav* stands together with the second *Nune*, representing the other half of the external level. The implication here would be that the *Nune*, the force of interaction within God's will that spawns the entire process of Creation, can only be reflected through duplication in the material, physical universe.

The *Tav*, the world, is encased in the verb root with the *Nune* on both sides. Giving is the process of the *Kav*. That is the inner mystery of giving. On an external level in the *Tav*, the universe, the *Nune*, the Divine Will in action, is replicated through giving. The universe then is the external product of the activation of God's Will on one side and the external environment for replicating it, through true giving, on the other.

This would be one way of understanding the root *NTN*, through meditation on the verb root within the context of the first three *Sefirot* of the Tree of Life. Another method of contemplating and meditating on a verb root would be through a linear method. In this method, one simply views the letters of the root as a sequence of forces in a specific gestalt.

THE VERB ROOT AS SEQUENCE

Here the viewpoint is somewhat different. In this approach, the three letters of a verb root constitute a linear pattern. Within this triad, a middle letter is being encased in between two external letters. The middle letter can be seen as the fulcrum that balances the two opposing forces of the first and last letter. The middle letter, in this meditation, is the center of gravity. The neutral point is the second letter. The first and third letters are the conjoined forces that are being balanced and allowed to manifest in the World of Doing, through the binding and harmonizing accomplished by the middle letter.

Take the root *Kaf-Tav-Bet*, "to write." The *Tav*, meaning among other things "the world," is the balance point and the grounding force for the *Kaf* and the *Bet*. *Kaf* means "palm of the hand" in Hebrew. One meaning for the *Kaf* on an esoteric level is that of potential. It is the ability to do something. One holds a tool in one's hand. One has to decide to do something with it and activate the force of will in that direction. But the potential is there. *Kaf* is also the first letter of the word *Koach*, "strength or power."

Bet is the second letter of the alphabet and is the number two. *Bet* refers to duality. Duality can manifest as opposition or ambivalence or dynamism. So on one side of the scale one has potential, force seeking to express itself, the hidden being impelled to manifest. On the other side, there is the duality of resistance and drive. What mitigates this potential stalemate? The *Tav*, the world. The physical universe, which on the Tree of Life is the *Sefirah* of *Malchut*, is totally receptive. The most central of the underlying principles of receptivity is that of need.

So, writing in this context can be viewed as follows. Writing is a response to need. It is potential waiting to be expressed. The expression could be held in stasis indefinitely, because of the duality of resistance and dynamism. What allows for writing to overcome the inertia of the writer? What conquers the external resistance to what is written? The needs of the world, the external environment and how it perceives itself. Writing is need-based, and it is very much based in this world. It can be proactive or reactive. It can change the world or be resisted by it. Either way, it has great power at its source. It aims at activating potential.

As a sequence of letters, the verb root can also be seen as exemplifying the process of expansion and contraction. The first, middle, and last letters of the alphabet are *Aleph*, *Mem*, and *Tav*. This root, *Aleph-Mem-Tav* (.MT), in Hebrew means "truth." The word formed from the first and last letters, *Aleph-Tav*, has no meaning in Hebrew. Yet it is an extremely important word. The word *et* is used in Hebrew to signal the listener that the next word in the sentence is the direct object.

It is highly significant that the two letters that symbolize the entirety of the alphabet, the beginning and ending letters, should spell the only word in Hebrew that has no meaning, yet produces the object of a thought. This is a reflection of the underlying concept of Creation manifesting from Nothingness. The alphabet is the medium for producing something, Creation, from Nothing. The alphabet represents the process of Creation unfolding and evolving.

When one adds the middle letter of the alphabet, *Mem*, in between the *Aleph* and the *Tav*, "truth" ('*e MeT*) appears. Truth is equated in Jewish literature with the Will of God and with Divine Law, the expression of Divine Will. Hence, any verb root with its three letters can be correlated to the unfolding process of revealed truth by association with the *Aleph-Mem-Tav* sequence.

The process of Creation is one of three-stage movement: expansion, contraction, and rest. If one wishes to experience and understand a realm of activity from the cosmological standpoint, one should connect the meditation on the verb root directly to the expansion-contraction-rest principle. Understanding how a force or action plays itself out on other levels of consciousness requires transcending the purely physical realm. That can most easily be accomplished by connecting the verb root, in meditation, with the breathing process.

In the verb root *Aleph-Mem-Tav*, the *Aleph* is the origin point. From it emanates the *Mem*, the process of Creation. From the *Mem* issues forth the *Tav*, the end, the final reality made manifest. That is the expansion. The contraction is the return to the Source. *Tav* withdraws back into *Mem*, which in turn will ultimately be reabsorbed by the *Aleph*. Then the process starts over again. This becomes a six-stage process of emanation and return. This reflects the six aspects of three-dimensional reality.

The letters of a verb root can be substituted for the *Aleph-Mem-Tav* in meditation. The process, however is the same. To begin with, the meditator takes a deep breath in, then exhales as he begins the meditation. One visualizes first the initial letter of the root. Then, after a moment, the second letter is envisioned as emanating from the first. This is all done while breathing out. One proceeds to rest, after visualizing the emergence of the final letter of the root. Continuing to visualize the whole root, one begins to inhale. During the inhalation process, the *Tav* is absorbed into the *Mem,* and in turn, the *Mem* is taken back into the *Aleph*. At the point where only the *Aleph* remains, the meditator pauses and rests. With the resumption of the exhalation, the process begins over.

One last meditation practice involves the expansion and contraction principle. It is based on a geometric pattern comprising a twelve-letter pattern. Twelve is the number of simple letters of the alphabet, which *Sefer Yetzirah* identifies as the letters of detail. This meditation pattern assists one in more clearly understanding the complex ramifications of any action.

If one accepts the kabbalist concept, emphasized in the structure of the *Aleph* itself, that what is above is as what is below and that the relationship between Heaven and Earth, like that of four- to three-dimensional reality, are mirror images of each other, a simple geometric pattern springs to mind. The relationship between Heaven and Earth can be portrayed geometrically as mirrored triangles. On a two dimensional plane, this would appear as an upright triangle over an inverted triangle.

If one were to create the pattern with dots marking the beginning, middle, and end points of each layer of the form, you would have twelve dots. One dot, followed below by a line of two dots, followed by two lines of three, succeeded by a line of two, and ending with one dot at the base. Altogether, twelve points, each point being a letter of the verb root in progressive unfolding.

In this meditation, the principles of emanation, along with that of expansion and contraction, and the principle of mirrored imaging operate jointly. This meditation begins by centering the focus of one's attention above the crown of the head.

For purposes of illustration, let us use the verb root for "faith," *Aleph-Mem-Nune.* After relaxing into a meditative state, picture the *Aleph* a sufficient distance above the crown of the head. Let the *Aleph* build energy. At a certain point an *Aleph-Mem* pattern will appear below the *Aleph.* In further meditation, a third pattern, that of *Aleph-Mem-Nune* will appear below the second line. Given time, a fourth line will appear below the *Aleph-Mem-Nune.* It will be an inverse pattern. It will be a line on *Nune-Mem-Aleph.* Then below it will appear a *Mem-Aleph* pattern, to be succeeded by the last line, a single *Aleph* again.

Draw energy from the final *Aleph* at the base of this structure. Draw in the energy through the very top of the head. Let the energy permeate your whole being. Allow the energy to overcome you and let yourself experience all of the ramifications of this force, until you are ready to stop. Then, release the energy back into the *Aleph.* The uppermost *Aleph* will, in turn, reassimilate all of the lower lines, line by line, and ultimately disappear from view. You may then experience a series of realizations or insights. Or the knowledge imparted during the meditation may reveal itself gradually over time, within the next several days or weeks.

In summary, it is important to understand that the verb root is the gestalt of an entire spectrum of activity. The actions that a verb root represents, work themselves out on all levels of Creation. As an action, a verb root has specific importance and wide implications in the physical universe. The realm of physical reality as we experience it is that of the *Olam Ha-Assiyah*, the World of Doing.

The meditations one can do using the Hebrew verb roots tap into the very foundational patterns and paradigms that govern our entire existence as created beings. That makes this type of meditation very broad in its ramifications and its consequences. The verb root is one of the greatest gateways to exploration of our level of Creation. As such, it must be handled with great care and must be treated with the uttermost respect and reverence.

9

A View from the *Zohar*:
The Dynamics of the *Sefirot*

It is now time to narrow the focus of discussion regarding the *Sefirot*. In order to do this, attention will be centered on selections from the *Zohar*. The *Zohar* is one of the most important, and one of the most basic texts within all of kabbalist literature. Published in the latter half of the thirteenth century by Rabbi Moses ben Shem Tov de Leon, the *Zohar* established itself as the core work of classical Kabbalah. It has remained one of the most authoritative and influential sources of kabbalist thought to this day.

The *Zohar* is structured as a mystic commentary on the Torah, the Five Books of Moses. Using the biblical text as a catalyst, the *Zohar*, through the use of commentary, explanation, story, and discourse, launches into deep exploration of a vast field of diverse mystic topics. The scope of the *Zohar's* purview encompasses a very wide range of esoteric subjects. Because the *Zohar's* insights are so poignant and so central to kabbalist thought, it is important to round out this study of meditation from the kabbalistic perspective by drawing on the text to help complete the picture.

It is in the *Zohar* that the concept of the Tree of Life received its fullest and most comprehensive exposition. In the *Zohar*, the Tree of Life in general and the *Sefirot* in particular serve as the basis for portraying, as well as for understanding, all of the workings of the universe. The Tree serves as a model of the interaction of the forces that produce Creation. Any subject discussed in the text is referenced, directly or indirectly, to the Tree and to the *Sefirot*. The nature of the *Sefirot* and their interplay serve as the context for explaining and understanding the inner, esoteric realities that underlie all of the dynamics of Creation.

The *Zohar* often describes inner realities as processes, that take place within the *Sefirot* and between them. Understanding any given interaction between the *Sefirot* immediately connects one to the internal process that produces and sustains some specific reality. For instance, if the *Zohar* is describing dreaming, it may be doing so in metaphoric terms. These terms correspond to several different *Sefirot*. The metaphor is speaking simultaneously of the nature of dreams, of the process of dreaming, and of the dynamics of interpreting dreams. On the level of dynamics, they are all the same. It is up to the reader to assimilate this information, by contemplating it, meditating on it, internalizing it, and becoming one with it. By so doing, one enables oneself to truly understand and to properly utilize the reality of dreaming a dream.

In this instance, the zoharic text is portraying a specific inner working of consciousness. It is describing the internal process by which dreams are generated. Since the Tree of Life is the paradigm for all of Creation, by talking about the process of dreaming and the nature of dreams the *Zohar* is also illustrating the cosmic, inner workings that go on at all levels of Creation. It is portraying the mechanism that produces the equivalent of dreaming on higher levels and in alternate states of consciousness. Hence, penetrating the inner meaning of a text is dependent on contemplation, meditation, and internalization. Such penetration leads to personal experience and to deeper intuitive knowledge. Upon this knowledge, greater cognitive understanding can later be built and expanded on.

One must go through these processes several times, first, to understand the text properly, second, to learn and to assimilate the processes thoroughly. One must repeat them in order to experience them fully and to come to know them intimately. The ultimate objective is to be at one with the cosmic reality of these universal laws and with the multiple dimensions in which they are expressed. Only then is one fully cognizant of them and in a position to assist others in reaching a true understanding of them.

The aim of this chapter is to gain a deeper, fuller insight, through selected passages of the *Zohar*, into the nature and purpose of the *Sefirot*,

by illustrating the dynamics of the Tree of Life's "Process of Unfolding."
Pay careful attention to the details of the process and to the sequence.
Rabbi Shimon [bar Yohai] said:

I raise my hands upward in prayer. When the highest Will [the *Ayn*],
beyond the beyond, infuses the unknowable and permanently incompre-
hensible Will, the most hidden source [*Keter*], this selfsame source [*Keter*],
gives forth that which it gives forth but is unknowable [*Hochmah*] and
illumines what it will illumine [*Hochmah*], though it is all concealed.

The desire of the Highest Thought [*Hochmah*] is to pursue it [*Keter*]
and to be illuminated by it. A curtain is parted and through the curtain, via
the movement of the Highest Thought [*Hochmah*], it [the light of *Keter*]
reaches and yet does not reach. (It reaches) up to the curtain, which illuminates, what it will illumine. Hence, the Highest Thought [*Hochmah*]
illuminates with a hidden, unknown illumination, since it itself is unknown.
Since the illumination of Thought [*Hochmah*] within the curtain, which is
itself illuminated by that which is unknown, unknowable, and unrevealed
[*Keter*], is therefore unknowable, so the unknowable illumination of
Thought [*Hochmah*] strikes the light of the curtain and together they give
off light from which the nine *Heichalot* [palaces] are made.

The *Heichalot* are not lights, or spirits, or souls. No one can stand in
them. The desire of all nine lights, which exist within Thought [*Hochmah*],
Hochmah itself being counted within their number, is to return to them
(to their sources in *Hochmah* and in *Keter*), all the while they exist in
Thought [*Hochmah*].

They are not comprehensible and are unknowable. They do not stand
in [share the nature of] either Will (Keter) or Thought [Hochmah]. They
reach but do not reach. [They reside in *Hochmah* but are not synonymous
with either *Hochmah* or *Keter*.] In them [the *Heichalot*] stand all the
secrets of faith. All of the lights from the secret of the Highest Thought
[*Hochmah*] on down are all called *Ayn Sof*. Up to this point the lights reach.
They do not reach and are unknowable. Here there is no Will [*Keter*] and
no Thought [*Hochmah*].

When Thought [*Hochmah*] is illumined by that which is unknowable, it is subsequently dressed and concealed in *Binah*. It [*Hochmah*]
illumines that which it will illumine [*Binah*]. One enters the other, until
all of them [*Keter, Hochmah*, and *Binah*] are inclusive of each other. In
the secret of the Sacrifice, when it rises, everything is connected to each
other, one illuminating the other. All are present in the ascent. Thought
[*Hochmah*] is crowned by Infinity [*Keter*]. The same illumination, by which
the Highest Thought [*Hochmah*] is illuminated, is called *Ayin*. From it
everything that bears light is founded, given existence, and illuminated.
On this everything stands. (*Zohar*, Section 1; *Noach*, page 65, Side 1)

In this selection, God's Will emerges. *Keter* is formed and seeks expression. *Keter* is infused with infinite possibility. This impetus produces *Hochmah*. *Keter* penetrates and permeates *Hochmah*, producing a sustained extension of itself. Yet, due to the separation of *Hochmah* from *Keter*, a boundary exists. Movement toward reconnection with *Keter* is initiated by *Hochmah*.

There seem to be two motivations for *Hochmah*'s initiative. On one hand, *Hochmah* wishes to retain its own existence and consciousness, but not at the expense of losing its connection with *Keter*. On the other hand, it is looking to receive illumination from *Keter*. That illumination would be the force that would allow *Hochmah* to expand and evolve.

From Nothingness (*Ayin*), God creates Infinity (*Keter*). *Keter* is All. By being infused with all potentiality, *Keter* is compelled to seek expansion and, by extension, produces *Hochmah*. It infuses within *Hochmah* the power of extension. In order for *Hochmah* to manifest extension, it needs to become Life Force. It seeks to accomplish that by acting back on its source, *Keter*.

This movement separates the curtain. The unknowable illumination of *Keter* fills the opening within the curtain. Within the curtain, the concealed light of *Hochmah* collides with and is merged with the unknowable illumination of *Keter*. The illuminations, though separate and distinct from each other, one having produced the other, are none the less the same, hidden and unknowable.

Hochmah's illumination is Life Force. Life Force is the result of Infinity extending itself. *Keter* extends itself and *Hochmah* emerges. Seeking to return, *Hochmah* initiates a movement that leads to a reunion of energies and the activation of the power of extension. *Keter* and *Hochmah* are inextricably linked together.

Keter is unknowable. So is *Hochmah*. So are their respective illuminations, their true natures. Yet, within the curtain, the very barrier that separates them, their illuminations merge as a result of the contact that takes place between them there. The result is an inner transformation within *Hochmah*. Nine *Heichalot* emerge within *Hochmah*.

These nine *Heichalot* are the inner dimensions of the nine *Sefirot* from *Hochmah* on down. These are core energies that are rooted within *Hochmah*. They are the seeds and the roots of all of the subsequent *Sefirot*. They are the roots within the unknowable that will become manifest and knowable. Their nature is more that of the later, emanated *Sefirot*. It is not that of the totally unknowable and concealed nature of *Keter* and *Hochmah*.

These nine inner dynamos are resident within *Hochmah*. They are not an actual part of *Hochmah* per se. They do not share the same nature as *Hochmah* and *Keter*. Yet *Hochmah* is referred to as Thought. In that regard, there is some relationship between *Hochmah* and the resident nine *Heichalot*.

Thought implies process. Thought awaits verbal expression. The *Heichalot* are produced within *Hochmah*, because they are the innermost imprints within the Life Force that await articulation. Their extension will become the cores of the various *Sefirot*. Not only will the existence of the *Sefirot* depend on them, but they will also be the continual source of the desire within the *Sefirot* to return to *Hochmah* and *Keter*. Because they are rooted in *Hochmah*, the *Sefirot* are aware of the hidden reality of their origin and so constantly desire to return to their source, the unknowable, unfathomable interaction between *Keter* and *Hochmah*.

Within *Hochmah*, the *Heichalot* are rooted seeds. As they extend into the *Sefirot*, as the *Sefirot* emanate, they become lights. They are produced by the interaction of the illuminations of *Keter* and *Hochmah*, but they are not the light of *Keter* and *Hochmah*. The illuminations of the top two *Sefirot* are completely and eternally hidden. As the lights of the lower *Sefirot* ascend, they can reach to *Hochmah*, but no further.

Why then are they referred to as the "lights of the *Ain Sof*" (*Keter*)? Clearly, they are not *Ain Sof* (*Keter*), since they do not share in its nature. It is unknowable and they are knowable. They are called the "lights of the *Ain Sof*" because of their desire to reunite with the ultimate source, *Keter*, via reconnection within *Hochmah*. *Hochmah* is often called, "the Light of the *Ain Sof*." These lights of the *Sefirot* seek to reunite with the unknowable source, *Keter*, by returning to the unknowable light of *Hochmah*, wherein their roots are resident. Within the light of infinity, they are the potential for differentiation and for reunion. That makes them both products of and agents of *Keter*, not the *Ain Sof* itself.

What, exactly, are the implications of what is being said here so far?

There are four general concepts that can be inferred from the *Zohar's* discussion so far. First, the interaction between *Keter* and *Hochmah* activates the Life Force, which is the illumination of *Hochmah* and sets the stage for the emanation of the *Sefirot*, by invigorating and empowering the power of expansion. The roots of this expansion of *Keter-Hochmah* into the Tree of Life are the nine *Heichalot* resident within the *Sefirah* of *Hochmah*. The *Sefirot* all derive their inner nature from these roots and they all lead back to the *Heichalot* in *Hochmah*.

However, though present in *Hochmah*, they are not part of *Hochmah* by nature. They are knowable and *Hochmah*, like *Keter*, is not. The implication here is that Life Force empowers the *Heichalot*, which extend out and empower the various *Sefirot*. That power gives life to the *Sefirot* and unites all of the *Sefirot* to each other. It also allows the energies of the *Sefirot* to ascend back to *Hochmah*.

What is portrayed here is an interesting dichotomy. The extension of Life Force sustains all of the *Sefirot*. It has function and is knowable. Yet Life Force itself, the essence of *Hochmah*, is totally unknowable. Hence, one can experience life and make purposeful use of it. But what lies behind it, Life Force itself, can never be known per se.

The second implication in the material is also clear. Though *Hochmah* emerges out of *Keter* and maintains a distinct identity, the two *Sefirot* are inextricable from each other. They are linked together by the interaction that occurs between them, within the curtain. This is the selfsame curtain that serves to separate them from each other. There is a qualitative difference between the two *Sefirot*, on one hand, and a very basic unity underlying them both. There is a difference between Infinity (*Keter*) and Infinitude or Endless Possibility (*Hochmah*). Yet both share the same nature, that of being infinite.

Third, within all the *Sefirot*, at their very core is the extension of Life Force, which both animates them and causes them to continually seek return to the source, *Keter-Hochmah*. Therefore, it is safe to say that the will to reconnect with the Source, with the Will of God and with Life Force, the Highest Thought, lies at the heart of all levels of existence.

Last, one is brought, via the inner forces leading back to the *Heichalot*, to the very gates of *Hochmah*, but no further. The *Sefirot* are all differentiated one from the other, below *Binah*. The return road toward the source leads back to the *Heichalot*, the roots of differentiation. That is the end of the line. *Hochmah* and *Keter* know no differentiation.

Here, the implication is that, one can only experience Beingness, through his own being. Beingness, Being itself, is beyond even the roots of our existence. Remember, the *Heichalot* are resident within *Hochmah* and they are not lights, nor spirits, nor souls. They are forces within *Hochmah*. No one can stand in them. That is, no one can experience their true nature. That is beyond the scope of any created essence.

Since the illumination of *Hochmah* by *Keter* is unknowable, it is the illumination received by *Binah* from *Hochmah* that allows the unknowable to become known. The illumination of *Hochmah* is concealed within *Binah*. It is clothed by *Binah*. The roots of the various forms that the lights of the *Sefirot* will take on are produced within *Binah*. This development results directly from the acceptance of the illumination from *Hochmah*.

At this point, within *Binah* all of the light-roots of the *Sefirot* become distinguishable. Though separated, they are all the same, illuminating each other and collectively rising back toward *Keter*. *Binah*'s role serves a dual function. It receives and gives form to the illumination from *Hochmah*. By doing so, *Binah* completes the process of emergence, initiated by *Keter*. The hidden light is received by *Binah* and redirected back to *Keter*. This completes the first stage of the Creation process, the manifestation of Will. The *Korban*, the Sacrifice, is completed. The World of Emanation now exists. Upon it, all is to be built.

The World of Emanation is referred to as the *Korban*, the Sacrifice, because the roots of both nouns, *Atzilut* (Emanation) and *Korban* (Sacrifice), mean "near" or "close." This harkens to the idea of being close to God, since one is dealing with the Will and Thought of God. The secret of the World of Emanation is that all three of the *Sefirot*, *Keter*, *Hochmah*, and *Binah*, are so tightly intertwined that they are, for all practical purposes, the same. They are all inclusive, even of each other. They are all interlocked and they all ascend together.

Keter illuminates *Hochmah*. The illumination merges and connects the two *Sefirot*. The nine *Heichalot* (core forces) are produced as a result. Within the concealment of *Binah*, as a result of the transmission of illumination from *Hochmah*, their energies are differentiated from one another. As *Binah* accepts the illumination, she becomes one with *Hochmah* and as a union, they both ascend to *Keter*, reforming a unity.

Throughout this process, all is concealed. All remains hidden. *Keter*, *Hochmah*, and *Binah* are an integral whole. As a whole, they are undifferentiated from each other. However, the potential for differentiation exists. That is the driving impetus for the emergence of the remaining *Sefirot* and for the formation of the entire Tree of Life. This potential is already articulated within *Binah*. Even though the World of Emanation stands as an integrated unity, the unexpressed differentiation, so necessary for the universe's existence, will fulfill itself with the emergence of the lower *Sefirot*.

The entire Tree of Life is based on the unity of the upper three *Sefirot*. They are the foundation of all that is. Everything depends on the World of Emanation. This World is the level of Divine Purpose and

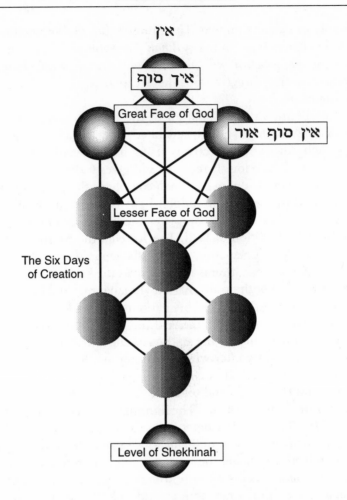

אין

איך סוף

Great Face of God

אין סוף אור

Lesser Face of God

The Six Days
of Creation

Level of Shekhinah

Will. It is very important to understand the indivisible unity of this level of the Tree. It is referred to as the *Arikh Anpin*, the Great Face of God.

The best analogy for describing the nature of the World of Emanation and the relationship of *Keter-Hochmah-Binah* is that of the brain. The brain has a right hemisphere, a left hemisphere, and a neuro-cortel net. Each has a different set of functions. The right hemisphere handles creativity, association, free flow of thought, emotion. The left brain is the center for logic, analytical thinking, for differentiation and for structure building. The neuro-cortex forms all the interlocking connections between the two hemispheres.

Though it is common in popular parlance to refer to the right and left brains, it is ridiculous to view them as independent entities. They are both component parts of the brain, not different brains. Though they are distinct from each other both physically and functionally, they are organically one whole. Right brain, left brain, cerebral cortex; these are separate, component parts of the brain, not independent realities. They function by interconnection and intensive interaction.

The same can be said for the three *Sefirot* of the World of Emanation. *Keter*, *Hochmah*, and *Binah* are all separate *Sefirot*. However, they are also all component elements of the Level of Emanation within the Tree of Life. They are different dynamics of the All, the great unity, the Will of God. They are Being, as it emerges from Nothingness. God's Will may have three stages of emergence, but it is the one Will of the one God. It is the organic Oneness, from which everything derives and upon which the universe is ultimately built.

What we learn about the World of Emanation in this selection helps us understand both the nature and intrinsic unity of the upper three *Sefirot*, and the relationship between this world and the remaining *Sefirot*. The implications in terms of meditation are very subtle and very important to bear in mind at all times. They are fundamental in understanding the role of meditation in exploring the Tree of Life and the *Sefirot*.

The World of Creation (*Olam HaBeriyah*) and the World of Formation (*Olam HaYetzirah*), the second and third levels of the Tree of Life, like the World of Emanation, are composed of three *Sefirot* each. The general pattern of the World of Emanation is replicated in the structures of the second and third worlds. Though the uppermost realm of Emanation is largely unknowable, it is not totally sealed off. One of the functions of *Binah* is to unite the *Keter-Hochmah-Binah* triad and make it an integral whole. The other major function of *Binah* is to give birth to all of the lower *Sefirot*.

Because *Binah* has a dual function and is the source for all of the knowable *Sefirot*, it too is knowable. By connecting with *Binah*, one has access to the link between the upper world of Emanation and the three lower worlds. Something of the nature of the upper world is reflected and knowable within *Binah*. Hence, in accessing *Binah* through a process of return via the lower *Sefirot*, one not only is able to reach the level of the "roots" of the *Sefirot*, one is also able to gain access to a level of experience that reflects something of the nature of the unknowable aspects of Creation.

One cannot come to know a famous painter from the eighteenth century. The artist is long gone and inaccessible. Yet, by studying his paintings, by becoming emotionally and spiritually intimate with his legacy, one comes to understand something about the artist's world view, emotional experience, reaction to life, and so on. If one were to read the artist's memoirs, a biography, reports about him from people he knew, one extends the process even further. One can come to know the artist on a limited indirect level, by way of reflection, as it were. Though the analogy is by no means a perfect one, it does illustrate the importance of focusing meditation on the *Sefirah* of *Binah* as a reflection of the Supernal Level of Creation, which otherwise is unknowable.

Binah not only unites all of the upper *Sefirot* into a unity; it reconnects directly with *Keter* in the process. That means that within *Binah*, one can meditate on the connection between the *Ayin* and *Keter*. *Binah* reflects the fundamental relationship between Nothingness and the Eternal Infinite. It mirrors the oscillation between Non-Being and Being. *Binah's* dual function of completing the hidden process of forming the unknowable World of Emanation on one hand, and giving birth to the process of Creation on the other, means it too oscillates. It ebbs and flows between being and becoming, which is a reflection of the oscillation between Non-Being and Being.

Focusing meditation within *Binah* allows one to center meditation on either of these oscillations. One can focus on alternating between Being and Non-Being or on moving up and back between the reality of being and the process of becoming. In the Meditation Appendix at the end of the book, one will find descriptions of practical meditations, designed to access both of these alternatives.

Please bear in mind also that even though the World of Emanation is unknowable, unrevealed, and completely concealed, the process of Creation that is implicit within it is replicated in the lower worlds. These lower realms are knowable. Though God's Will and Thought are not directly knowable, the process by which they manifest absolutely is. That is one of the major premises behind all of kabbalist thought.

One cannot ultimately connect directly with the Supernal Unity of *Keter-Hochmah* and *Binah*. One cannot know their essence. However, by focusing on the interrelationship of the *Sefirot* in the lower worlds and understanding their dynamics, one can most certainly connect with the process of Creation. Connecting with the process is tantamount to becoming one with and understanding the intent of the uppermost world.

One comes to understand the motive through the reflection. The impetus is understood through experiencing the process of unfolding.

The upper world of Emanation is not a focus for meditation, for no one can stand there. No one can know it. Rather, the Supernal World, the Great Face of God, is the objective of meditation. In this realm of intimacy with God, one cannot stand with God. Here, one can only be with God.

To reach this realm, one must access *Binah*. Rabbi Bar Yohai bases his whole discussion here on the concept of "raising one's hands in prayer." Several important clues are given regarding reaching the level of *Binah*.

The "raising of the hands" implies acknowledging the limits of duality. Our two hands reflect both our ability to get things accomplished in this world, and the very dual nature of all of reality within Creation. We are advised to raise up our hands, to expose them openly. We are instructed to surrender, to admit the farthest extent to which duality can reach, and to acknowledge that there is something beyond it.

The motion of raising one's hands is that of an upward sweep. That which we do must be directed upward toward God. All of our work, all of our actions, and all of our accomplishments must be elevated by focusing on the Will of God, not our own wants and desires. If we elevate our focus, then we exalt our actions. If we look beyond our limitations and view our actions as offerings to God, then we can approach communion with God.

The World of Emanation is called the *Korban*, the Sacrifice. In sacrificial ritual, one draws close to God by the process of surrender and release. One is offering up something very valuable and dear to them. That offering and release creates space. What was held on to is burned and no longer exists. Space is created. Within that sacred space, nearness to God becomes possible. The *Zohar* states here that the secret of faith is the connection between Knowingness and the Unknowable.

The focus of faith leads to reaching the World of Emanation. Arriving there is the outcome of a process. One journeys through the replicated patterns of the lower worlds and becomes ultimately familiar with the supreme paradigm of the uppermost world, through experience. One travels toward closeness via the lower realms. When one arrives, one no longer seeks closeness. One is close. The holy journey is the act of sacrificing. The World of Emanation is the sacrifice. Sacrificing is a process. The sacrifice is a state of Being.

Rabbi Shimon said:

How wonderful are the words of the Torah. Happy is one who occupies himself with them and knows to walk in the way of truth. "And the house as it is being built" (1 Kings 6:7). When the Will of the Holy One, Blessed Be He, was aroused to provide [a place of] honor for His honor, the will arose within Thought [Hochmah] to expand, and it expanded from the place that is Hidden, Unknown Thought, until it reached and dwelt in the House of the Throat [Binah], a place where the breath of life always flows secretly. So when Thought expanded and came to dwell in this place, Thought called it, "The Living God," as it is said, "He is the Living God" (Jeremiah 10:10).

"It [God's Will] wanted to expand further and be revealed. From there [Binah] emerged fire, wind, and water together, all inclusive [as a unit]. Jacob [Tiferet] emerged, a complete man [as a complete system; Hesed-Din-Tiferet]. One voice went out and was heard. From this point, Thought, which was hidden and silent, was openly heard. Thought extended even farther in order to be revealed. Voice struck and pushed on the lips [activating itself, the world of Creation, Hesed-Din-Tiferet, replicated itself, producing the world of Formation, Netzach-Hod-Yesod]. The result was the emergence of Speech [the physical universe, Malchut] that completed everything and revealed everything.

"The significance here is that everything is [ultimately] Hidden Thought, that was within. Everything is One. [Everything is at root, the unified Will of God, whole, undifferentiated, and unexpressed within Hochmah.] When the expansion (of God's Will) reaches the point of making Speech [Malchut] through the power of Voice [Hesed-Din-Tiferet] one has "the house as it is being built." For it is not written, "was built" [or "is built"] but rather, "as it is being built," meaning that it is a step by step process. (Zohar, Section 1; Noach, page 74, Side 1)

The Sefirah of Binah is referred to as the "breath of life" [Ruach Chayim] and the "living God" [Elohim Chayim]. Both of these terms are meant to say something about Binah. Both terms emphasize life [Chayim]. It is Binah that accepts and encompasses the Life Force of Hochmah. Binah is also the efficient source of life as it is understood and experienced within Creation. Binah embraces Life Force on one hand and gives birth to the lower Sefirot on the other. Binah, therefore, transforms Life Force into life.

The first terms in both Hebrew phrases, that is, Ruach and Elohim, are parallel to each other. Binah is referred to both as Ruach Chayim [the breath of life] and as *Elohim Chayim* [the living God]. If you remove the word "life" [*Chayim*] from these parallel names, what remains is the term *Ruach Elohim* [the Spirit of God]. Genesis 1:2 states that "the Spirit of God sweeps over the face of the waters."

The waters, or the deep, in the view of the *Zohar*, refer to the *Sefirot* from *Hesed* through *Yesod*. The waters are the six *Sefirot* that comprise the creative process, that leads to the Creation, the *Sefirah* of *Malchut*. *Binah* is the Great Mother. She is the emanating source of the *Sefirot* below, and also the sustainer and support of them all. The relationship between the Will of God, the six *Sefirot* of the process of Creation, and Creation itself, the realm of *Malchut*, is unstained and managed through the agency of *Binah*.

In this regard, *Binah* is the source of expansion downward from the World of Emanation. The second triad, that of *Hesed-Din-Tiferet*, emerge from the World of Emanation as a unit. The central focal point of this second world, the World of Creation, is the *Sefirah* of *Tiferet*. At this level, there is also unification, but in a different mode. Whereas in the World of Emanation, the *Sefirot* of *Keter-Hochmah-Binah* are an integral whole, in the World of Creation duality emerges. *Hesed* and *Din* are opposing forces that must be brought into balance and harmonized. *Tiferet* performs this function and, therefore, becomes the focal point for the triad. The difference is that at this level the unity of the World of Emanation is replaced in the World of Creation by the unification achieved by *Tiferet*.

The World of Emanation is described as the base upon which all is built. The World of Creation and its counterpart, the World of Formation (*Netzach-Hod-Yesod*), constitute the building process. This is a different reality. Unity is supplanted by duality. Duality, in order to continue to exist, must be harmonized and balanced. These two worlds are maintained by the work of unification accomplished by *Tiferet* and *Yesod* respectively.

Tiferet is called the "Voice." *Yesod* is called the "Lips." *Malchut* (the physical universe) is called "Speech." In the broad sense, when one speaks of *Tiferet*, one is referring to the World of Creation, which is consolidated and held together by it. Similarly, *Yesod* can be used to signify the World of Formation that it balances.

Voice is the ability to communicate, the power of speech. Lips represent articulation, that is the deliberate, meaningful formulation of sound into pattern. Speech is concrete expression, the externalization and communication of thought. What was totally unmanifest and deeply concealed within *Keter-Hochmah* is now given the power of expression in *Tiferet*, articulated in *Yesod*, and finally openly externalized and disclosed in *Malchut*.

There is the sense here that as *Hesed-Din-Tiferet* emerge as a unit, so does *Netzach-Hod-Yesod*. As the World of Creation emanates from the World of Emanation, so too does the World of Formation emerge from the World of Creation. The power of sound and expression and that of articulation are intimately interwoven with each other. *Tiferet* and *Yesod*, sound and expression, unification and harmonization are two sides of the same process. They are interlocked realities. They are distinguishable from each other by function but are inseparable in terms of the process.

That which imparts reality to the energy and substance of anything is the final, external form that emerges and gives it concrete definition. That definition is the end product of the process. The end product of the process of Creation is the universe, the World of *Malchut*.

Malchut emerges from *Yesod* as both a unit, as a *Sefirah*, and also as a unity, the universe. It is an external reflection of the ultimate unity. This unity mirrors *Keter* on one level. On another level, it reflects as the uppermost triad of *Keter-Hochmah-Binah*. *Malchut* is speech. That is, it is thought becoming manifest. The universe is the concrete expression of the hidden Will of God.

In Hebrew, the term for speech, or speaking (*dibbur*) comes from the same verb root as the term for thing, or something (*davar*). At the level of *Malchut*, the physical world, thought is perpetually becoming manifest. The world is in essence expression being expressed at all times, continually.

The *Zohar* calls *Malchut* "the house as it is being built." Physical life is the external expression of the process of life. The house is continually being built. Being built is an unending process, of which physical reality is the articulation. That is, the house, the universe is both a construct and in a state of being constructed, simultaneously. It is both the reflection of the process of creation in progress, and the end result of the process, Creation, all at the same time.

The Divine Will, the process of creating, and the constant evolution of the universe are all different dimensions of the eternal moment. They are different aspects of a unified whole, the reality of existence. The unknowable and the knowable are both expressions of the totality, which is God making manifest His Will.

In terms of meditation, two principles are crucial to understand. First, is the reality that oneness, the Will of God, underlies everything. God's Thought is unknowable, yet has two dimensions by which it is knowable and by which it comes to know itself. One is through creative process, and the other is through the structure of the universe.

Any process, be it the process of creating or producing something, the artistic process, the thought process, physical or psychological processes, is a replication of the flow pattern of the *Sefirot* within the Tree of Life. To become one with a process, by doing, by feeling, by thinking, by contemplating, or by meditating, is to experience the Creation process directly. It is to understand it and become transformed by it. Doing and producing make us cocreators with God. We become the reflection of God and thereby fulfill our essence, as the beings made in the image of God.

Meditation and contemplation on the *Sefirot* and the Tree of Life bring us face to face with the inner processes of the cosmos on all levels. Any process reflects the universal Process of Unfolding. Deep immersion on any level of a process connects one to the Process, the inner dynamics of the eternal moment of Creation.

Immersion in a process of thought, emotion, or action is like riding a river. To one extent, a person is driven by the currents. To another extent, he or she navigates them. The river is a journey, bringing one to and passing through many places. The river is vitality. It gives life and it sustains it, always driving forward. The river is also experience itself, the very foundation of life. Being on the river and flowing with it, one is guided down a set course. Moreover, one is transported in a manner unknown to those who choose to remain perpetually on land. Bear in mind, it is only the river that leads to the sea. Where the land, river, and sea meet, there one finds the horizon, the vista of the continent, the melding of the waters. Here one stands at the juncture of the revealed and the hidden.

Second, one can also access through study, contemplation, and meditation the structure of Creation. The concepts of building, the eternal process of Creation, and that of the house, the physical universe, both imply structure. A process is structured. It occurs in stages. The universe is a construct, structure taking form. The two again are intimately related. Only in something's external manifestation does its structure become apparent. The structure of something is implicit in its design. Only in the process a design takes on to work itself out is the structure fully perceptible, with the emergence of its final form.

Structure is the result of the stages of the building process unfolding and being completed. The World of *Malchut*, the universe, is both the end product of the creation process and a perpetual reflection of the process that produces and sustains it. Creation on all levels, is both the expression of the Divine Will and the vehicle for containing it. Hence, process and structure are two facets of the same thing, that which underlies all that is, because it is Creation.

Through meditation on the *Sefirot* and on the Tree of Life, one accesses both process and structure. Through the Tree, one connects with all levels of reality. Since all worlds are interlocked, being infinite replications of the same eternal and universal model of Creation, focusing on the *Sefirot* and their interrelationship through meditation allows for the unknown to become known. The All is revealed through penetration of any of its parts, for they are all predicated on the same pattern, the Tree of Life.

In contemplating and meditating on the *Sefirot*, as well as on the flow and geometry of the Tree, a very specific focus is suggested here.

Malchut is the *Sefirah* that is the external manifestation of the hiddenmost *Sefirah*, *Keter*. The principle enunciated here is that the beginning is revealed in the end. The motivation behind any action is clearly perceived in the event as it plays itself out. This being the case, *Sefirot* meditation can be used to diagram the internal dynamics of an event or situation, thus exposing its structure, process, and motive.

During meditation, place a picture of an event or situation before you. This can be an image of the event, or merely the elements of an event or situation that are of concern or interest. Then, visualize the Tree of Life and prepare to place the event picture within the Tree. The event or situation is placed in the *Sefirah* of *Malchut*. The unknown motivation and/or motive is visualized as being concealed in *Keter*.

By meditating, through progressive stages, on the intermediate *Sefirot*, one comes to see, to experience, or to understand all of the dynamics involved in the event or situation. Meditation on these *Sefirot* will reveal to the meditator the previously hidden structure, content, and interplay that is producing the event or situation in question.

The important concept here is that structure illustrates process. Both the inner and outer structure of something reflect the process by which it was or is being produced. Therefore, form speaks of content. Viewing something through the lens of the *Sefirot*, through the universal form of the Tree of Life, one begins to perceive the universal content, the deep inner meaning concealed within it.

10

The Harmony of the *Sefirot*:
The Conjunctive Points

From the standpoint of meditation, one of the most important realities to understand about the Tree of Life is that the key to meaning is structure. The dynamics of the Tree explain all of Creation, its origins, processes, ramifications, and effects. These dynamics are illustrated by the geometric patterns within the Tree. All of Creation is a result of the infinite interactions that take place within the Tree. The geometry of the Tree of Life reflects and illustrates the interrelationship of all the *Sefirot* to each other and to all the processes within Creation.

Meditation on the *Sefirot* involves not only focus on the *Sefirot* themselves and their essence, but also on the pathways between them, the corridors that connect them, the letters of the alphabet. Yet even that is not the whole picture. The broadest view is that of the geometry of the Tree. When one sees the interrelationships that exist, one begins to perceive both the structure of Creation and the Creative Process, the Great Flow.

BINAH AND THE ZEIR ANPIN

From the contraction, the *Tzimtzum*, that takes place within *Binah*, the Void is created. The Void, when filled by the light of *Hochmah*, gives birth to the seven lower *Sefirot*, the *Zeir Anpin*, the Lesser Face of God. It is *Binah* who guides, sustains, and empowers all of these *Sefirot* perpetually. As the Great Mother, *Binah* channels the flow of Life Force from *Hochmah* to all the lower *Sefirot*, on a continual basis. Hence, *Binah* is the provider for the *Sefirot* below.

Binah is also the source of structure as well as sustenance. The four letters of the word *Binah* (BYNH) can be rearranged to spell *Beniyah* (BNYH), meaning "building" or "the building process." With the directed flow of received Life Force being sent downward, comes the power to build and the force of construction. The result of *Binah's* work and relationship to the lower *Sefirot* produces support in both senses of the word, namely, provision and structure.

In its relationship to *Keter* and *Hochmah*, *Binah* completes the *Arikh Anpin*, the Great Face of God, and as such is not knowable directly. For this reason, the relationship of the lower *Sefirot* to *Binah* takes on extreme importance. The structure of the Tree of Life is the work of *Binah*. The roots of the Tree's composition and pattern are buried deep within *Binah*. These hidden roots are part of *Binah's* relationship to *Keter* and *Hochmah*. The structure of Creation emerges from *Binah* but is the result of the manifesting of the Divine Will.

It is only through the manifested structure of the Tree that we, as created beings, have any means at all of accessing and comprehending the infinite Will of God. On the physical level of *Malchut* we experience life. Life in the physical universe is a reflected reality. True reality is that which is formed through the structural interaction and process of construction taking place among the six interceding *Sefirot* of *Hesed* through *Yesod*. On the higher levels, we come to experience existence by coming to know energy flow and structure.

By accessing through meditation the upper realm, that of the "six days of Creation," we can begin to know what otherwise is completely unknowable. We can understand the manifestation of Creation and what lies behind it on the one hand, and we can sense the unknowable Will and Thought on the other, by connecting with the structure of Creation that links the two together.

According to the *Zohar* (part 1, Genesis, page 2, side 1), in order to initiate the process of revelation, *Keter* creates a point (*Nekudah*). This point, called Thought, is the *Sefirah* of *Hochmah*. Within it, *Keter* engraved all the patterns that would be the *Sefirot*. From *Hochmah* emerges the Holy of Holies, the *Sefirah* of *Binah*. *Binah* is given the name *Mi* (Who), implying *Binah's* function of defining essence.

As the power of delineating essence emerges within *Binah*, the building process commences. *Binah* seeks to manifest Creation. *Binah*'s essence and reality is only fully manifest with the completion of the Creation. To use an analogy, a woman is not a mother until she has children. The potential is not the same as the reality. One cannot be a provider or support if there is nothing objectively to provide for. Just as *Binah* is the receptor for the light of *Hochmah*, giving it a reality, so too the *Zeir Anpin* must exist. It produces *Malchut*, who in turn receives from *Binah* and makes *Binah*'s reality complete.

Seeking to wear the light of Creation, to make it manifest and to fulfill its role practically, *Binah* creates the lower seven *Sefirot*. These *Sefirot* are collectively referred to here as *Eleh* (These).

The term *Eleh* (*'ELH*) illustrates just how intimately connected these lower *Sefirot* are. The seven *Sefirot* of the *Zeir Anpin*, the Lesser Face, are referred to jointly as "these." The implication is that they are a set, a collective reality. They are interdependent elements of a group process.

From this standpoint, there are just two components in Creation. One is the Hidden Process, the inner dynamics of the *Arikh Anpin*, the movement deep within God's Will. This process is concealed and unknowable directly. It is an eternal present. The other, the *Zeir Anpin*, is the flow of the Revealed Process, the evolution of pattern and structure.

What then is the connection linking these two, and what does it mean from the standpoint of meditative accessing?

The *Zohar* states that the seven lower *Sefirot*, when they rise, reintegrate with *Binah*. Hence, the lower *Sefirot*, the *Eleh*, merge with *Binah*, the *Mi*, and the letters of the names combine to form the general name of God, *Elohim*. The name only truly exists when all of the letters that form the names of the *Zeir Anpin* and of *Binah* merge and become one. Upon this secret does the universe exist and endure.

Binah is the point of unification and completion within the Tree of Life. It is *Binah* that separates from *Hochmah* in order to contain its hidden light. At the same time, *Binah* fulfills the *Keter-Hochmah* relationship. *Binah* accepting *Hochmah* reunites with *Keter* and creates the unity that is the World of Emanation.

From the other direction, *Binah* also gives birth to the lower *Sefirot* and serves as their point of reintegration and reunion. The seven *Sefirot* of the *Zeir Anpin* return to *Binah* during their ascent and are reabsorbed. *Binah*, in turn, in its union with *Hochmah*, ascends and is reintegrated into *Keter*. *Binah* serves as the completion agent for the World of Emanation on one hand, and as the origin and completion point of the lower seven *Sefirot*, the worlds of Creation, of Formation, and of Doing. Moreover, *Binah* is clearly the connection point linking the uppermost world of Divine Will with the lower worlds of Creation.

In terms of meditation, it is important to remember that *Binah* is referred to as the Holy of Holies. In the ancient Temple in Jerusalem during biblical times, the Holy of Holies was the core element of the Temple. It was within the Holy of Holies that God's Presence in its most concentrated and intense form dwelt. This was the great sacred chamber that was the point of intimate contact between man and God. This was the link connecting Heaven and Earth.

We, as created beings, cannot become God or be God. However, we can know God by connecting with His Will and Presence. This is done through movement upward via the *Sefirot*. The ascent allows us to take something of each *Sefirah*'s essence upward with us, until we reach the great connection point, *Binah*. There, all is merged together. Distinctions disappear. Unity is achieved through unification. The arrival at *Binah*, from the standpoint of meditation, is the achievement of *devekut*.

Devekut, attachment and adhesion, is the act of bonding with God. It is the ultimate objective of meditation, prayer, and life itself. At the point of integration in *Binah* one has completed himself and his processes. All elements of one's being become united and fulfilled. One is at peace. At the same time, the soul becomes connected directly with the Presence and Will of God in Creation. The meditator is at one with himself and with God simultaneously, because the levels being reached are the exact same point, *Binah*.

The name *Elohim*, according to Rabbi Joseph Gikatilla in his work *Shaare Orah*, is the name of God associated with the entire left side of the Tree of Life, which has *Binah* as its source and its guide. The *Sefirot* of *Din* and of *Hod* emanate from *Binah* directly. Each *Sefirah* on the left side of the Tree carries a name of God, connected with *Elohim*. *Binah* bears the name of *YHVH Elohim*. *Din* is called *Elohim* proper. *Hod* carries the name, *Elohim Tz'vaot*.

Binah is the objective and ultimate destination of meditation. It is the point of mystic union with God and with Self. To achieve this, one must pass through all of the lower *Sefirot*, absorbing their essence and thereby unifying them during the course of ascent. Since all of the *Sefirot* on the left are reflections of *Binah* exclusively and those of the right pillar conversely are extensions of *Hochmah*, travelling a route upward that focuses on the left or right is not necessarily appropriate. There is no balance, if one is focused on the left or the right. One must reach *Binah* with balanced energy.

In Part Three, Section *Ha'azinu*, page 290, side one, the *Zohar* tells us that when *Keter* extended and created *Hochmah*, male and female were implicit and unified within *Hochmah*. When *Hochmah* extended and produced *Binah*, male and female came about, balancing each other as the "Great Father"and the "Great Mother." Out of their united light comes the World of Emanation. Without this balance, the universe would not exist. Balance is the key principle of the Uppermost World.

According to the *Zohar*, *Hochmah* and *Binah* form the first two letters of God's articulated Name, the *Tetragrammaton* (YHVH). They are the Y and the H. Their light gives birth to the light that illumines the universe, the letter *Vav* (V). The letter *Vav* is the *Sefirah* of *Tiferet*, at the very heart of the Tree of Life. The last letter of the Great Name, the *Heh* (H), is the last *Sefirah*, *Malchut*, which is the physical universe and the World of Action, of Doing. It receives the light of *Tiferet* and reflects it back toward God.

In part 2, section *Terumah*, page 164, side 1, *Tiferet* is portrayed as the *Vav* of the Great Name of God. *Tiferet* unifies Heaven. That is, it balances and harmonizes the opposing forces of *Hesed* and *Din* that are to the right and left above it. *Hesed* and *Din* are the direct extensions of *Hochmah* and *Binah*. The *Hochmah-Binah* unity, of which *Binah* is the key element, becomes the *Hesed-Din* duality. *Tiferet* reestablishes balance and harmony by a process of unification. That produces the source of light for the physical universe.

The *Zohar* tells us here that all of the seven lower *Sefirot* are empowered and governed by *Binah*. It is impossible for the *Sefirot* per se to go further back than this. (They would have to be totally reintegrated into *Binah*, for only *Hochmah-Binah* reenter *Keter*.) We are instructed that meditation should focus on the *Sefirah* of *Yesod*. Within *Yesod* are ten *yeriot*, coverings, that correspond to the *Sefirot*. They are the appropriate focuses of meditation.

What is being suggested here is that the first stage of meditation aimed at reaching *Binah* is mediating on the ten *Sefirot* first within the realm of *Yesod*. *Yesod* represents the core of the World of Formation, the world of archetype and of pattern. It is *Yesod* that transmits light, energy, and form for all things to the physical universe of *Malchut*, below.

THE ASCENT TO *BINAH*

So, based in *Malchut*, we begin our ascent by exploring and assimilating the imprints made by the emanated forces of the upper worlds upon the *Sefirah* of *Yesod*, which transmits them to and sustains them in our world of physicality. We are specifically warned not to utilize in meditation *Hod* or *Netzach*, the *Sefirot* to the left and right.

If in our meditative ascent toward *Binah* we cannot utilize the left or the right, then we must follow the path of God's Great Name. That will take us directly to *Tiferet*, which is on the central pillar directly above *Yesod*. We began at *Malchut*, the final H of the Great Name, stopped and passed through all of the sefirotic imprints within *Yesod* directly above it, and then moved on to *Tiferet*, the *Vav* of the Great Name. It stands over *Yesod*, at the heart of the central pillar and in the center of the entire Tree.

Tiferet encompasses both *Hesed* and *Din*. In an identical manner to the work of *Yesod*, *Tiferet's* energy embodies the core of its world. To know *Tiferet* fully is also to know *Hesed* and *Din*. Moreover, to know *Tiferet* is to know the entire Tree, since it is the very heart and harmonization point of the entire Tree of Life. Meditating on *Tiferet* is of primal importance. One comes to understand the form and content of all the *Sefirot* by meditation on them within *Yesod*. One comes to experience their essence, energy, and interrelationship by *Tiferet* meditation. This is made clear in the *Zohar* as well.

Section *Terumah*, page 175, side two, comments on verse 27 of Genesis 25, "And Jacob is a simple man, a dweller in tents." The *Zohar* points out that it does not say that Jacob dwells in a tent but rather in tents. Jacob is a name used for the *Sefirah* of *Tiferet*. The term used above, *yeriot*, coverings, can also be translated or understood as "tents." Hence, the *Zohar* expresses that all of the *Sefirot* are encompassed, from a certain standpoint, within *Tiferet*.

Just as all of the *Sefirot* leave an imprint of themselves within *Yesod*, all of the *Sefirot* impact *Tiferet*. All of the energies of the *Sefirot* can be experienced within *Tiferet*, because it acts as the collection and rerouting point of all their energies, as they interact with each other in the Tree.

The term *Eesh Tam*, normally translated, "a simple man," can also mean, "a complete man." The *Zohar* emphasizes that here. *Hesed* and *Din* emanate as extensions from *Hochmah* and *Binah*. *Tiferet* unites and unifies *Hesed* and *Din*. *Tiferet* is inclusive of *Hesed* and *Din*, which are extensions of *Hochmah* and *Binah*, the Supernal Unity. Hence, *Tiferet* completes the two opposing *Sefirot* of *Hesed* and *Din* directly and thereby indirectly supports the Highest Unity of *Keter-Hochmah-Binah* by finishing the work begun at that level and by providing the base upon which the archetypical and physical universes are established.

As the *Zohar* puts it, Jacob (*Tiferet*) is inclusive of Isaac (*Din*) and Abraham (*Hesed*). They become a unified whole through *Tiferet*. That unity of Abraham, Isaac, and Jacob is in turn inclusive of all the *Sefirot*. In other words, *Hesed-Din-Tiferet*, the World of Creation, has *Tiferet* as its core. The unified nature of the World of Creation is the direct product of the unity of The World of Emanation above it.

It is also the source for the subsequent replication of its pattern. The unified triangulation, characteristic of the World of Creation, will become the pattern for the World of Formation. Ultimately, the World of Formation will establish the Physical World.

The World of Creation stands at the center of the four worlds. It is the energy core of Creation itself. At the core of the World of Creation is the *Sefirah* of *Tiferet*. *Tiferet* anchors the World of *Beriyah*, the World of Creation. *Beriyah* powers and lies at the center of the entire Tree, at the core of all four worlds. Hence, *Tiferet* is all inclusive, because it is the heart of the entire system that produces the universe.

Within the Tree of Life, thought and emotion are intimately tied together. The central *Sefirah* of *Tiferet* is not only the core of the World of Creation (Thought), but also the emanation point of the World of Formation (Emotion). As the heart of everything, *Tiferet* is both the source of reflection and of feeling, as well as the center of their interaction.

The World of Formation, in terms of human life, is the level of the emotions. The World of Creation is the level of thought. Yet the core of the World of Creation is *Tiferet*, the heart. Moreover, the World of Formation is a replica of the World of Creation. Structurally and functionally, it is a duplicate model. It is the World of Formation, the world of emotion, that imparts form, structure, and content to the physical.

This suggests that the core of our existence on the physical level is emotionally based. There is an emotional fulcrum on which our whole reality as beings in this universe is balanced. All of the *Sefirot* are encompassed by *Tiferet* and regulated by it. *Tiferet* is the Thought-Emotion nexus. *Tiferet* is the central focal point for the operation of the entire Tree. Will, energy, form, and content are balanced at this vital junction.

The right pillar within us comprises the pole of emotionality. It is that part of the Tree that emotes. That is different from emotion itself. Emotionality or emotionalism is the manner in which we handle and experience our emotions. Emotion per se is the capacity itself, the very ability to feel. Emotion, like thought, is within the middle pillar. It is centered in *Yesod* and is epitomized in *Tiferet*.

The left pillar of the Tree is the pole of thinking. Here too, thinking is not the same as thought. Thinking is a process. It is application. It is the process of definition, delineation, ordering, and structuring. Thought, however, is knowing and understanding. It is more a state than it is a process. It can, though, also be viewed as the state of processing. It too is in the central pillar, in the *Sefirah* of *Tiferet*.

The extensions of *Hochmah* and *Binah*, *Hesed*, and *Din*, both the right and left sides of the Tree, are brought together, merged, and balanced by *Tiferet*. *Tiferet*, in turn, gives birth to the triad of *Netzach*, *Hod*, and *Yesod*, the World of Formation, the world of emotion. *Tiferet* solidifies and produces the World of Creation, the world of thought, and gives birth from itself to the world of emotion.

Emotion is first the product of the merging of energies within the World of Creation, the realm of thought. Then, when emotion extends itself, it produces a whole world of its own, the World of Formation, the realm of emotion. This world is culminated and brought into full existence by *Yesod*. *Yesod* is the world of archetypes, the world of the delineated blueprints of Creation. It in a very real sense is the epitome of thought form. So, as it solidifies the realm of emotion, it does so by reflecting the culmination of thought.

In the structure of the Tree, thought and emotion are carefully interwoven. Like the Eastern symbol of the yin-yang, the core of both thought and emotion are their counterpart. The seed of yin is yang. The seed of yang is yin. In the Tree of Life, the core of the Thought World is concentrated emotion and the center of the Emotional World is intensified thought.

This concept is particularly useful in meditation. It is crucial in understanding the objectives of meditation in Jewish tradition. This is particularly true if viewed from the standpoint of spiritual development. The principle involved here is that the end result of a meditative process manifests as a concentrated experience, revealing itself as its own compliment.

When using meditation to process through emotion, one should eventually reach its core, which will be revelation. Revelation is a deep, cognitive understanding. The emotional process is truly understood, cognitively. Conversely, when processing thought meditatively, the end result will ultimately be enlightenment. Enlightenment is emotional breakthrough and a sense of inner knowingness.

Moreover, moving up through the central pillar, one sees the exact route toward spiritual integration and fulfillment. *Malchut* represents physical processing. First, one has to be grounded and must deal with processing day-to-day reality. To become grounded and balanced physically, one has to work through his or her issues in practical life on all fronts and thereby to seek balance.

When that is achieved, one is to move to *Yesod* and to process the emotions. This processing will eventually lead to the emergence of a clear mental picture. The cognitive conclusion of the emotional processing leads to a concise image of what the set of emotional experiences being worked through actually means. Revelation takes place. Emotional processing leads one to cognition. One suddenly recognizes the pattern. He/she is in position to acknowledge it, because it can finally be seen.

At that point, one is led to processing the intellectual ramifications. By thinking through the details of the picture, the implications of what you have come to understand emotionally, one eventually comes to the point of enlightenment. The meditator no longer merely sees. Rather, one understands. Intellectual processing leads to emotional realization, to breakthrough. One suddenly feels the totality of the pattern and the experiences it produced. The structure of one's emotional experience becomes completely self-evident. This is the process of *Tiferet* meditation.

The last stage in the process is the movement back to *Binah*. At this point, one reconnects with the Divine presence within oneself, the level of soul. The process at this level is a reentry into the womb, so to speak. One must go into a self-contraction. This is the process of emptying. It is the process of humility.

One must release all emotion and thought. They are the province of the lower *Sefirot*, the lower worlds. They are the emanated reality of oneself. They have to be relinquished in order to reenter the world of the spirit, the level of the soul, the undifferentiated World of *Atzilut*, nearness to God.

The interlocked duality of Thought-Emotion cannot enter the realm of unity. Beyond the gates of *Binah*, there are no answers nor are there any questions. There is just being itself. Thought and emotion are movements of the soul, not the soul itself. They are attributes of soul development. Reentry into the World of *Atzilut* is a transcendence. It is beyond evolution. It is pure being. One passes from the realms of understanding and knowledge to that of knowingness, knowing Self and knowing God. That is the ultimate centering, the supreme balance point. One is no longer in a state of becoming. One simply is.

To reach this threshold, one must humble oneself totally and must release fully. One must empty out completely. All the garments that the soul wears must be removed. Hold on to nothing and enter into the realm of totality. The key to this process of *Binah* meditation is the meditation practice described earlier as Nothingness meditation.

This entire process, first rising through the emotions and through thought to the point of self-realization, then centering within the soul, and finally via *devekut*, connecting with God, is very dependent on the physical level. Grounding and balance on the physical plane and emotional thought processing are equally essential, if we are to reach the spiritual level. The *Zohar* suggests that psychoemotional processing must be centered on and grounded in physical reality and daily life. We need to continually keep these two realms intimately united or else *devekut*, spiritual cohesion, will not be attainable.

In part 1, page 35, side 1 of the *Zohar*, *Tiferet* is referred to as the Tree of Life, because the entire Tree is dependent on it, structurally and functionally. Without *Tiferet*, there is no Tree of Life. Being in the middle of the Tree, *Tiferet* distributes the *Shefa*, the Great Abundance, the Life Force of God's Will and Intent, to all the *Sefirot* below. It draws it down from above and nurtures all of the *Sefirot*.

In the parlance of the *Zohar*, the waters of *Bereshit*, the Beginning (*Hochmah* and *Binah*), irrigate the mountains (*Hesed* and *Din*) and then reach the Tree of Life (*Tiferet*). From there the waters spread out below it to all sides (to *Netzach* and *Hod*). *Yesod* draws in the water from them. The six *Sefirot* from *Binah* to *Yesod* are referred to as the Cedars of Lebanon. Their energies are to be transmitted to *Malchut*, called the Tree of Knowledge. For this reason the upper *Sefirot* are termed the "six days of Creation."

Part 3, page 239, states that the World to Come (*Binah*), gives birth to the Tree of Life (*Tiferet*). She nurtures it, tends it, and sustains it perpetually. *Tiferet* is the principle of unification. From *Binah*, the Tree of Knowledge (*Malchut*) also emanates. However, it is not nurtured directly by *Binah*. Rather it is watered and cared for by *Tiferet*. Both Trees are linked directly to *Binah*.

However, the flow is such that *Malchut* is dependent on *Tiferet*, who in turn is dependent on *Binah*. It is the unification of both Trees that allow for access directly back to *Binah*. In practical terms this means that the physical world is the training ground and base of operations for processing the emotions and the thought. Meditative work, therefore, cannot abstract emotional processing and thought processing from the realm of physical or from practical experience.

SPIRITUAL ASCENT AND THE MIDDLE PILLAR

Meditation, if it is to lead to either spiritual development or spiritual transcendence, has to be grounded. It must focus on the immediate here and now. The Kabbalah teaches that each of the *Sefirot* has a complete tree within itself. One must first, in meditation, access the physical level. That can be done through the body or through an experience. Every part of our physical body corresponds to one of the *Sefirot*. Every event we experience, along with the feelings and thoughts that accompany it, is an expression of one of the *Sefirot*.

The entry point or initial stage of any meditation along the lines of self-exploration or the climb to transcendence needs to start with a physical focus. The beginning meditative focus can be a physical object, an event, a personal experience, a set of feelings, a part of one's body, a bodily process, a clearly stated idea. The possibilities are numerous.

The point here is that one's meditation needs to begin with something tangible and must be connected to one's own immediate reality. To do otherwise is to cut a lifeboat loose to drift on the open seas. One loses connection with Self and is caught helplessly in currents that he can neither control nor navigate. One is left floating without much possibility of rescue. One has put oneself in very grave danger, voluntarily and for no good purpose.

Meditating on abstract thoughts, undefined or vague emotion, hypothetical possibilities, or other people's realities will not impact one's own life nor in any way advance one's own self-development spiritually. Such meditation has no anchor nor any true foundation. It only serves to energize illusion, distraction, confusion, and self-destruction.

The Kabbalah refers to disconnecting the physical world from the upper worlds as "the cutting down of the Tree." This severance of the lower world from the upper ones can be accomplished by totally withdrawing and denying the upper worlds. By focusing exclusively on the physical and by relinquishing psychological and emotional self-exploration and spiritual self-development, one creates a severe and dangerous psychic rupture. One risks a similarly disastrous break if one focuses totally in the realm of the mind or the emotions to the complete exclusion of the physical. Either way, the result of the "cutting down of the Tree" is deadly. The consequences involve death on some level. To avoid these consequences, direct connection to life and experience is imperative.

Meditation on the ten *Sefirot* within the physical level, *Malchut*, are the gateways to their counterparts on other levels of consciousness. They are the grounding necessary to provide stability and structure, to meditative and spiritual ascent. That is why *Malchut* is referred to as the Tree of Knowledge. One gains the first, primary knowledge of reality through physical experience. That serves as the basis for approaching these forces on higher levels of consciousness. The intimacy of experience, gained within the physical world, grounds one physically, emotionally, and intellectually for spiritual connection and development.

Meditation on the *Sefirot* within *Tiferet*, the Tree of Life, accesses the dynamics and interaction of the upper worlds of Formation and Creation. In Genesis, the Tree of Knowledge is called "the Tree of the Knowledge of Good and Evil." It is the knowledge of the workings of duality within Creation. *Tiferet* is the point of harmonization between light and dark, mercy and judgement, expansion and contraction. It is the balance point between open-endedness and limitation, between essence and definition.

Here within the depths of *Tiferet*, the secrets of the upper worlds are penetrated, explored, and assimilated. Whereas *Malchut* is the Tree of Knowledge, the realm of learning, *Tiferet* is the Tree of Life, the realm of experience. The roots of both Trees lead back to *Binah*, that contraction which is the gateway to transcendence, the realm of spirit.

First sequentially in *Yesod*, and then in harmony in *Tiferet*, one explores the imprints and workings of the *Sefirot*. One comes to understand the entire structure and function of Creation from both of these vantage points. Only then is one brought to the threshold of spiritual oneness and communion with God.

The *Zohar* insists that *Tiferet* encompasses and reflects all of the *Sefirot*, as the core of the World of Creation, as the reflector of the World of *Atzilut*, and as the parent of the Worlds of Formation and of Action. As such the *Sefirah* of *Tiferet* is rightly called the Tree of Life.

The core of our existence as souls in the universe, then, is *Tiferet*, the psychoemotional nexus. This means that our reality has at its center an emotional fulcrum. All the aspects of our existence hinge and revolve on this central axis. All the *Sefirot* revolve around it and are interconnected through it. True health, completion as human beings, then, is predicated on the reality of *Tiferet's* nature, which is emotional balance and psychological neutrality.

Tiferet is not emotional processing. Nor is it intellectual construction. It is psychoemotional transcendence. It harmonizes and balances the right and the left. It is at the center of the middle pillar of the Tree. All of the seven lower *Sefirot* of process and experience are gathered together in *Tiferet* during the ascent toward spirit. Having assimilated all experience and knowledge, *Tiferet* ascends into *Binah*. Together with *Hochmah*, *Binah* ascends into *Keter*. There *devekut*, communion with Self and with God, takes place.

According to the *Zohar*, part 2, page 239, when *Hochmah-Binah* ascends into *Keter*, it becomes perfumed by its contact and so gives off a fragrance. This fragrance is imparted through *Binah* to all of the *Sefirot*. Though *Keter* is unknowable, unification produces the scent of Creation that is ultimately reflected in all of the levels of Creation represented by the *Sefirot*. Though one may be in a room and not see the beautiful woman who is the owner of the mansion, one is none the less aware of her existence due to the lingering fragrance of her perfume.

On a physical level, scent, the activation of the olfactory nerves, stimulates emotion. This activation is critical for the interconnection and proper functioning of both hemispheres of the brain. What is more, the sense of smell also directly affects short-term memory.

The implications here are very important. Short-term memory reflects our ability to focus on and deal with the immediate present. The immediate present is our conscious life. Our direct experience of life, the here and now, is influenced heavily and regulated by the psychoemotional nexus that unifies the right and left brain.

Psychological and emotional balance achieved in *Tiferet* harmonizes both right brain, emotional processing (*Hochmah-Hesed-Netzach*), and left brain, thought process (*Binah-Din-Hod*). They are nurtured and regulated via *Tiferet* and its subsidiary, *Yesod*. *Yesod* in turn produces the patterns that manifest on the physical level.

Hence, *Tiferet*, psychoemotional balance, is the key to being a complete person. All aspects of being are integrated through this process. *Tiferet* is the mechanism by which the full structure of the *Sefirot* is built, directed, and sustained. Through *Tiferet* all the *Sefirot* are united, all life experience is integrated, and all of one's being is centered spiritually.

The achievement of this balance and integration, leading to spiritual ascent and transcendence, occurs through the interlocked workings of both lesser trees, *Malchut* and *Tiferet*, for ultimately they are two manifestations of the same Tree of Life. Referring to Song of Songs 2:3, the *Zohar* (part 3, page 74) asks why the *Sefirah* of *Tiferet* (the Tree) is referred to as an "apple tree."

The *Zohar* answers as follows: First, an apple is healing. The *Sefirah* of *Tiferet* is the level of healing. Second, *Tiferet* is Heaven. Heaven, like an apple, has an exceptional color. Moreover, Heaven is goodness, which is symbolized by the taste of the apple. Finally, the apple tree has the most distinct scent of any tree.

Tiferet is Heaven and *Malchut* is Earth. What occurs in one *Sefirah* directly affects the other. When the righteous multiply on Earth, Heaven is strengthened by the spiritual proximity created. God blesses the Earth and its surface shines brightly. Conversely, when evil increases, the Heavens reject the Earth and the face of the Earth darkens.

Here again, the *Zohar* emphasizes the intricate and critical relationship between physical reality and the psychoemotional nexus. Heaven and Earth and their interrelationship are being compared to three senses, those of sight, smell, and taste. Sight represents the eyes, the gateway to the mind. Smell and taste are related directly to emotions. All three of the senses involved are facilitated through organs in the head.

The level of spiritual consciousness, the Great Face of God, is accessed through the psychoemotional nexus of *Tiferet*, which encompasses all of the seven *Sefirot* of the Lesser Face of God. Clearing up psychoemotional blockages, through meditation and processing, through therapy and by constant connection and work with the physical realm, brings balance to all levels. That balance, then, opens up access to spiritual experience and growth.

The equation of *Tiferet* with the image of an apple also points to a meditation process that furthers the end of connecting life experience directly with higher levels of consciousness. This meditation propels one continually upward, through the worlds, fueling spiritual evolution.

In two-dimensional reality, the concepts of totality, wholeness, and completion are represented geometrically by a circle. Brought into three dimensions, the circle becomes a sphere or globe. In four-dimensional reality, a globe becomes a hypersphere. A hypersphere from our three-dimensional viewpoint appears as a doughnut of seven colors that is in constant motion, all its sides continually revolving through the hole in its center.

An apple can be seen as a metaphor for the hypersphere, also known as the torus. The skin and the pulp of the apple, which constitute its shape, represent the energy movement of the torus or hypersphere, which gives it its form. The stem and core of the apple, on the other hand, represent the neutral center around which the energy flows.

The core of the apple is both delineated by the pulp around it and is the guiding force behind the growth and development of the apple. The core of the apple is the point of emanation. Without it, the apple would have no base and no structure. Following the line of the stem, the growth pattern of the apple is established and consistently maintained. Moreover, the core of the apple houses the seeds. From the original seed, the core emerged and formed the basis for energy movement and growth. That led to the production of the apple and ultimately to the emergence of new seeds. The core of the apple is the Alpha Omega, the point of beginning and end. It is the seed and the fruit simultaneously.

The apple image, or the "doughnut" model, are three-dimensional representations of the hypersphere, the torus. These models of the hypersphere/torus are indicative of the Tree of Life in motion. The neutral core of the torus is the middle pillar of the Tree. It is the balanced movement from *Keter* to *Tiferet*, to *Yesod*, to *Malchut*, and back again. It is around this basic core that the right and left pillars interlock and interact. The right and left pillars revolve around the neutral central pillar. Hence, the interconnection of the right and left pillar creates the two halves of the apple or doughnut.

Two distinct movements center around the neutral core of the middle pillar. Together, they produce both the substance and the form of the Tree of Life and of Creation. First, each pillar pulsates with its own energy. This directional movement, upward and downward, produces each of the pillars and maintains their integrity. Second, a perpetual, circular motion by the two pillars is produced by the principle of attraction and repulsion. This revolution of the two external pillars, centering on the neutral core, the Middle Pillar, produces the form and substance of the torus.

The perpetual movement of the Tree is the constant "becoming" that is Creation itself. As it continues to move, it continues to exist, both redefining itself constantly and maintaining its basic integrity at the same time. The interaction between the right and left pillars around the central pillar, in conjunction with the simultaneous oscillation of each pillar from above to below and back again, produces the "doughnut," within the eternal moment of the "now."

The image of an apple cut in half is identical with the image produced by scattering iron filings around a bar magnet. The magnetic field around the bar magnet is that of a halved apple. What one sees here is two distinct, interlocked halves, centering around a neutral core. The magnet itself is an integral whole, yet it is comprised of two polar opposites. Also visible are some faint lines, representing the magnetic fields, that emanate upward from the top pole and downward from the bottom pole. This suggests that there was a magnetic field before the one being

Energy Flow Three: Oscillation

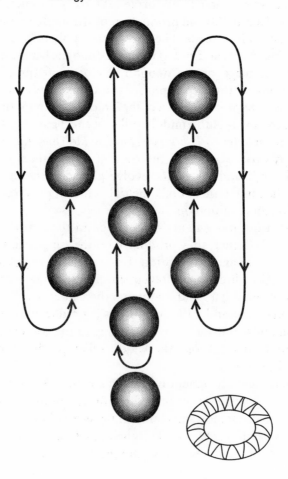

viewed and one that will emerge from it in the future, though they are all the same in actuality. The implication here is that Creation is the "now" and constitutes the "was-will be" as well. Creation both is, was, and will be, simultaneously.

Duality and the harmonization of opposites are the core dynamics of worlds of Creation and Formation. Duality is the basis for dynamism. The unification of the opposing forces around a neutral core creates form and movement. The motion of the form continually defines, sustains, and evolves. This unity of Was-Is-Will Be is the very essence of the Tree of Life. It is implicit in *Tiferet*. It is observable within the very structure of the Tree of Life. Moving through the physical realm leads one back up to the "Six Days of Creation," the worlds of *Yetzirah* (Formation) and *Beriyah* (Creation). Through their exploration, one is brought to the World of *Atzilut*, the level of spiritual awareness.

Reaching this state of knowingness is entry into the realm of spirit, of true knowledge of Self and of Communion with God. It is the ultimate goal and the central objective of meditation in the Jewish tradition.

Epilogue

The intent and objective of this brief work is, in essence, threefold. First, it is the desire of the author to provide the reader with a clear and consistent understanding of the ultimate aim and purpose of meditation in Jewish tradition. The goal of meditative practice is ultimately reconnecting with one's Self, reaching the level of soul and the realm of inner knowingness. Through this realm of spirit, one comes to know oneself and to draw close into communion with God.

Second, it is important to see the close, inner connection that exists between the Kabbalah, Jewish mystic thought, and meditation. Meditation practice is the truest and most important application of mysticism in the Judaic tradition. The active practice of this mystic discipline leads to a deep, profound, personal understanding of Kabbalah and kabbalist thought.

In these chapters, great attention has been placed on trying to illustrate the process of extracting concrete, usable knowledge in terms of meditation and practice. From a careful reading of the sacred texts themselves, much information regarding spiritual practice and meditation can be reconstructed. Much of the wisdom of Kabbalah and many of its doctrines are not merely intellectual formulations. Rather, they are the results of revelation, insight, and enlightenment that have come directly out of meditation.

Meditation often leads to the experience of altered states of consciousness. It opens the inner gates of awareness to alternate realities and to higher realms of existence. Meditation, subsequently, provides the basis for contemplation, which in turn allows one to come to understand and assimilate the experiences and to garner the knowledge that can be drawn from them.

Since few books have ever been written in Kabbalah that actually detail meditative practices, it is imperative that people develop the skill of extrapolating these techniques from the mystic doctrines in which they are imbedded intellectually. To do this unites both elements so crucial to Kabbalah, thought and action. When one can study the texts of the Kabbalah both as theology, cosmology, and sacred science, on the one hand, and as a handbook on meditative practice and discipline, on the other, the full intent of Kabbalah is fulfilled.

Meditative practice leads to revelation and insight. They are the fruits of experiencing other realities and exploring other levels of self. Experience opens into knowledge. Exploration fosters contemplative soul-searching. The contemplation of meditative experience transforms one's knowledge into knowingness. Knowingness brings one to the center of self, the soul. Being centered in the soul unifies one with God. At the base of this entire process lies the same constant, namely, meditation.

The central and primary objective of this work is quite straightforward. It seeks to provide the reader not only with some very basic concepts that lie at the core of Jewish meditation, but also with an array of practical, detailed techniques to help reach the goals of meaningful, mystic experience, inner enlightenment, and connection to God. The spiritual objective of this material is to empower the meditator, through an expanded understanding of the founding principles of Jewish meditation, as reflected in Kabbalah.

The pragmatic goal of this work is to assist the reader in developing those skills necessary in the pursuit of spiritual growth, through an active use of the Kabbalah. This book, first and foremost, is intended to strengthen the knowledge base of anyone who chooses to delve into the Kabbalah. It seeks to empower the meditator, on a very practical and sustainable level, by introducing and detailing specific meditation practices derived from Kabbalah.

The discipline of kabbalist meditation brings both knowledge and experience. The key to spiritual commitment and development is the practical application of the meditative techniques, alluded to in the Kabbalah, in a consistent manner. As was indicated by the Israelites, who stood at the foot of Mount Sinai, doing and understanding, knowledge and action, are inextricably interwoven when it comes to serving God and humanity.

With that in mind, it is only fitting that this volume be concluded with an appendix. Within this last chapter, a series of graduated meditations will be presented to the reader. They are keyed to a number of the concepts and ideas explained in the preceding chapters. The appendix begins with very simple meditations and ends in more advanced ones. The techniques involved increase in complexity in accord with their objectives.

Not all of the meditations will suit everyone. A meditative path is as distinct as the individual meditator. One should work through the meditations progressively, focusing and becoming proficient in those with which one resonates the most. Worked with long enough, the meditations one has chosen to focus on and assimilate will over time become second nature. They will also lead the meditator in new directions of meditative exploration.

May these meditations be a lamp, illuminating your way and furthering your spiritual quest. May you find healing and growth. May you be led back to your spiritual center. May you find the joy of being at one, with Self and with God.

Appendix

Graduated Meditations

GENERAL MEDITATIONS

I. Increasing Light and Reaching Equilibrium

A. Visualize a seven-branched menorah with seven candles in it. The candles are all even, with a dominant candle in the middle and three candles flanking it to the left and to the right. The middle candle is already burning. The others remain to be kindled.

B. Starting with the candle on the farthest right, imagine the first three candles being lit, sequentially, by the central candle. These candles are the aspects of your daily outer life. Your relationship to career, community, and society is candle one. Your relationship to friends and acquaintances is second, and the third candle is your relationship to family.

 As you light each candle, focus on what is currently happening in all of these relationships. Get a sense of the light you are generating for others in their lives, and the light that others are generating in yours.

C. Now light the three candles on the left side, from left to right. These three candles are your inner lights. They represent your

189

hopes and dreams, your thoughts and feelings, and your sense of self. As you light these candles, let the light of these internal realities affect you. Feel where you are at with all these levels and accept them.

D. Now replace the central candle. Focus your attention on the flame. Feel the warmth and bask in the light. Let its light be expanded and surrounded by the illumination of the other six flames. This candle is the light of the Soul. It is the core of your being. Bring yourself to a point of balance and inner peace. Center your light and be with it. Be thankful for the light and honor it. This is the Sabbath of the Soul.

II. Meditating on the Eight Lights of Hanukkah

Here in meditation one focuses on the different lights within oneself. The objective of this meditation is to expand one's awareness of eight inner dimensions of Self. The goal is to better understand the forces of self-awareness and self-expression as they operate within us. Through clarity and focusing on them, we increase the influence they have on our daily life.

One should meditate independently on each candle and its meaning, in succession. Then take in the light as a unified whole. Surround yourself with it and become energized and protected by it.

Here are the meanings of the individual candles.

A. The Shamash Candle is that of God's Presence, guidance, and protection in one's life.

B. The first candle (far right) is self-awareness, the experience of oneself as one lives his/her life.

C. The second candle represents one's view of himself/herself. It is the light of self-esteem.

D. The third candle is the flame of interpersonal relationship. This candle is that of our interaction with friends, family, and loved ones.

E. The fourth candle is the candle of grounding. It is one's sense of being present and of belonging.

F. The fifth light is that of impact. This candle represents reaching out and touching others.

G. Candle six is the light of accomplishment. This is the energy generated by achievement and the resulting satisfaction.

H. Completing one stage leads most often to embarking on a quest for greater achievement. Hence, this seventh candle is the torch of hope and aspiration.

I. The last light is that which brings us back full circle to self. The final taper represents our connection with God in this world. It is the light of higher purpose, the light of our obligation to God to fulfill our potential during this life.

III. A Mandala of One's Individual Relationship to God

Meditate on the visual image of this letter progression. You may do so by first studying the image. Next, contemplate how the energy of the pattern strikes you. What feeling do you get from it? Then, by contemplating each line in sequence, focus your attention downward, one row at a time, on the letters and on the words formed. Gain a sense of the movement from one line to another and the progression of meaning.

The next step is to let the energy of the pattern generate itself in wave motion, beginning with the top letter and undulating, row by row. Finally close your eyes, and holding the image of the pulsating pattern, become one with it and with its energy.

$$\aleph$$
$$\aleph \quad \ell$$
$$\aleph \quad \ell \quad \text{י}$$
$$\aleph \quad \ell \quad \text{ה} \quad \text{י}$$
$$\aleph \quad \ell \quad \text{ה} \quad \text{י} \quad \text{ם}$$

Meanings: Line One. *Aleph*. The Self. One.
Line Two: God
Line Three: My God
Line Four: My God and God of my Ancestors
Line Five: God, the Creator

IV. The Six Stages of Ascent

A. *Stage One.* Niggun *(a tune without lyrics)*

Close your eyes and begin to meditate. Sing or chant a simple meditative tune of your own choosing. Focus your attention exclusively on the tune and the flow of the melody's energy. This process should take you into a meditative state of equilibrium.

B. *Stage Two.* Hagah (*Meditative Focus*)

Focus on a visual image of something important to you, a scene, an event, a symbol, a person, or whatever. You may choose to focus on something more abstract instead, a feeling, an issue, or a Hebrew letter. Continue to chant the *niggun*, while centering your attention on this new meditative focus. A connection will emerge between you and the object of meditation.

C. *Stage Three.* Ranen (*Singing for Joy*)

Begin to flow with the energy being generated. Continue singing the *niggun* with increasing intensity. Allow more enthusiasm and emphasis to emerge with each refrain. Allow joy to fill your heart and your being. Let this momentum carry you upward.

D. *Stage Four.* Nogah (*Reaching the Light*)

As you continue to experience the joy and the song, light will surround you. It will fill you entirely. You will become lighter and lighter. You will feel an increasing sense of peace and harmony, joy, and exaltation.

E. *Stage Five.* Siach (*The Great Flow*)

You will float ever upward. Allow yourself to drift higher and higher, into new realms and new levels of light. Ride with the currents. Sing a new song or speak what needs to be expressed in an internal dialogue with God.

F. *Stage Six.* Sha'ashu'a (*Ecstacy*)

Let yourself oscillate between light and dark, between expansion and contraction, between joy and peace. Flow freely with the movement and the experience. Let it take you to the level of transcendence, the level of pure joy beyond time and space, beyond cause and effect.

When ready, count down from 32 to 0. Return through your body. Center in your heart and reach a focus in your feet at the count of zero.

V. Visualizing Biblical Paradigms

Biblical stories and biblical motifs often function, very effectively, as models of psychological and spiritual change. By meditating on a story, or on the major component elements of the story, one becomes attuned to a specific experiential pattern that can produce a psychological and spiritual shift. Through self-identification with the process, in meditation, one resonates with the pattern. By so doing, the meditator takes on the imprint of the event and is affected by the replicated results.

One vivid example of such a paradigm would be the story of the Exodus from Egypt. Jewish tradition tells us that we all, throughout the generations, must retell the story and refocus our attention on it yearly. We are commanded by God to reexperience the Exodus. All generations, it is said, past and future, were redeemed from Egypt and were present at the Giving of the Law at Mount Sinai. Meditating on the story of the redemption from slavery helps release one from the inner patterns by which the individual has been enslaved.

ALPHABET MEDITATIONS

I. Letter Energy

   A. Once in meditation, picture a vast field of energy before you. Carve a Hebrew letter in the energy field. Once done, the letter will turn black and the energy field will remain white. Both the letter and the energy field will pulsate with burning energy, black flame on white flame.

   B. Concentrate first on the white flame background. Then shift to the black flame letter. Study the structure of the letter. Get a feeling for the letter. Embrace the energy.

   C. Picture the letter as a hollow created in the energy field of white. This letter is one of the twenty-two primal building blocks of reality. It is a great doorway to a specific aspect of the fabric of reality. Let the formatted energy, created by the emergence of this letter, pass through the doorway and reach you.

   D. You may feel the urge to utilize the energy. If so, you will know instinctually what needs to be done with it. Or you may simply wish to experience the energy and then release it back to its origin point.

II. *Atbash* Pillars

In the Kabbalah, an ancient method of coding was developed, which is a form of letter substitution. This system of letter correspondence is known as *Atbash*. Each letter of the Hebrew alphabet is considered to have a sister letter at the other end of the spectrum. This sister letter can be substituted for the original letter, since both are direct counterparts of each other.

The primacy of duality, in the process and construction of Creation, is emphasized frequently in the Kabbalah. The birth of opposing forces, the continual tension between them, and their subsequent harmonization and balance, characterize the basic dynamic of the structure of the universe.

Therefore, that the Hebrew letters, the very building blocks of Creation, should also have a form of dual reality is not at all surprising. The difference here is that duality on the level of Creation manifests as opposites, left and right, up and down, good and evil, and so on, whereas with the alphabet, the energy blocks of the creative process, duality manifests as the interrelationship of the hidden to the revealed.

In *Atbash*, the Hebrew alphabet is grouped as eleven sets of two letters each. The first and last letters of the alphabet, *Aleph* and *Tav*, are paired (A,T), the second and second to last, *Bet* and *Shin* (B,Sh), and so on. The *Aleph* can potentially be changed to *Tav*, and the *Bet* can be substituted with a *Shin*. One is revealed, the other is hidden. Hence, an *Atbash* letter represents the concealed reality of its sister letter. *Tav* is the hidden potential within *Aleph,* and *Aleph* is correspondingly the concealed inner reality of *Tav.*

This principle of letter substitution is very useful in meditation, when it comes to the Hebrew alphabet or Hebrew language. For example, the letter *Aleph* refers to the Self, the core of one's being. The *Tav*, its counterpart, represents physical manifestation. On the level of human experience, the *Tav* would signify one's personality, ego, and physical presence in the world. Meditating on the *Aleph-Tav* duo connects one directly to the interrelationship between the inner Self and one's outer personality. This particular pair of letters exemplifies, both in one's daily life and on the level of Life Purpose, the intimate connection between life experience and the core of one's existence, a very fertile field for exploration.

Another powerful *Atbash* technique is to take a Hebrew word and convert it into *Atbash*, substituting all of the letters for their sister letters.

Once accomplished, one meditates on the new letter pattern in order to
tap into the hidden dimensions of the reality the original word represents.
For point of reference, here are the eleven *Atbash* sets:

א-ת ב-ש ג-ר ד-ק ה-צ ו-פ ז-ע ח-ס ט-נ י-מ כ-ל

III. A Hebrew Letter as Mandala and Mantra

Exercise A

1. Relax into a meditative state. Picture a field of white, in the form
   of a blank wall reflecting sunlight, in front of you. Allow a letter of the alphabet to emerge on the wall. It is large and very
   dark. It is quite distinct and detailed. Focus on the letter carefully. Let the letter take effect on you.
2. Spend some time contemplating the meaning of the letter. Let
   it suggest what it will to you. Let it speak to you.
3. Examine the physical structure of the letter. Move your focus
   along its lines. Inspect its construction. Feel the flow. Explore
   the letter's angles and the geometric relationships within the
   letter. What does this tell you?
4. As you visually explore the letter and sense the flow of energy,
   allow the energy to be absorbed into your heart, then into your
   mind, and finally into your soul.
5. Now let the letter affect your very soul and inner being. Chant
   the letter with the following vowel pattern:

   $$x \; \dot{x} \; \ddot{x} \; x \; \dot{x} \; x \; \chi$$

6. When ready, visualize the letter, holding it within you, while
   you chant a *niggun* (any wordless melody that comes to you).
   Continue to chant the *niggun* and focus on the letter until your
   consciousness takes you somewhere else or you feel ready to
   exit the meditation altogether.

   If you are taken somewhere in the meditation, experience
   what is there fully, before completely exiting the meditative
   state.

Exercise B: A Hebrew Word as Mandala and Mantra

1. Pick a Hebrew word to meditate on. Some powerful focus words
   to use in this meditation would include: *Kodesh* (holy), *Shabbat*

(Sabbath), *Shalom* (peace), *Hesed* (grace, loving-kindness), and so forth.

2. Pronounce or chant the first syllable as you picture it in your mind. Then, picture the first and second syllables emerging underneath the first and pronounce or chant both syllables in sequence. Finally, picture the entire three-letter word appearing under the second tier. Pronounce or chant the entire word, syllable by syllable. Then, reverse the process. This will produce a diamond pattern as a mandala as well as a specific mantra to accompany it.

If you chose the word *kodesh*, the pattern of visualization would be as follows:

```
          ק
        ד   ק
      ש   ד   ק
      ש   ד   ק
        ד   ק
          ק
```

Visually, this pattern is a mandala. To use it as such, relax and let your eyes flow freely from letter to letter. The eye can flow with the movement of the structure in a number of different ways. There are a lot of geometric patterns that connect the letters to each other. Create paths, by wandering from one to the other. Cluster them in groupings. Where are the lines, the squares, the circles, the triangles, the diamonds, and so forth? At a certain point in the process, when you feel the energy within you reach an apex, close your eyes and release your mind. Just float and be carried to another level of consciousness.

This pattern also serves as a mantra to chant or sing. Here, one verbalizes each line of the pattern progressively. Start at the top of the pattern and work down. Chant each line clearly and at a comfortable tempo. When you reach the bottom of the pattern, use the letter there as the beginning point of the chant, reversing the process. Continue the chant, moving down and then back up continually, line by line, until you feel ready to close your eyes and release your consciousness into free float.

At the end of the meditative experience so induced, you will awaken to full normal consciousness.

The pattern above, is that of *Kodesh*, holiness. Line by line, it would sound like this from the top down:

KO, KODE, KODESH, KODESH, KODE, KO.

Then, from the bottom back up to the top, the pattern would sound the same.

An alternate progression could also be constructed, which would look and sound like this:

```
            ק
      ר   ק
   ש  ר   ק
   ש  ר   ק
   ש  ר
      ש
```

Read: KO, KÓDE, KODESH, KODESH, DESH, SH.

Here are a few other patterns to try.

Shalom. Peace

```
            ש
      ל   ש
   מ  ל   ש
   מ  ל   ש
      ל   ש
         ש
```

Read: SHA, SHALO, SHALOM, SHALOM, SHALO, SHA

or

```
            ש
      ל   ש
   מ  ל   ש
   מ  ל   ש
   מ  ל
   מ
```

Read: SHA, SHALO, SHALOM, SHALOM, LOM, M.

Hesed. Loving-kindness

```
            ח
      ס   ח
   ד  ס   ח
   ד  ס   ח
      ס   ח
         ד
```

Read: HE, HESE, HESED, HESED, HESE, HE

or

ח

ס   ח

ד   ס   ח

ד   ס   ח

ד   ס

ד

Read; HE, HESE, HESED, HESED, SED, D

One can also create a pattern that uses two words that are often used together in the same context. A simple example would be *Hanun* and *Rahum*, gracious and compassionate. Such a pattern would look like this:

ח

נ   ח

ן   נ   ח

ם   ח   ר

ח   ר

ר

Read: HA, HANU, HANUN, RAHUM, RAHU, RA.

IV. Verb Root Assimilation

As has been mentioned earlier, most of the Hebrew language is based on the verb. Nouns, adjectives, adverbs, as well as verbs, are all built on the verb root. The verb root, in Hebrew, comprises three letters. To understand the inner dynamics and to probe the deep internal, hidden meanings of any aspect of life or reality, one must be able to see and experience the primal force behind it, from the inside out. This is done by meditating on the verb root. The method used is simple.

    1. Select a verb root. Here are a few possibilities:
        A. To be courageous, to overcome, to strengthen, intensify:

גבר

        B. To bless, to be blessed, to kneel, to congratulate:

ברך

        C. To know, to be intimate with, to inform, to comprehend, to be known, to be conscious of:

ידע

D. To reign, rule, to illustrate, to tell a parable or proverb:

משל

E. To see, to perceive, to show, to appear, to be apparent, to demonstrate:

ראה

2. Cup your hands and visualize holding the letters of the verb root.
3. Close your eyes. Picture lifting up the verb root and placing it approximately two to three inches above the crown of your head.
4. As you meditate, picture the verb root becoming an inverse triangle of letters, like this:

ה   א   ר

א   ר

ר

All of the energy of the verb root is condensed into the first letter. Allow the single letter at the bottom of the pattern to pulsate with energy.

5. When the pulsation reaches its climax, the letter will begin to oscillate, disappearing and reappearing alternately. When the letter disappears, during this cycle, feel it being drawn into you through the crown of your head.
6. The condensed verb root energy will begin to permeate your entire consciousness. Release yourself to the flow. Allow the energy to fill you. Let it lead you to an inner understanding of some of the multitude of meanings and realities encompassed by this facet of Creation. Understand the force and the potential from within, both from within it and from within you.
7. You may exit from this meditation when it runs its course, or at any juncture, by counting backward from four to zero.

V. Meditating on the Meaning of the Letters

Each letter in the Hebrew alphabet has various intrinsic meanings. The letters all have names, most of which mean something and therefore symbolize a certain aspect reality, with all its implications. Each letter, moreover, has a numerical equivalent, since the letters are also used as numbers. Numerologically, numbers have specific meanings. Therefore, each Hebrew letter has a numerological meaning. Numbers are often the reflection of geometric relationships, as well, so another level of meaning in the letters is their relationship to geometric form and to structural interconnection.

Presented below is a simple table of basic meanings for each letter of the alphabet. One can meditate on any letter by focusing on an aspect of its general meaning.

א

Aleph: Unity. Self. Oneness. Above/Below. Singularity. Infinity.

ב

Bet: Duality. Domicile. Environment. Inner Being. Structure. Definition. A Line.

ג

Gimmel: Extension. Movement. A Route. Transport. Destination. Expansion. Triangle.

ד

Dalet: Transit. Transition. Exploration. Connected Realities. Gateway. Opening. Interdimensionality. Solidity. Square.

ה

Hey: Divine Force. Spirit. Spiritual Reality. Divine Presence. Hidden/Revealed. Determinative Force. Definition. Authority. Pentagon/Star.

ו

Vav: Conjunction. Unification. Connection. Linkage. Male/Female. Union. Love. Attraction. Heart. Interplay of Divine and Human. Star of David/Hexagon.

ז

Zayin: Tool. Power to Fashion and Build. Masculine force/Energy. Assertion. Assertiveness. Seven. Sabbath. Transcendence.

ח

Het: Field. Cultivation. Sustenance. Fertility. Receptivity. Feminine Force/Energy. Boundary/Limit.

ט

Tet: Internalization. Introspection. Journey within. Soul-searching Opening oneself. Spiritual Pursuit.

י

Yud: Hand. Ability to Do/Make. Self-expression. Interaction in the World. World of Senses. Primal Matter. Creation.

כ

Kaf: Palm. Potential to Do/Make. Coordination. Control. Strength. Destiny.

ל

Lamed: Learning. Teaching. Experience. Growth. Rapid Change. Shift. Altered Viewpoint.

מ

Mem: Water. Transformation. Hidden/Deep Emotion. Birth/Life. Immersion. Purity.

נ

Nune: Fish. Regeneration. Rebirth/Renewal. Fluidity. Flow. Creativity. Interplay of Life Forces.

ס

Samech: Circularity. Cycles. Evolution. Development. Regularity. Support. Trust. Empowerment. Authorization.

ע

Ayin: Eyes. Sight. Vision. Perception. Viewpoint. Perceptual Shift. Revelation. Theory. Reflection of the Soul. Internal Gateway.

פ

Pey: Mouth. Expression. Articulation. Communication. Ideas. Interchange. Absorption. Business/Commerce. Internalization/Eating. Externalization/Exposition.

צ

Tsaddi: Righteousness. Justice. Morality. Intercession. A Saint. Charity. Channeling Divine Light and Energy.

ק

Kuf: Spontaneity. Love of Life. Exuberance. Community. Fulfillment. Spiritual Emergence. Spiritual Energy.

ר

Resh: Head. Thought. Mind. Intellect. Mental Energy. Beginning. Origin. Initiation.

ש

Shin: Soul (*Neshama-Ruach-Nefesh*), Fire. Emotion. Emotionality. Life Purpose. Individual. Individuation. Teeth. Biting Through.

ת

Tav: Note. Sound. Vibration. Unexpressed Becoming Expressed. Manifestation. Realization of the Original Thought. The Physical World. End. Completion. Culmination.

VII. The *Gematria* (Numerology) of a Hebrew Word.

Since all Hebrew letters of the alphabet have numerical equivalences, any word in the language has a numerical value. Hence, any word can be understood numerologically, which is the basis for further meditation.

Let us take as an example the full names of the three Mother Letters, *Aleph*, *Mem*, and *Shin*. Written out fully, they appear as follows:

אלף מם שין

Checking the Table of Equivalents, we find that the eight letters have the following numerical values:

Aleph=1, Lamed=30, Final Fey (Pey)=80, Mem=40, Final Mem=40, Shin=300, Yud=10, Final Nune=50. If you total all the numbers, the grand total, that is the full value of the three names, equals 551.

The Hebrew word Resha'im (heads, sources) totals 551 as well.

These three letters are the Mother Letters, the sources upon which all of the alphabet is built and from which all other letters derive their existence. Interestingly, 551 is also the numerical value for the word Morasha (legacy, heritage).

Once a word or phrase is reduced to a numerical total, several operations can be done to reveal connections and patterns that serve as substantive kernels or gestalts upon which to meditate. Here are a couple of different techniques:

A. Exploring the Meaning of the Letter Sequence

The word Yir'ah means "awe," also, "to be in a state of awe." It is frequently used in biblical literature to describe the appropriate relationship to God. In Hebrew, it is spelled,

יראה

The sequence of letters in the word is Yud, Resh, Aleph, Hey. A pattern for meditating on the deeper meaning of the word would be to meditate on each letter sequentially. When focusing on a letter, center your concentration on the meaning of each letter. Gain a feeling and some insight into the nature of this reality from the flow of one concept into the next.

The conceptual flow of our example of Yir'ah (Yod-Resh-Aleph-Heh) could be interpreted as follows:

Yud, Doing/Making, is the molding of primal matter. The beginning of the process of experiencing awe is to rework one's relationship to physical reality. Reduce it to a primal level. Assume nothing. Discard all old frames of reference. This leads to the Resh.

Resh is mind and it is beginning. Reconnect with the beginning. Elevate yourself to the level of thought and will. Open yourself up to the possibility of new paradigms and new ways of understanding. Once this is done, the Aleph emerges. You then reexperience Self. You become reintegrated with the deepest part of your Being. You unify yourself with God. You ultimately experience the *Hey*, spiritual transformation.

B. *Meditating on the* Temurah *(words with equal numerical value)*

The word *yirah*, "awe," has a total numerical value of 216 (Yud=10, Resh=200, Aleph=1, Hey=5, Total=216).

The assumption in Kabbalah is that there is a deep mystical connection and hidden identity between any two words or phrases with the same numerical value. Therefore, one can juxtapose two words of equal numerical value. Meditating on each of the two words separately at first and then on both together will reveal to the meditator the hidden connections between them. What will become clear will be the internal realities and inner dimensions connecting the two. Ultimately, great truths will emerge as a result.

Here are some other words of phrases in Hebrew, that also total 216:

בחרו, חברו, יראה, ידבר, וייקץ, ברוח, בחור, גבורה

(Translations: They Chose, They Combined, He Will See, He Will Speak, And He Will Awaken, With Spirit, Young Man, Courage)

GEOMETRIC MEDITATIONS

The term *Gematria* refers to Hebrew numerology and the use of numbers in connection with interpreting the secret meanings and interrelations of Hebrew words. Technically, *Gematria* is the Greek word for Geometry.

It is accepted in Kabbalah that letters arranged in geometric patterns yield deeper insight into reality. This is due to the intrinsic meaning of structure and form themselves.

All of the patterns described below are geometric patterns formed from words or from verb roots. These geometric constructions are built from words, phrases, or connected terms. They are meant to be used as visual mandalas, sacred meditation patterns.

Meditation on these patterns can take several forms, depending on the inclination of the meditator. There are choices. One can focus on the image as a whole, or on the structural progression and flow of the letters. One may instead seek to center on the overall structure of the form, or on the various interconnections between the letters.

1. A Line of Initials. Process.

(This line of letters is comprised of the first letter of each word of Proverbs chapter 10, verse 29: "The Way of God is a stronghold for the blameless, but ruin for the evildoers.")

מלדימלא

A line of letters represents a progression, movement from one point to another. This pattern focuses on a concept or objective.

2. A Triangle. A Concept Emerging and Expanding.

(This illustration is based on the Hebrew word, *Shalvah*, "Tranquility.")

```
            ש
         ל   ש
       ו   ל   ש
     ה   ו   ל   ש
```

A triangular pattern represents the flow of the divine energy downward. God's sustenance of the universe.

3. The Square. The Field of Choice and of Will.

(This pattern is built on a pattern of sixteen letters, four times four. The choice represented in this example is the acceptance of the Law at Sinai. Hence, the sixteen letters used below are those of the names of Moses, Aaron, Miriam, and Torah [the Law].)

```
א   ה   ש   מ
נ   ו   ר   ה
מ   י   ר   מ
ה   ר   ו   ת
```

4. The Pyramid. Purpose, Regulation, and Accomplishment.

(The pyramid, three-dimensionally, is the relationship between three and four. Four triangles are united by a square base. On a two-dimensional plane the pyramid is a square with a point at the center. The extension of divine force into the field of will and choice opens up the possibility of purposeful activity, doing, making, and achieving. Five is the number of the senses and the fingers of the hand. In this example, the word *Avodah*, meaning "work" (also, "worship"), is being used.

עַ בַּ

וַ

הַ דַּ

5. The Star of David. The Interaction of Divine and Human Will.

(This is a thirteen-letter pattern, comprising all the points of linear intersection and the center point. The letters being used here are those of the names of three patriarchs, Abraham, Isaac, and Jacob.)

אַ

מַ הַ רַ בַּ

חַ צַ יַ

קַ עַ יַ קַ

בַּ

6. The Circle. The Totality of Concept.

A circle represents wholeness and completion. It also offers the most opportunity for exploring different vantage points. All points within a circle are equal. One can stop and focus on any of them, and not change the totality or shape of things at all. What changes is the perspective one has on the whole. This is because the position from which it is being viewed has altered. In this meditation, take a meaningful sentence and transcribe it as a circle of equally spaced letters. First, focus on the beginning letter of the phrase or sentence. Meditate on the meaning of the sentence. Then, move to different points on the circle and meditate on each point in sequence. See how the perspective has changed and with it the very meaning of the concept.

MEDITATIONS ON THE *SEFIROT*

I. Using the *Sefirot* as a Process of Introspection, Meditation 1

1. Enter the meditative state by balanced breathing, in and out rhythmically to the same number of counts or heart beats.
2. Picture before you ten concentric circles. The first circle, the largest, on the periphery, is the dimension of *Malchut*. *Malchut*

represents your ego experience. Concentrate your attention on the area between the outer circle and the next circle inside. This is your ego field. Take some time to explore aspects of your ego.

3. Moving inward one level, you reach the realm of *Yesod*, that of the subconscious. Here, life experience is processed and assimilated. This is the realm of dreams, inner experience, and your internal relation to external life. Take some time and explore your hopes, dreams, and inner understandings.

4. The next two levels, as you move inward, are *Hod* and *Netzach*. *Hod* is the level of thought, planning, programming. *Netzach* is the level of aspirations, desires, and conscious drives. Together, these two *Sefirot* are the level of prophecy and of archetype. This level is that of reward and punishment, cause and effect. When focusing on this level, let your instinct be your guide. Sometimes you may feel the need to focus on one *Sefirah* field or the other. At other times, the impulse may be to focus on both fields together or on each field alternately.

5. The next realm, the fifth circle within, is that of *Tiferet*. This area of yourself is your "hub." *Tiferet* is the frontier between mind and emotion, between the subconscious and unconscious. The interdimensionality of consciousness is most acutely experienced and most readily accessible to you at this point within. *Tiferet* is also the level of imprinting. It is here that all of the patterns which affect your thought and actions have been established and assimilated and are stored. All of the subconscious, subliminal programs that influence and pattern your conscious reality are established here. This is an extremely important area for meditation and focus.

6. When passing from *Tiferet* deeper within, you reach the levels of *Din* and of *Hesed*. Now, you are entering the realm of the unconscious. You are accessing mind itself. This is the level of primal energy, the power sources within. *Din* is the realm of discernment, separation, self-definition. How you understand reality and how you see yourself within reality is the domain of *Din*. *Hesed* is the realm of compassion, involvement, and commitment. *Hesed* is the realm of passion and of the sheer joy of life. Here is where one feels the pulse of life, and where one comes to experience the Grace of God.

It is best, to focus your meditation on both of these *Sefirot* together. Each of these *Sefirot* are enormously powerful in their own right. The dynamics between them can prove to be very volatile if each is dealt with individually. So they should be handled together as a unit.

7. Moving to the second and third circles around the center, you arrive at the area of *Hochmah* and *Binah*. This is the realm of the superconscious. Focusing on these areas takes one out of the confines of normal consciousness. This is the portal to transcendent experience. In focusing on these two circles, you view reality from the perspective of above and beyond.

   These two levels need to be worked together. In essence, they are a unit and need to be handled as such. You will need to maintain clear focus and sustained concentration at these levels. In the early stages of practicing this meditation, you may find yourself falling asleep or fading out at this juncture, until you become more adept at holding the focus.

8. As you reach the center, the innermost circle, you have arrived at the level of Self. This is the core of your Being. It is the point of pure existence, of consciousness itself. This innermost element is the connection between you and your innermost Being. It is the bridge between you and God. Explore this sacred space with reverence.

9. When ready to exit the meditation, count backward from twenty-two to zero.

Meditation 2

An alternate method of accessing these same levels is to picture the *Sefirot* as a tunnel. You enter the tunnel from *Malchut*, the level of conscious, everyday life. You exit the tunnel into Self.

As you proceed in the tunnel, you will encounter doorways. Each gateway opens into a different color field. Each color field is a different *Sefirah*. You are free to pass through any field to the next doorway, or to spend some time experiencing the *Sefirah* and its influence on your life.

Within each color area in the tunnel you may encounter additional doors. These are areas of exploration within the *Sefirot* themselves. An analogy would be that of a house. The gateways are the doors from one room to another, from one *Sefirah* to another. The doorways are closets, hallways, alcoves. That is, they are significant, auxiliary dimensions of a specific area of your life.

You should traverse the tunnel in both directions. You do not, in any given meditation, have to reach all the way to *Keter*, to the Self. You can stop at any juncture you feel comfortable. However, you do need to retrace your steps and exit from the tunnel at *Malchut*, the entrance. That will bring you back to full conscious reality. In returning back through the tunnel, you simply progress through the color fields. There is no need to dwell in any of them on the return trip.

II. Meditation on Releasing the Past

1. This meditation utilizes the concept of the Four Worlds within the Tree of Life, so the focal points of meditation will be *Malchut* first, *Yesod* second, then *Tiferet,* and finally *Keter*.
2. In meditation, picture a large Tree of Life above your head. The central pillar is aligned directly above the crown of your head. In a series of stages, you will move up through these four globes above your head.
3. First, picture yourself rising and centering your attention on the lowest *Sefirah*, that of *Malchut*. Here, you will encounter scenes, events, images, or cognitions drawn from your present life experience. This is the realm of the now. It is important to explore this level very carefully, because it will show you an area of your life that needs attention, or at least some understanding and focus.
4. Moving up to the *Sefirah* of *Yesod*, you will see and feel the ramifications your conscious experience is having on various areas of your life or on other people. This knowledge is not that of which you would normally be cognizant. Pay close attention to this information.

   Focus on this level will also portray what will likely develop next. In other words, the event shown in the *Malchut* level will be fast forwarded on the *Yesod* level. You will see where it is going and what both the long-term and short-term effects will be.
5. In the next level up, in *Tiferet*, the past history of this tendency within you is replayed. Anything that is happening in a given area of your life is not something which is simply spontaneously generated. It has a history. For a full and complete understanding of what has occurred, you need to focus very carefully in *Tiferet*.
6. To come to terms with the cause of this pattern within your life, you need to move to the highest *Sefirah*, that of *Keter*. Here, you will experience the deep, underlying causes that have produced and sustained this behavioral pattern and this reality in your life.

It is in *Keter* that you can release the past and alter the future. This is accomplished by centering on the light and joy, which is the essence of *Keter*, the essence of Self. By so doing, you will reconnect with the purest level of Self. This is a level beyond that of comprehension, thought, emotion, or desire.

Joy connects you to Self, to God, to Life Purpose. Once focused on the pure essence of Self and the Joy that is inherent in it, the lower levels of past, future, and now are automatically rectified and reformatted. This does not mean erasure. Releasing the past is not a matter of obliterating what has been. It is a process of redefinition. Connection to the past pattern is released. The past is de-emotionalized. The present and future are reconstituted along purer, more inwardly guided patterns, stemming from the deepest part of Self.

7. To exit the meditation, simply glide downward through the *Sefirot*. When you reach *Malchut*, you will reawaken to full consciousness.

III. Imprints and the *Sefirot*

An imprint, as has been discussed above, is an internalized pattern that molds the experiences of one's life. Events and our emotional reaction to them create templates, patterns of perception, that become implanted within us and shape the events of our lives. This most often happens on a subconscious level.

Something happens to us that is a highly charged event. We respond to the experience on many different levels. This response pattern, because it is a subconscious reaction, becomes internalized and often permanent. It is as if we respond to intense situations by creating colored glasses for ourselves. We choose to wear these tinted lenses, in order to avoid seeing the event accurately, often because we are not in a position to emotionally or psychologically handle the experience properly at the time.

Once a psychoemotional response pattern has been created, it serves as a filter or template that molds our subsequent thinking, emotional responses, and behavior. Utilizing the structure of the *Sefirot*, our internal imprints can be viewed, understood clearly, and consciously changed. Being able to see the patterns we carry with us provides us with an enormously important opportunity. We are then able to access areas of blockage and obstruction within ourselves. We can evaluate them and change the models. By reformatting the patterns within, we restructure all of our subsequent life experiences. Through meditation on the *Sefirot*, we can access, view, and alter the patterns to which our life experiences conform, thereby inducing healing and improving the quality of our lives.

Viewing an Imprint

1. Select a specific area of your life that you feel needs work on. Next, select a scene to keep in mind, that typifies this area of your life. Preferably, it should be a scene that has taken place in your experience. However, you may wish instead to create a typical scene, if that is more comfortable emotionally. Picture the scene clearly, with as much detail and as many specifics as possible.

2. Now, picture in front of you a Tree of Life consisting of ten large glass globes. Within the bottom one, *Malchut*, place the selected image that you have held in mind.

3. Move at this point to the uppermost *Sefirot*, *Keter-Hochmah-Binah*. This is the *Arikh Anpin*. This is the level of super-consciousness. Activate the energy of this level. Picture all three *Sefirot* being filled with crystal clear, white light. As the light gets stronger, the whole triad will begin to pulsate with energy and to glow.

4. Let the energy that has built up in the upper triad of *Sefirot* filter down and energize the six middle *Sefirot*. As they fill with light and are activated, images will appear in most, if not all, of these six *Sefirot*. What is being portrayed are the various dynamics and inner dimensions of the imprint. The basic imprint itself will appear portrayed in *Tiferet*. How it is affecting your life in general will appear in *Yesod*. The other four images are the underlying dynamics of the imprint. What is being illustrated here are the causes, effects, ramifications, and component parts of a specific pattern within your life.

5. While in meditation, observe and study the images carefully. Much of this information can only be grasped intuitively. Sense from the images what it is you need to know and understand. Take it to heart.

6. When emerging from the meditation, write down the images, the feelings and cognitions, and the *Sefirot* in which they appeared. Do so immediately, with as much detail as you can. At a later time, go back over the notes, recall the experience, and contemplate the information. Make it a point to write down any

insights, flashes, or understandings that the contemplation produces.

Changing the Imprint

1. In meditation, recall the original image. This time, instead of putting it in *Malchut*, place the image in one of the six *Sefirot* from *Hesed* to *Yesod*. Intuitively, you will know where it belongs.

2. Once placed in the correct *Sefirah*, view the image carefully from this perspective. Meditate on allowing the image to change, in accord with the deeper understandings you have of it from the previous meditation and from contemplation. Let the image reformat itself.

3. Once the process is finished, transfer the transformed image, the new paradigm, from the *Sefirah* it is in to *Yesod*. Allow the image to be charged with energy by *Yesod*. When the energy becomes intense enough, let *Yesod* send energy downward and replicate the new pattern in *Malchut*. Once this link is completed, the imprint has been changed and will remain so, until you choose to repeat this process and alter it again at some point in the future.

IV. The Well of the *Sefirot*: Levels of Self- Awareness

If one visualizes the *Sefirot* as being arranged in a vertical line, with *Malchut* being at the top and *Keter* at the bottom, a tool for self-exploration and self-analysis emerges. This vertical shaft is the Well of Self.

The deeper you move into the well, the further you explore the very depths of your inner being and inner reality. The process is quite simple. You move downward through the *Sefirot* until you reach the level you are seeking to explore or experience. As if you were in water, you float downward, seeking the proper level to be on. Each level of the well is a different color of blue. Each depth is a specific *Sefirah* and a particular, unique experiential reality.

These levels of personal experience are as follows:

Malchut = Memory, Recall, Actualized Experience.

Yesod = Comprehension, Viewpoint, Decision-Making.

Hod = Considered Action, Analysis, View of Self.

Netzach = Reaction to Life, Strength, Self-Esteem.

Tiferet = Inner Experience, Psychoemotional Process, Integrity.

Din = Self-Control, One's Limits, Judgment.

Hesed = Love, Joy of Life, Compassion.

Binah = Life Purpose, Self-Awareness, Emergence.

Hochmah = Creativity, Knowingness, Wholeness.

Keter = Oneness, Unity, Spirit, Self.

V. Diagnosing Experience through the *Zeir Anpin*

The broad patterns of our lives are most often apparent in the significant, individual events of our daily reality. By examining a noteworthy
event or experience through the lenses of the seven lower *Sefirot*, one
can gain not only a deeper understanding of the internal dynamics and
inner realities of the event, but also a far fuller picture of the general
gestalt that lies behind it.

The seven lower *Sefirot* are referred to in the Kabbalah as the seven
days of Creation. Keeping that in mind, there are a couple of underlying
assumptions here. The first is that all of our experience as created beings
is a perpetual process. That is, we live our lives experiencing reality as
an unfolding of events. We actualize our reality, we mature, and we
evolve by going through the process and playing it out.

Second, we gain understanding and reshape our definition of reality
by contemplating an experience after the process has actualized. Going
through the process is not enough. We must also come to terms with it to
derive meaning from it. In essence, these two aspects of reality take place
simultaneously. We play out events and we learn from them by reflecting
on them. Living the process and coming to an understanding of the mean-
ingfulness of the process are inseparable and intertwined realities.

The Tree of Life represents the ten *Sefirot* in a dual relationship to
each other. The *Sefirot* are a process of Unfolding on the one hand, and a
Structure of Existence on the other. They evolve one from the other and
interact with each other. They also constitute a set construction of inter-
related realms. They are distinct domains, standing in a predetermined
relationship to each other. Together, the *Sefirot* form the structure of reality.

Using this concept, the seven lower *Sefirot*, the *Zeir Anpin*, can serve
as a set of meditative focus points that allow one to diagnose and to ana-
lyze the consistuent realities that underpin any specific life experience.

Each of the *Sefirot* can be viewed as a specialized lens, clarifying a specific area of one's life. The lower the *Sefirah*, the more precise the focus.

One way to approach a deeper understanding of an aspect of your life is through the worlds of *Assiyah* (*Malchut*), *Yetzirah* (*Netzach-Hod-Yesod*), and *Beriyah* (*Hesed-Din-Tiferet*). *Malchut*, which is by itself, the world of *Assiyah* (Doing), is the level of the actualized event or experience itself.

If a person is working on an art project, for example, and is having difficulty completing it, the difficulty itself will be manifest in *Malchut*. Should this individual meditate on seeing the project in *Malchut*, he will reexperience all the difficulties and frustrations on multiple levels. This may be of considerable benefit, since it could assist him in working through the blockage in an accelerated and more intense manner. It may, however, not be enough.

To understand the conditions that are producing and sustaining the difficulties, one needs to move up to the *Yetzirah* level. This is the level of cause and effect. By focusing on the project through the lens of *Yesod*, one sees the conditions that are producing the friction and blockages. Refocusing the project on *Netzach* and *Hod* will reveal the causes and the effects. The relationship between these two *Sefirot* will show the meditator the interplay of forces that are producing the pattern by which the project is currently playing itself out.

The *Netzach-Hod-Yesod* triad portrays the mechanics of what is transpiring. They illustrate the efficient causes and the resulting pattern of events being experienced. *Netzach*, *Hod* and *Yesod* are the "domino effect" in operation, as well as the gestalt it creates.

Should one wish to understand the driving forces of the situation, not merely the mechanics, he would need to move up to the level of *Beriyah* (*Hesed-Din-Tiferet*). This is the level of dynamics. Here, within this triad of *Sefirot*, the forces of motive and drive operate. Within *Hesed* are the influences, both inner and outer, that propel what is happening. In *Hod*, assumptions are being made, reactions are taking place. Between the two, within *Tiferet*, the vast set of potential options are generated. *Tiferet* epitomizes the interrelationship of thought and emotion, desire and action. It is the level of motivation.

Focusing the art project on the level of *Beriyah* allows one to view the dynamics, the motivations, desires, and possibilities. This series of lenses provides the basis for not only understanding the deepest undercurrents of what is transpiring, but also what the original motivation is and what other possibilities exist.

VI. Understanding Influences Using the *Zeir Anpin*

By meditating on each of the *Sefirot* of the *Zeir Anpin* in ascending order, one can gain access to information, feeling, and experience that will provide the meditator with a greatly expanded view of the various levels of consciousnes. It will also illustrate how these inner realms are presently influencing a given area of one's conscious reality, one's everyday life.

Below is a list of each of the *Sefirot* in ascending order. Indicated next to each name are the different aspects of conscious reality that can be perceived through the focus of that *Sefirah*. One can picture an event, visualize a pattern of behavior, examine a feeling, or focus on an emotional gestalt or process. Move into each *Sefirah* sequentially. Meditate on what has been brought within the context of the *Sefirah*. See what feelings, intuitions, insights, and knowledge are yielded from meditating on an event, image, or pattern within a *Sefirah*. Then move up to the next.

One need not always dwell on each and every *Sefirah*. Within a specific meditation, some *Sefirot* will have much more appeal and power than others. Focus most on those. Move through the others expeditiously, touching base and moving on. Within any given meditation session, move as far as feels appropriate. It is not always necessary to traverse all seven levels.

LEVEL ONE: Malchut. Physical Reality. Focus is on the body, on a concrete reality, or an event.

LEVEL TWO: Yesod. Patterns of Reality. Emotional Center. Present Time. Focus is on feelings, creative flow, and one's view of self.

LEVEL THREE: Hod. Pattern of Definition. Past. Focus is on emotional impact and inward flow of emotion, and on the effects of growth impetus.

LEVEL FOUR: Netzach. Pattern of Growth/Evolution. Future. Focus is on emotional influences, on outward flow of emotion, and on the impetus to grow and evolve.

LEVEL FIVE: Tiferet. Experience of Reality. Mental Center. Mind-Emotion Nexus. Focus is on perception, on centering one's being, and on self-awareness and self-development.

LEVEL SIX: Din. Ability To Contain Experience. Focus is on mental impact from experience, on analytical thought, and on thought process.

LEVEL SEVEN: Hesed. Ability To Experience. Focus is on the capacity to experience and perceive, to grow and evolve, on mental stimulation, on free flow, and on associative thought.

VII. A Meditation Pattern on the *Sefirot* as Aspects of Self

KETER: The Self

HOCHMAH: The Subconscious Mind

BINAH: The Conscious Mind

HESED: Ability To Give

DIN: Ability to Recieve

TIFERET: The Emotions

NETZACH: Self-Esteem

HOD: Self-Definition

YESOD: Experience

MALCHUT: Personality

Bibliography

Ashlag, Yehudah. *The Book of the Zohar With the Sulam Commentaries.*
    Jerusalem: Am Olam, 1975.

The Book of Formation. Jerusalem: Lewin Epstein Inc., 1968.

The Book of the Zohar. Jerusalem: Am Olam, 1967.

Gikatilla, Yosef. *The Gates of Light.* Jerusalem: Sifriat Dorot, 1970.

Kaplan, Aryeh. *Meditation and Kabbalah.* York Beach, ME: Samuel
    Weiser, 1990.

Rabbi Saadiah Gaon. *The Book of Beliefs and Opinions.* Tel Aviv: Israel
    Offset, 1969.

Schatz-Openheimer, Rivka. *Dov Baer of Mezeritsch's Maggid Devarav Le
    Yaakov.* Jerusalem: Magnes Press Hebrew University, 1976.

Yizhak, Levi. *Kedushat HaLevi.* Bnei Barak: Heichal HaSefer, 1988.

Index